KU-395-237

Terms of Work for
Composition
A Materialist Critique

Bruce Horner

Foreword by
John Trimbur

STATE UNIVERSITY OF NEW YORK PRESS

Published by
State University of New York Press, Albany

For information, address the State University of New York Press,
State University Plaza, Albany, NY 12246

Production by Kristin Milavec
Marketing by Anne M. Valentine

Library of Congress Cataloging-in-Publication Data

Horner, Bruce, 1957–
    Terms of work for composition : a materialist critique / Bruce
Horner : foreword by John Trimbur.
        p. cm.
    Includes bibliographical references and index.
    ISBN 0-7914-4565-8 (alk. paper). — ISBN 0-7914-4566-6 (pbk. :
alk. paper)
    1. English language—Rhetoric—Study and teaching—Social aspects—
United States.   2. Academic writing—Study and teaching—Social
aspects—United States.   3. English teachers—Social conditions—
United States.   I. Title.
PE1405.U6H67 ·2000
808'.042'07—dc21   99–40966
                                                                        CIP

10 9 8 7 6 5 4 3 2 1

To my parents, Robert Horner and Shirley Oakes Horner,
who taught me the value of work,

and to
Min-Zhan Lu, a true worker

Contents

Foreword
John Trimbur

For academics, the very notion of work poses some vexing difficulties. Despite the popular view that college teachers have cushy jobs and get the summer off, it's not that academics don't work hard. Styling oneself as "overwhelmed" by the sheer volume of work, after all, has surely become one of the most common (and, to my mind, least attractive) responses to the apparently innocent enough question "How are you doing?" that faculty members routinely ask each other passing in the hall or around the mailboxes. In my department, people sometimes don't even answer. They just wag their heads and sigh as though a great weight rested on their shoulders. Or they'll tell you about how they can't get "caught up" or "out from under" the piles of work and that they can't wait until the end of the term—when, oddly enough, they say they can really get to work. Once, that is, work stops and vacation starts.

Such exchanges, of course, can be overheard on one level as the kind of everyday presentation of self typical of professionals in the workplace, acts of self-aggrandizement about the courses, student papers, advising, committee meetings, reports, memos, editorial work, publishing deadlines, and conference presentations that academics must take on as part of their normal workload. To be "overworked" or "overcommitted," in this sense, is a sign of value and a bid for status (and perhaps a preemptive strike to fend off requests to do further work). In another sense, however, this casual conversation about "my" work and all that it calls on me to do reveals how profoundly privatized and contradictory work in the academy actually is.

Everyone knows you have to be productive to get ahead in the academy—to get tenured and promoted—but one question the conversation I'm imagining we've all overheard raises is what, exactly, is it that gets produced when we say we have a lot of work to do. The dominant fiction in academic self-fashioning holds that the main product of work is a person's career, the curriculum vitae that tells the story of a life's work. Certainly, we take our work seriously and personally, through deep affective and practical investments in our various intellectual and pedagogical projects. Doing so, we realize our labor in the form of service, credentials, publications, recognition, and standing. The main arena of this work may be the actual place where we are employed—the program, department, and institution. As often, it is the "field" of study in which we've specialized, a purified world of inquiry and like-minded individuals set over against the "real" world of FTEs, bottom lines, "outcomes," and the growing cry from politicians and policymakers for accountability.

To put it as bluntly as I can, the fantasy of academic work is that of unalienated labor, where you get paid for doing what you really want to do, in loose affiliation with others who share your passion. In this idealized vision, life and work merge together in a seamless whole, interrupted only by the conventional acknowledgment in a book preface that you've neglected your family to pursue your intellectual obsessions (which, of course, only reinforces your stature with readers in your field as a warrant of sincerity that you cared *that* much about your work). This is the view of work as "free" labor, undertaken willingly in classrooms and over intersession or summer vacation, when, as the opening conversation suggests, academics can "get back" to what really matters to them.

And yet, for all the standard professions that work is the uncoerced expression of an individual's personality, the prevailing logic of academic work is also calculated and entrepreneurial, in which each of us figures as a small start-up enterprise where we function as the owners and operators, seeking our market share and our piece of the action. If anything, a cynic might say that given the process of professionalization, we wind up investing our time and energy in precisely what we can capitalize, loving what sells, which is, well, us. Faculty members work this out in various ways. Some do research, some trade on their reputations as teachers or administrators, while others throw around their weight as campus politicos. Many combine some or all of these activities. This, at any rate, is the view of the academic as a rational, self-interested actor, maximizing benefits and cutting losses, straight out of classical economics, with a little image-packaging from the postwar organization woman and man thrown in.

One reason academics have such difficulty thinking clearly about the nature of academic work is that the notions we have available are themselves caught between the traditional (and idealized) ideology of intellectual work as the free expression of the individual's genuine predispositions and the (equally ideological) commonsensical view of a faculty member's work as the rational calculation of cost-efficiency and personal advantage. These are obviously quite different (yet coexisting) representations of work, and the fact that they are always entangled with each other helps explain why, as in the opening conversation, work is persistently getting in the way of work.

The problem of understanding academic work, however, is not really a matter of removing the terminological tangles and finding a persuasive definition everyone can agree to. Instead, as Bruce Horner shows throughout *Terms of Work for Composition*, the problem begins with the surplus of meanings that have attached themselves to the notion of work and exert their special pulls. For Horner, work is "simultaneously an activity, the product of an activity, and the place of its practice" (xvii). The fact that academics keep getting these various senses mixed up (as in the opening conversation) is not so much a sign of muddled thinking as an evasion of the material conditions and social practices of work.

To my mind, what makes *Terms of Work* such an important book is the way Horner develops a cultural materialist perspective, from Raymond Williams and Anthony Giddens, in order to re-read old issues and debates that have been floating around the various institutional histories and critiques of composition and English studies. I am especially impressed by Horner's persistent efforts to read closely both professional and student texts and to connect them, in consequential and non-reductive ways, to the material social processes that determine their production, circulation, and use. If anything, many of the standard topics compositionists seem to debate endlessly and entropically, such as why teaching is undervalued, how we think about students, the politics of teaching writing, the contradictions of professionalism, and so on, take on new complexity—and, best of all in my view, become thinkable again in helpful terms.

As Horner suggests in the Introduction, *Terms of Work* can be read in virtually any order, for the keyword that names each chapter resonates and ramifies its meaning across a deftly cross-referenced design. Readers will, no doubt, find their own paths. I leave you with what I found to be one of the most provocative lines of analysis in the book, namely the way Horner handles the persistently perplexing problem of how the "real world" figures in the writing classroom.

There can be little question, as Horner notes, that students are typically identified by writing teachers "as non-workers preparing for subsequent status as 'productive' professionals in a service economy" (xxi–xxii). But if this is the dominant representation of who students are (and I think his assessment is correct), the question of what writing teachers should do about it has produced polarized responses: to escape (or delay entrance into) the "real world" through the development of authorship in the protected space of a writing workshop, or to embrace the "real world" as the subject of writing instruction, whether academic discourse, collaboration, workplace writing, contact zone encounters, or community service learning. Horner's point is a simple yet audacious and devastating one. In his view, both sides reify writing by substituting textual forms external to the classroom for the possibility of the real work students can do *as students* producing writing in order to investigate the material conditions and practices of writing. In other words, to put it more formulaically than Horner does, there might actually be something to study in the writing classroom, a "content" that goes beyond the writing samples, readings, paper topics, prompts, and research assignments that characteristically make up the syllabus—and that is the work of writing and the work Horner imagines writing teachers can do with their students.

Academics tend to be wildly ambivalent about the "real world," veering between resistance and subservience to its pressures, attractions, and demands. To be "in the world but not of it" is the traditionally preferred position. The great virtue of *Terms of Work* is that it helps us see that the "real world" is not somewhere else but is very much and inescapably here, right before us, in classrooms and in the work we do.

Acknowledgments

A Drake University Undergraduate Research Assistantship Grant enabled me to benefit from the research of Kevin Hedman in writing this book. Work on this book was also supported by grants from the Drake University Center for the Humanities. Joseph Lenz has encouraged me in my research leading to this book in the best ways available to a department chair.

I am grateful to the National Council of Teachers of English for granting permission to reprint material from my essays "Students, Authorship, and the Work of Composition," *College English* 59 (1997): 505–29; and "Traditions and Professionalization: Reconceiving Work in Composition," *College Composition and Communication* (Feb. 2000). Thanks also to the editors of *JAC: A Journal of Composition Theory* for granting permission to reprint material from my essay "Resisting Traditions in Composing Composition," *Journal of Advanced Composition* 14 (1994): 495–519. Thanks to all my students for working with me and for allowing me to use their writing here.

Priscilla Ross, my editor at SUNY Press, gave early crucial support to this project and, with Jennie Doling's and Kristin Milavec's expert assistance, helped see it through to completion. SUNY Press reviewers gave insightful comments, criticism, suggestions, and encouragement. David Prout provided the index. My Drake colleagues, Bruce Martin and Elizabeth Robertson, read and provided useful commentary on earlier drafts of most of these chapters. Thomas Swiss and Joseph Harris were generous enough to read through and help edit the entire manuscript. Thanks especially to Min-Zhan Lu, who patiently read, criticized, and reread every word of every draft of this book, and put up with me during the writing of it. And thanks, finally, to Yvonne Hsu, for providing occasional serendipitous reminders that there is more to life than work.

Introduction

Should English teachers wish to change English teaching, they
will have to understand the interrelationships of English teaching
to American work.

—J. Elspeth Stuckey, *The Violence of Literacy* 12

This book presents a cultural materialist critique of how, in
Composition, we talk about work, both in the professional discourse
of "composition studies" and in the talk of composition conducted in
classrooms, in the hallways outside classrooms and outside conference sessions, and in the popular imagination.[1] I carry out this critique by examining the meaning of work in Composition in relation
to five other recurring terms: *students, politics, academic, traditional*, and *writing*. While no set of terms could exhaust or define
the parameters of such talk, I focus on these because, in the inflections given these terms and those with which they are associated, I
identify a tension between Composition's desire for disciplinary status and its material location(s). This tension (and ambivalence) is
felt in how we understand and name who we are, what we do, with
whom, and our reasons for doing so. In short, these are often the
terms by which we understand and engage in the work of composition. In each of the six chapters, I trace the ways in which a specific
term operates as a site for competing constructions of Composition's
identity. Using texts from local institutional discourse—for example, course catalog descriptions, curriculum vitaes (CVs), university

newsletters—as well as published scholarly writings and popular discourse, I show how such constructions attempt either to evade the material location of work in composition or to insist on the determinant effects of that location in defining that work. Against either move, I argue for redefining these sites in ways that confront their materiality, acknowledging both the power of existing material conditions to shape the work we do in composition and the historicity of those conditions—that is, their susceptibility to changing consciousness and action.

This book is motivated by my dissatisfaction with existing perspectives that equate an improved disciplinary status for Composition with a rejection of its material practices. This equation has led to a series of ethical and conceptual dilemmas, framed as sets of impossible choices founded on discrete, hierarchized oppositions: either abolish freshman composition courses and lose Composition's institutional base, or consign Composition to a low "service" status within the academy; either insist that schools staff composition courses only with tenure-line Ph.D.s in rhetoric and composition (thereby putting their chances of tenure at risk), or exploit part-time and adjunct faculty and subject students to unsound pedagogies; either define Composition as the scholarly study of classical and modern rhetorical theory and eliminate its concern with meeting the immediate needs of students and society, or devote composition only to training students to succeed in business and industry (thereby putting aside any concern over the ethics of reproducing existing social practices and power relations). In response, my argument throughout is that these dilemmas result from a failure to confront the materiality of all work in composition, including that work deemed "theoretical" or "scholarly." I trace the roots of this failure to the class interests maintained by the ideological distinctions between work and labor, art and craft, literature and writing, thought and experience, distinctions sustained in how we use terms like *work, students, politics, academic, traditional,* and *writing.* Unacknowledged by hegemonic discourse in Composition are the physical demands and materials of writing and composition scholarship, the conscious theorizing that informs the "lowliest" aspects of teaching practice, and the counterhegemonic potential of conventional forms of writing instruction. To recover these will require an acknowledgment of the complex, often conflictual class interests of both teachers and students, a recognition of what Raymond Williams has termed "practical" consciousness, and a material as well as conceptual redefinition of the work of composition addressing its location in the academy, its value and constituency, and its practice.

Raymond Williams' concept of the materiality of culture forms the basis for my argument as a whole. In keeping with that concept, my use of the term "materiality" conforms to the Marxist tradition of *historical* materialism, in which the mode of production is understood to include social relations as a significant "productive force" (see Marx and Engels, *German Ideology* 18). In a critique of how base-superstructure relations, productive forces, and art have been conceptualized in Marxist thought, Williams observes that the error in such conceptualizations resides not in materialism but in a failure to be materialist enough (*Marxism* 92). For example, the view of the work of art as reflecting material concerns suppresses "the actual work on material—in a final sense, the material social process—which is the making of any art work" (*Marxism* 97). As a result of that suppression, the work of art—and, by extension, intellectual work generally—is separated from the material social conditions of its production, and so imagined as, at most, acting autonomously on, against, or in spite of but not with and within such conditions. The material means of such work are elided, as are the processes of its distribution and consumption, the interaction of these in its production, and the social relations enabling and constraining it.

My focus on work as point of entry into debate in Composition is meant to draw attention to this materiality. For work—denoting simultaneously an activity, the product of that activity, and the place of its practice—encourages us to think of what we do as located materially and historically: as material social practice. Further, this identification of composition as work, so understood, also encourages us to think of it in relation to other places, activities, and social forces, responding to and conditioned by them, and shaping them in return. It can accentuate the materiality and historicity of our work, and so enable us better to understand the specific and changing delimitations governing it and its real potentialities.

In insisting on seeing the work of composition as material social practice, there is a danger of appearing to invoke an abstraction in the name of a specificity: to repeatedly assert work as "material social practice" without identifying, exactly, what kind of material social practice it is. The difficulty, however, is that no representation of work in composition locating it in its historical, material specificity can serve as proxy or portrait of the full range of that work across time and space. There is a politics engaged in representations of that work that cannot be evaded. In presenting a cultural materialist critique of discourse on Composition, I confront in this book an inevitable tension, then, between, on the one hand, identifying the materiality of such work in specific instances, and recognizing the contingent nature of such identifications. I engage the politics of such identifications in defining and choosing which demarcations of what constitutes the "materiality" of our work are to be addressed.

Consider, for example, how we might identify the materiality of writing. That materiality may be understood in terms of writing technologies, an attribute of writing now being given renewed attention because of the recent shift from the technologies of paper and pen to computer software and hardware (see, for example, Haas). Or it might be understood more broadly to refer to a host of socioeconomic conditions contributing to writing production, such as the availability of certain kinds of schooling, number of students in writing classrooms, student financial aid (and the need for it), public health, access to time and quiet. Yet more broadly, the materiality of writing might be understood to refer to networks for the distribution of writing, controls over publishing (in whatever forms), and global relations of power articulated through these (see Canagarajah). And it may be understood to include the particular subjectivities—the consciousness—produced by the conditions of "postmodern," "post-Fordist," or other sociocultural conditions (see, for example, Faigley). Similarly, the materiality of writing may be understood to include social relations—say, between students and teachers in the composition classroom; relations of race, gender, class, ethnicity, sexual orientation, generation, and region, among others within the classroom and/or in the larger social realm; "personal" (e.g., familial) relations—and the lived experience of the history of these relations to which any act of writing may be seen as responding. The materiality of the work of teaching composition can be understood to include physical classroom conditions (size, heating, furniture, lighting, number of students); the teacher's physical health and office and library resources; clerical support, teaching load, salary and job security; intra- and interdepartmental relations between composition staff and other faculty; characteristics of the student population; relations between the academic institution and state and commercial institutions; relations among members of the Composition "profession" and between those members and other organizations and constituencies; and teachers' lived experience of the history of these relations to which any act of teaching may be seen as responding.

As these lists suggest, no representation of teaching or writing can exhaust the full range of their materiality but must be understood as focused, and thus partial and selective in all senses. Which demarcations of their materiality one emphasizes will inevitably place into the shadow other possible demarcations. The partiality of the focus I present will, I hope, invite others to test my reading of compositional work against what is cast into the shadows by the demarcations of materiality I have emphasized. But recognizing the materiality of culture, however demarcated, is crucial in preventing slides into either structural determinist or individualist errors. I use social theorist Anthony Giddens' theory of the duality of structure as a model for avoiding such slides. As Giddens argues, both structural determinist and individualist tendencies remove structures from their instantiation in time, eliding their material historicity. As a consequence, individual agency is either denied or inflated, and both agency and structure are imagined as discrete and opposed rather than material, historical, and interdependent. Giddens' theory of the duality of structure addresses this by recognizing the interdependence of agency and structure and their location in time. This enables us to identify the limited effectivity, and so the potential for changes to and within, both agency and structure. From this perspective, work is the occasion for both reproducing and revising material social relations. Applied to writing, in Fredric Jameson's formulation, the work of writing can be seen as "always entertain[ing] some active relationship with the Real. . . . bring[ing] into being that very situation to which it is also, at one and the same time, a reaction. It articulates its own situation and textualizes it" (81, 82).

Insisting on the materiality of social relations can also prevent slides into structural determinist or individualist arguments by focusing attention on the specific interrelations and interactions between and among the various levels of material social realms, such as those noted above. Otherwise, it is all too easy to leap from a set of global relations—as in the "global" postmodern economy, say—to the sensibility detected in a student paper: finding in a student paper the "turbulence" of postmodern sensibility without examining the relation of the specific, local, material conditions of the production of that paper to more general "postmodern" conditions. Such leaps constitute a throwback to mechanical "reflection" models of the relation of base to superstructure against which cultural materialist arguments are posed. To identify the specific means and modes of articulation between different levels of the material social process, I draw on Pierre Bourdieu's conceptualization of economic, social, cultural, and symbolic capital and the production of and conditions of exchange between various forms of these within and between different sociocultural sites. Such a conceptualization makes it possible both to identify delimitations in the kind and degree of significance to be attached to specific practices while recognizing the socially and historically contingent nature of those delimitations.

Each chapter of this book proceeds by reviewing competing definitions for a given term in published and unpublished discourse on Composition. I examine how these competing definitions resituate Composition in relation to specific historical, material, institutional pressures and show how they operate to reproduce specific practices in Composition. While I intend the book chapters to be read in order, it is possible to read individual chapters in isolation, as each presents an argument about the relation of our work to one of the key terms of our discourse, terms whose meanings overlap. As a result of that overlap in the meanings of the terms and the common discourse on which I draw, discussions of several issues recur in different chapters—for example, the use of service learning pedagogies, the professionalization of Composition, collective bargaining, institutional relations between Composition and literary study, the commodification of writing and pedagogy, the relation of academic to nonacademic literacy practices. Consequently, individual chapters include cross references to other chapters containing such discussions.

Chapter 1, "Work," locates the idea of academic work more specifically in relation to such terms as "labor," "art," and "craft." Commonplace identifications of teachers' work in Composition not with teaching but with writing intended for publication (work with which one's teaching and administrative duties are thought to interfere) signal Composition's adherence to currently dominant academic identifications of non-manual work with the production of reified texts having cultural capital. Such identifications compete with institutional designations of the work of composition with the managed processing of quantified units—for instance, courses, students, and credit hours—and the production of abstract writing skills. Uniting these views, however, is a reification of academic work into institutionalized forms, whether published essays, books, and papers or credit hours, courses, and students ("FTEs"). This reification thereby obscures the material practices and conditions of the production of these forms. The competing identifications of composition work mark Composition's location on the periphery of the academy. The economic capital it ostensibly produces in the form of writing skills, for which it is valued outside the academy, serves only to secure the marginality of its status within the academy. Meanwhile, both the academic and non-academic spheres refuse to recognize, and so devalue, the cultural capital represented by compositionists' attempts to achieve professional academic status through the production of abstract knowledge. Because both the move to professionalize and the move to unionize fail to address the full sense of the materiality of work in composition, both risk the alienation of composition workers from their work, whether through succumbing to bureaucratization of the production of academic knowledge or through proletarianization of the labor of teaching.

Chapter 2, "Students," considers how students are mapped in their relations to nonstudents (e.g., workers), teachers, and the academy and further as specific student types. Building from Marguerite Helmers' analysis of the transhistorical representation of students and teaching in Composition "testimonials," I argue that these identifications fail to recognize the material location of these students and their relation to other students and to the academy, their desires and needs, and the location of the teaching practices and conditions intended to address these. Above all, students are identified in relation to work as non-workers preparing for subsequent status as "productive" professionals in a service economy. Implicit in such identifications is a valorization of certain kinds of work to which the students are expected to aspire and a neglect of the work in which they engage as students, in "student work." After exploring the relationship of the often lamented asocial positioning of these students to the subjectivity and material practices expected of service-economy professionals, I present how we might understand the work in which students engage in their writing as material social practice. I do so by considering a student essay and classroom discussion of that essay, and by reviewing the potential in the structural position students occupy *as* students for the work they perform in "service-learning" projects.

Chapter 3, "Politics," considers how debate over the "politics" of Composition retains dominant, stark conceptions of both power and the possibilities for changing relations of power. The chapter examines debate over four sites for "politics" in Composition: the classroom, the institution, the profession, and the relation of the institution to larger social formations. These debates often retain institutionalized reifications of the sites of compositional work as discrete—the course, the institution, the profession, "society"—rather than seeing the interdependence and convergence of practices and relations of power among and between these sites. Arguments to engage Composition in politics typically accept dominant conceptualizations of what does and does not constitute work carrying "political" significance. In so doing, they frequently accede to the dominant's ascription of powerlessness to alternative practices, thereby giving greater sway to the force of hegemonic pressures on Composition. Using the debate over Elizabeth Ellsworth's account of an explicitly "politicized" course, I show how understanding the political effectivity of work within a course must take into consideration the ways in which that work is articulated not only in the relations between teacher and students and among the students but in the relations between students in a course and outside the course, the course and the curriculum, the course and the institution, and between the teacher and these sites. Reviewing debate on the "professional" politics in Composition in arguments over the use of part-time and adjunct faculty, I show the interaction between the material conditions and positioning of faculty and their pedagogies, suggesting that tracing the convergences between the debate over professional politics and the politics of pedagogy may contribute to better understanding and addressing the politics and (and the politics of) the practices of both.

Chapter 4, "Academic," examines how hegemonic notions of academic work and Composition's location on the academic periphery limit its views of writing, institutions, and individuals deemed "academic." Composition's ambivalence about its "place" in the academy is mirrored by its ambivalence towards all things academic and its expressions of nostalgic desire for non-academic experience, writing, and institutions. Specifically, by conceiving of what is "academic" in dematerialized ways, Composition ends up mistaking the reductive, fixed forms in which what is "academic" is officially recognized for the full range of academic work and its interrelation to work at other, "nonacademic" sites. I examine debates within Composition over academic discourse and the academic institutional structural forms of curricula, programs, and disciplines to show the operation of such reductions. I use my analysis of that debate to suggest not only how we might resist such reductions but also how we might recuperate the counterhegemonic potential of work carried on at such sites, despite their close association with the hegemonic. Arguing against "functionalist" views of such academic institutional structures as basic writing, freshman composition, writing-across-the-curriculum, and service learning programs, and such academic disciplines and projects as English, cultural studies, and rhetoric, I show how locating academic discourse and institutional structures in their material instantiations can enable us to recognize and engage the contingent nature of the effects of these forms. We may thus avoid false hopes of the effects of affiliating with or abolishing Composition's affiliation with such structures. More importantly, we may learn to exploit the potential residing in those practices and structures commonly dismissed as merely "academic," making use of the relative autonomy and material resources of specific academic sites.

Neglect of the counterhegemonic potential of such sites, I argue in chapter 5, operates in dominant conceptualizations of what is "traditional" in Composition, particularly in recent histories of Composition as a field of knowledge in which "tradition" represents the Other against which the professionalization of Composition struggles. Identified with pedagogies deemed unacceptable and with what North terms "Practitioner lore," "traditional" often carries the sense of being unreflective, inert, involving a passive transmission of beliefs and practices imagined in terms of transfer of knowledge. But this sense of what is traditional overlooks the active processes by which traditions are in fact reworked by their practitioners in the very process of being sustained. I use a tradition of teaching at Amherst College and the relationship between the work of David Bartholomae and William Coles to suggest the possibility of this more active sense of tradition and to argue for how Composition may both value and tap the potential of such traditions.

This more active view of what is traditional in Composition parallels the perspective on "writing" for which I argue in chapter 6. Whereas writing is typically identified with the texts produced or with a process abstracted from material conditions, I argue for Composition to redefine the work of writing as material social practice. Such a definition runs counter to ideological distinctions between art and craft, and even between "writing" and the denigrated "composition." Nevertheless, it promises to help resolve the dilemmas Composition confronts as it increasingly faces pressures both from the "high" culture of academic literary study and from forces outside the academy to betray its commitments to teaching and learning the practice of writing in the material world. I use debate over the use value and exchange value of the writing of students, theorists, and ethnographers—often framed in terms of the relative abstractness or concreteness of that writing—to show both the potential within commonly derided commodified forms of writing and the susceptibility of other forms of writing to commodification. I thus highlight the need to locate the potential of writing not in its abstracted forms or histories but in the specific and various uses to which it may be put. Illustrating this potential in a discussion of some examples of student writing, I suggest some ways in which writing may be taught as material social practice. I also suggest how such a view of writing provides an alternative to limitations in critical theorists' elevations of the "text" of writing at the expense of the "work" of writing, and the work of composition.

This book is aligned with the turn in Composition studies to the history of Composition theory and practice.[2] It attempts to extend a growing critique of the professional discourse of Composition to which such historical studies have contributed,[3] and it participates in scholars' increasing attention to the social and political location of writing and writing instruction.[4] More specifically, it is intended to complement and further recent feminist critiques of work in Composition and education highlighting the ways in which gendered constructions undermine that work, denigrate its workers, and serve to justify and perpetuate its poor material working conditions.[5]

To this extensive body of scholarship I hope to contribute a decisively materialist perspective. Like much of that work, this book critiques discursive constructions of Composition. However, critiques of the epistemologies underlying dominant theoretical perspectives, pedagogies, and scholarly methodologies in Composition often neglect the material circumstances in which these have operated. Like other critiques of Composition discourse, I look at a set of terms key to Composition and consider the history of contesting constructions given these terms in Composition. However, because I am concerned with the material construction of Composition as a profession or discipline in relation to other academic "fields" and to non-"professional" sites and concerns associated with locations outside the academy, I do not restrict my focus to the terms of professional discourse in Composition studies or the inflections given them in the profession. For example, while I critique dominant conceptions of "tradition," a term of great contention within the scholarly literature of Composition meriting consideration by its scholars, I incorporate my critique of these scholarly conceptions of tradition within a more general critique of the common cultural resonance of the term "tradition" in popular discourse. While such a broadening of focus admittedly risks obscuring the various specific perspectives on terms current in debates within Composition studies, it may foreground the larger material social context in which such debates take place and to which they must ultimately respond.

My focus arises in response to the increasing pressure on the work of composition, as well as on academic work generally, from that larger context. One sign of that pressure is the increasing interest among compositionists, as well as among college faculty generally, in the strategies of unions and unionizing, strategies I consider in chapters 1 and 5. Those considerations and others have led me to explore the application of insights from ethnographic studies of industrial and postindustrial work and from studies in industrial relations to the situation of compositionists, both to address unionizing specifically and to better understand dominant attitudes toward work, types of work, and workers. While I argue for far more attention to the strategies of unionizing, an argument specifically for or against unionizing composition teachers is well beyond the scope of this book. In making work the focus of my critique, however, and in the approach to work that I present, I do hope to contribute to, or at least to provoke, the formulation of a labor theory of the work of composition crucial, I believe, to considerations of such strategies. In this sense, this book may be of use to all those interested in thinking through the relation of our work to professionalism and unionizing, literacy, the work of others, and class. And while this book is addressed primarily to those in Composition, its delineation of the relation of work in Composition to work in English, the academy, primary and secondary education, and "work" in non-academic spheres should interest those located in these other educational fields as well. It is my attempt to contribute not only to recent studies of work in and the professionalization of college-level "English studies" but also to ongoing debate on the current conditions, problems, and possibilities of education.

Chapter 1

WORK

Within the "field" of Composition, *work* has three distinct usages. First, in a usage closely aligned with a general trend in the culture to restrict the term's meaning to "paid employment," it is invoked in debate over the *conditions* of teachers' work: class size, teaching load, salaries, office facilities, clerical support, library resources, use of adjunct and part timers, withholding of tenure and tenure lines for composition faculty, and the "feminization" of composition teaching evidenced by such conditions (Williams, *Keywords* 281–82).[1] Second, in much scholarly debate in Composition, *work* is used almost exclusively to refer to written texts. The question "What are you working on," for example, typically refers to the texts one is producing rather than to any other activities in which one might also be engaged (E. Watkins 11, 12, 85; see also Varnum 9, 114, 212). A third meaning refers to the actual concrete activities of teaching, as in the "work" of teaching. Significantly, however, this meaning is distinctly subordinate to the second and commonly subsumed by the first: teachers who daily spend hours interacting with students in classrooms and writing responses to student writing speak of their "own work" as something with which these activities compete: *their* work is the texts they produce when not engaged in such activities, which are understood as labor benefiting others, exchanged for pay—that is, as "paid employment."

It would be tempting to see these different meanings as pointing to disparate issues: the first, a matter of fair employment practices; the second, a matter of quirks in a profession's self-identification, the third, an issue of the "craft" of teaching and its lamentably low status. I would argue, however, that we can effectively address issues of working conditions, referred to in the first usage, only by confronting contradictions in the second and third definitions of academic work evidenced in the subordination of the activity of teaching to the production of scholarly texts. This subordination and subsumption of the work of teaching to the production of written texts constitute the playing out at the site of Composition of contradictions in more general conceptions of work. These contradictions are manifested in the distinction between intellectual and non-intellectual labor and in the commodification of intellectual labor. The distinction between intellectual and non-intellectual labor denies the location of "mental" labor in the material conditions of available technological and other material resources (e.g., computers, libraries, office space, writing materials, communication facilities, time, quiet, and the funding for these; as well as conditions of bodily health), and the social relations of the production of "mental" work (e.g., at the most immediate professional level, networks, institutions, training, rank; and at more general levels, the relations contributing to the institutionalization of such work). And that distinction denies as well the "intellectuality" of "manual," "unskilled" work.

Labor is commodified when the value of the product of that labor is identified as an objective property of the product itself (see Marx, *Capital* I, 153–54). In the academy, intellectual labor, in the form of "scholarship," is deemed to be one's *own* work, treated as divorced from material social conditions, a product of the autonomous scholar. It is thereby commodified, simultaneously with commodification of the scholar herself. In contrast, the value of the product of teaching is more clearly tied to material social conditions—which students, what class size, what school, what term, taught in what facilities and with what resources. Because these ties make the work of teaching resistant to such commodification, it tends to be viewed within the academy not as work at all but as labor, exploited by the institution. The work of Composition, insofar as it is identified with teaching, thus is in a double bind: it is less readily susceptible to traditional academic forms of commodification because of its ties to student bodies and institutional resources and conditions. At the same time, its attempts to valorize its work threaten either to deprive it of its identity as Composition by removing it from teaching, or to seal its fate as alienated labor owned, and exploited, by the institution.

In this chapter, I begin by examining the operation of these contradictions in academic representations of work generally. I then turn more specifically to the negotiation of these contradictions in representations of work in English and in Composition. Composition's location on the border between the realms of the academic and the social, as these are conventionally understood, lead it both to experience and respond differently to such contradictions in its work. To illustrate, I examine different strategies either contributing to or resisting the commodification of Composition's work in its treatment of pedagogies and in its efforts at "professional" organization.

Work in the Academy

The peculiar relegation of *work* to designate only the production of academic texts, far from being restricted to Composition, is endemic to discussions of academic activities within the academy (see, for example, Guskin 5; Varnum 219). Characteristic features of the genre of the academic curriculum vitae (CV) illustrate this conception of work, as do institutions' promotional literature. (A column on "Faculty News" in my own institution's biweekly newsletter *OnCampus*, for example, is devoted almost entirely to brief notices of faculty publications and conference presentations.) A typical academic CV consists of a series of lists of accomplishments categorized by type: publications (or categories of publication), conference papers, invited lectures, grants, "manuscripts in circulation," and, significantly, "work (i.e., writing projects) in progress." One's teaching is, at most, represented in lists of courses taught, ideally those which the individual has developed. Other activities, lumped under "service," are identified by committee name or position held.

One common criticism of this way of representing academic work, especially within Composition, highlights the relative emphasis given scholarship in comparison to teaching. Lists of publications and other presentations of research, for example, are often given more prominence in CVs than the lists of courses taught or services rendered. Insofar as Composition's identity is more closely tied to teaching than other disciplines, this devaluing of teaching would appear to threaten the status of Composition itself. A second, closely related criticism, often originating outside the academy, emphasizes the inverse relation between the work given prominence in the academy and the social utility of the work. The obscurity of academics' research topics makes academics the butt of late-night talk show jokes; legislators asked to fund academic work increasingly complain about universities' lack of emphasis on teaching and service to the community (see Plater).

One leftist response to such criticisms argues that tailoring one's work to serve the needs of an unjust society is to perpetuate such injustices: we cannot in good faith direct our efforts to training students to be exploited, alienated workers (see C. Freedman 80). Thus it might be argued that to de-emphasize those activities over which we have least control and which respond most directly to the demands of capital is part of a conscientious refusal to perform the task assigned to us by capital, to revel defiantly in the "unproductive," unreified work of scholarship (see Ebert; Hansen 260). Evan Watkins notes the attractiveness, for example, of arguments that "the 'value' of literature' is finally how it has neither value nor use," for such a valuation establishes literary study as a means to escape "the relentless colonizing of behavior that characterizes the expansion of industrial and then postindustrial capitalism" (164). Such arguments present the choice of a career in English literary study as a moral one of sacrificing lucre to pursue an ideal of individual, imaginative freedom (210). However, as Carl Freedman has argued, while the "unproductive" work associated with scholarship does appear to operate under conditions of significantly greater freedom over time, place, and pace of work, work content and significance, "[t]he price exacted for this freedom is more severe intellectual subjection to capitalist relations." In fact, even more than the manual laborer, the intellectual worker is "in certain respects the most completely imprisoned by the commodity structure" (Freedman 79). It may be true that intellectuals "own," in some sense, at least some of the means of scholarly production: in the form of knowledge and skills and control over the time and specific focus of their concrete labor (though, as suggested above, they do not control the full panoply of material resources that make their work possible and shape that work). However, the social relations of their work require its commodification. Such arguments, in other words, confuse a degree of apparent freedom in concrete labor practices with freedom from the extraction of exchange value from those practices, ignoring the larger social location and organization of scholarly labor.

The ways in which the work of both teaching and scholarship (as well as service) are represented in academic CVs demonstrate such imprisonment in the commodity structure: not simply what is included, but how it is represented, and about what it is silent. For all such work is represented precisely as a commodity, prized for its exchange value, as is the individual herself (cf. Faigley 142). Publications, courses, grants, even service positions are identified as items somehow belonging to, or in the possession of, the CV author, and so part of the "package" acquired through hiring that author (see Lunsford and Ede 168). Teaching is identified not in terms of the number of times a section has been taught, or how many course sections the faculty member has taught per term, but the names of the courses taught. A course developed by the author, and so ostensibly belonging to her, carries more exchange value than a course repeatedly assigned to her by an institution. This valuation is illustrated by my own institution's form for faculty to use in preparing their annual "Professional Activities Record," used to determine salaries, which allows faculty to highlight only that teaching which involves a "new" course or "innovative methods." Experience in teaching a course counts for little, just as teaching a large courseload counts for little, and just as a large number of years devoted to a single intellectual project not represented by publications is not advertised. The fact that one has been thinking about a given topic for ten years, far from demonstrating work, can suggest inefficiency, a lack of "productivity," just as to say one has been teaching an assigned course for ten years or teaching four sections a term may suggest not one's work but either one's staleness or one's subordinate position to the institution assigning one's tasks.

In this light, the much-decried devaluation of teaching in the academy has less to do with any actual specific commitment, or lack of commitment, among faculty to teaching instead of research.[2]

For "commitment" is not seen as a relevant criterion. Rather, it may have more to do with the difficulty of claiming courses as individually produced commodities (cf. E. Watkins 218–20). Courses remain commodities, but they are more commonly the product of—owned by—institutions rather than individuals, and are advertised as such—for example, in universities' course "catalogues." Indeed, one argument made against teaching "on-line" is that the process of placing coursework on-line not only restructures that work, allowing for greater control and scrutiny of faculty performance and course content and intensifying the work of teaching, but it also better enables institutions to claim ownership of those materials and take possession of faculty's knowledge and course design skill embodied in the course materials. On-line teaching thus may pose a threat to faculty jobs (Blumenstyk; Guernsey and Young; Noble 46–47; see also Rhoades chapter 5).[3] The identification of courses by title, number, and credit hours abstracts courses from their social historical locations, leading to a kind of false advertising in which courses are listed that may never, in fact, be offered, and obscuring differences between those sections of a course that are. On the other hand, while institutions advertise courses as products to entice student-consumers, the institutional origin, location, and production of courses argues against an individual academic advertising his labor in teaching them unless he can highlight the specificity of his labor as his. For example, if I want to claim any individual credit for teaching an English composition course students are required to take and I am required to teach, I must somehow document, for my "Professional Activities Record," that "my" teaching uses "innovative" methods for which I can claim authorship; I can't simply say I, rather than someone else, did the teaching.

Courses are clearly institutional products (of the specific college or university, or are "institutions" themselves, such as the ubiquitous Freshman Comp), and thus firmly grounded in material social conditions of time and place. By contrast, scholarly writing—associated with freedom from constraints of time and place and subject—is also commonly *dis*sociated from any specific institution, thus obscuring the materiality of such work. Scholarly writing is made to appear to be the product of purely individual mental labor, the result of being a careful, insightful thinker rather than being the product of appropriate time and access to specific people, books and computers, and an institutional position. While research grants might appear to highlight the dependence of scholarship on material resources, this relation of dependence is obscured by the common practice of identifying grants as in themselves discrete manifestations of the scholar's intellectual worthiness, listed in CVs as accomplishments, not explanations for how the scholar has managed to produce so much. The more the materiality of scholarly work is denied, the more the scholar can claim his work as "his own" rather than as made possible by specific material social circumstances.[4] That same denial of materiality is effected by academic institutions through their efforts to give their physical plants a "bucolic" appearance, and by professors' fabled absent-mindedness and indifference to material pleasures (see Fish, "Unbearable").

The practices I've described are so commonplace, so pervasive as aspects of both academic culture and late twentieth-century Western culture generally, as are the ideological assumptions driving them, that it is worth risking a restatement of the obvious to point to the contradictions embedded in the ways of defining work that these practices embody. There is, first of all, the ideological distinction between intellectual ("mental") and non-intellectual ("manual") labor, a distinction underlying the division of labor whose appearance Marx identifies as the moment at which all true division of labor arises (Marx and Engels, *German Ideology* 20). This distinction overlooks both the materiality of intellectual labor and what we might term the "intellectuality" of so-called manual, or "unskilled," labor (see Hull 16). More specifically, it overlooks, first, the location of intellectual labor in the conditions of material social history; second, the fact that those called out and self-nominated as intellectuals represent "only a particular sector of intellectual labor" (excluding, for example, journalists, technicians, managers, administrators, clergy, etc.; see Guillory 122, 131); and, third, the intellectual abilities called for in the practice of work deemed (by those not engaging in it) "unskilled" (see Kusterer). Accusations of the "politicization" of the academy (whether by the left or the right) depend on a prior denial of the location of the work of academics in material social history (see Horner, "Discoursing" 203; Nelson 140;

Mines; Soley). The designation of "intellectual" is restricted to workers who can credibly maintain just such denials. Richard Hofstadter, for example, claims that academics whose "ends are set from some interest or vantage point *outside* the intellectual process itself" don't count as intellectuals proper; rather, he brands them "zealots" or "mental technicians" (27).

The distinction between intellectual and non-intellectual labor underlying derisions of the intellectual abilities of those populations working outside professional realms is now being challenged by studies of "everyday cognition" operating in the seemingly most mundane of tasks (Kusterer; Lave), and by identifications of what Houston Baker has termed "vernacular theory" and Michel Foucault has called "subjugated knowledges" (see McLaughlin 5–7). As Shoshona Zuboff argues, "action-centered" skills, which she distinguishes from "intellective" skills, nonetheless incorporate significant knowledge, but because this knowledge remains necessarily tacit, it is not recognized (186–88). Charles Darrah, in his study of work on the production floor of a California manufacturer of computer workstations, found that while production workers, management, and engineers all saw the work of computer assembly and testing as "simple" (256), analysis of actual workplace activities revealed not only that workers who lacked ostensibly "required" skills remained valuable employees, but also that they possessed many other skills important to their work unrecognized by management (263–65). Similarly, Jean Lave concludes from studies of people's everyday arithmetic practices in specific settings that cognition "is distributed—stretched over, not divided among—mind, body, activity and culturally organized settings" (1). And Thomas McLaughlin argues from his analysis of the theorizing of various non-"theorists" that "it isn't only 'theorists' who raise important questions about the premises that guide cultural practice" (5). So, just as work deemed "intellectual" is inherently material in its location, involving far more than purely "mental" activity and capacities, so work deemed "non-intellectual" involves significant, if commonly unrecognized, "mental" capacity and activity.

The distinction between intellectual and non-intellectual work persists, however, because of the class interests it serves. For the distinction designates some labor, and so some laborers, "higher" than others by reason of the ostensibly greater intellectuality of their work, deserving of both greater status and rewards. Indeed, within this discourse, to designate academics as "laborers," or even "workers," seems counterintuitive, suspect, or perverse, for it implies a link between those officially distinguished as intellectuals and others that the distinction is intended to obscure (cf. L. R. Pratt 36–37; E. Watkins 11; Rhoades 127). My point in highlighting this link, however, is not to encourage an anti-intellectualism, to propose eliminating the category of "intellectual," or to overlook the material differences between those designated intellectual and those not. What matters is the purpose for which the category of "intellectual" is being invoked. The materialist approach to intellectuality I am advocating would insist on the material specificity and historicity of the kind of mental and material work involved in any intellectual practice. We can grant the "self-determined" character of work Hofstadter sees as distinctively intellectual, but only if we understand that "self," and so that self's intellectual work, as inherently social, material, and historical, no less than the work of, say, meatpackers. Intellectuals, in this sense, as Gramsci pointed out, differ from non-intellectuals not by their innate possession of an intellectual capability foreign to others but by their social position as people paid to do a kind of work called "intellectual" (304). Rather than denigrating or praising what passes for intellectual work for its intellectuality, we need to insist on the material social conditions making that work possible and shaping it; we cannot use its "intellectuality" as a basis for denying its materiality.

The distinction between intellectual and non-intellectual labor is embodied by the commodification of intellectual labor, which belies the location of that work in time as ongoing, processual, and social. While I'll have more to say about the specific commodification of writing in chapter 6, here I'll simply recall that, for example, even that intellectual work given prominence in academic CVs appears in reduced, reified form: as individual items removed not only from the material resources making the work possible (listings of grants, for example, are kept separate from listings of publications) but also from the ongoing activity of writing and thinking and the contributions of those other than the "author" to that writing and thinking—contributions both to its formation and to shaping its reception. Or, to point to the institutional commodity of "the course," the contributions to the work and very constitution of any course

made by individual faculty, specific students, and less easily identifiable factors of institutional, regional, and national history and circumstance are erased in course catalogues, as are the specific
meanings that specific actors in actual course sections take from
the concrete activities in which they engage for "the course."

"Work" in English

Within English, we can see evidence of attempts both to
counter and conceal these contradictions embedded in the commodification of academic work in "Making Faculty Work Visible," the
1996 Report of the MLA Commission on Professional Service. While
making gestures to recognize the material social conditions contributing to the production of academic work, the report contains
those gestures by its commitment to a meritocratic ideology opposed to recognizing either the contribution such conditions make
to that work or the social relations responsible for establishing the
criteria by which that work is evaluated. Responding to increasing
tensions between universities' teaching and research missions and
increasing demands on faculty to engage in "service" (7–8), the report argues that not only scholarship but also service and teaching
represent sites for significant intellectual work, and so ought to
merit reward (12–13, 20, 29). As the Commission explains, "the degree of intellectual work [in a site] is not in some predictable way
intrinsic to the task or activity but is a function of both circumstance and choice" (19). These observations suggest an attempt by
the Commission to blur common distinctions between "intellectual"
and "non-intellectual" work by insisting on the intellectuality of
those faculty work activities traditionally deemed to lack it. The
Commission observes that "the present model of faculty work conceals and thereby protects from criticism a set of tacit equations between the type of work done (named teaching, research, or service)
and the specific character and values attributed to that work" so
that research has come to serve as "metonym for intellectual work"
(11), at the expense of recognizing the intellectual demands of work
at the other sites.

Despite the report's efforts to revalue teaching and service, its
central concern with how to reward faculty members leads it into

contradictions. First, in pursuing that concern, it insists that faculty work that can be shown to be "intellectual" merits greater reward than work that cannot be shown to be intellectual, even if the latter contributes crucially to intellectual work, as the report acknowledges many activities do (14, 15): "What matters for assessing and rewarding faculty work," they warn, "is whether it is viewed as intellectual work or professional citizenship" (24). In other words, while recognizing that intellectual work occurs in activities other than traditional scholarship, and that such work depends on a host of other labor activities (e.g., of "professional citizenship") and material social conditions, the Commission still insists on maintaining individual faculty members' intellectual "property rights" over the work made possible, in fact, by that other, presumably less "intellectual" labor and those specific material social circumstances. These other tasks may be labor and time-intensive, but if they do not make sufficient conceptual demands to qualify as intellectual work, they merit less reward (26). On the other hand, the relative time and labor intensity of work deemed intellectual is not broached, since to do so would be to acknowledge the materiality of intellectuality. Thus labor and time intensity of a task are not considered legitimate criteria for evaluating merit, only a commodified intellectuality. We can see this insistence on the criterion of commodified intellectuality in the care the report exerts to distinguish the intelligence called upon in "intellectual" work as qualitatively different from the intelligence called upon in everyday activities. Some intellectuality, it seems, is more intellectual than others. As it warns,

> For the purposes of faculty rewards, significant intellectual work should be recognizably an outgrowth of faculty members' professional expertise, rather than simply of their general knowledge and skills as educated, intelligent people. . . . [Moreover,] [i]ntellectual work as understood in the academic setting is not simply any intelligent behavior or activities and accomplishments that demonstrate a certain degree of professional skill and knowledge. (16)

Thus the Commission insists on distinguishing intellectual work not only from the intelligence of "educated, intelligent people" but also from intelligence demonstrating "a certain degree of professional skill and knowledge." And the purpose of these distinctions is, as the report indicates, to determine merit. To honor these other manifestations of intelligence would necessarily undermine the variable both by which faculty generally are deemed more meritorious than non-faculty and by which some faculty or work activities are deemed more meritorious than others. Further, it would require acknowledging that this extra degree of intellectuality may be attributable not simply to the faculty member exhibiting it, as a commodity herself (like a better-quality television commanding a higher price), but to a different set of material circumstances. Like whites denying the role their privileges as whites have played in their successes, faculty—and academic institutions generally—resist drawing attention to the role specific material circumstances have played in producing "their" intellectual accomplishments.

This denial has now put the academy, and the humanities in particular, in crisis. The academy's commitment to an ideology of intellectual meritocracy valuing intellectuality for its own sake increasingly hampers its ability to persuade the "outside" public to fund it (see Plater 23; L. R. Pratt 36–37). There is simply less and less of a market for the kind of cultural capital it has traditionally produced: intellectuality, as a commodity, no longer sells. And within the academy, faculty committed to a view of their work as located outside the realm of material conditions find it difficult even to conceive of arguments against administration efforts to increase work expectations. At my own university, for example, *faculty* proposals to intensify faculty work in general education or advising, say, rarely consider what faculty will be expected to do less of in order that they may devote more attention to such matters. The very question would frame the issue as one of labor, and faculty cannot recognize their work as labor without putting at risk the class cultural status they enjoy as professional academics engaged in ostensibly non-material work. While faculty are and have always been vocal about feeling pressured, their commitment to their own status as non-laborers whose work is located outside the material realm both accounts for that pressure—when taking on projects, they often fail to consider the material demands, most obviously time, that such projects will require—and stands in the way of offering much resistance to it. John Guillory describes faculty thus straddling a "theoretical torsion" in class position between the alternatives of capitalization and proletarianization:

> the torque embodied in intellectual labor can be released in [either] direction. . . . This is to say both that knowledge, like money, is only capital when it is capitalized, when it produces the effect of *embourgeoisement*; and conversely, that knowledge can be devalued in such a way that its possessors become indistinguishable from wage-labor—a process of proletarianization marking the history of, for example, primary-school teachers and secretaries. (125)

This torsion is felt particularly by humanities faculty, thrown into crisis, Guillory argues, not because of the "politicization" of the humanities but because of their increasingly marginal role as instruments of ideological reproduction. There is, he observes, "a certain inverse relation between the organic significance of sectors of intellectual labor to the process of production [of the socioeconomic system] and the measure of work autonomy (and thus potential intellectual autonomy) granted to those sectors" (128). If humanities faculty are granted greater work and intellectual autonomy, it is because their work appears to be organically insignificant to such (re)production.[5] The explicitly political stances taken by some members of that faculty can thus be understood as an index of that inverse relation (Guillory 128–29; cf. Kramnick 90). What now places the humanities in serious crisis, according to Guillory, is the declining value of their cultural capital. While earlier humanists were responsible for producing and maintaining a useful (to the dominant socioeconomic order) ideological distinction between bourgeois and lower classes, that distinction is now effected not through that status hierarchy but through the ideology of "productivity" and "upward mobility" (134–35).

In response, humanities faculty have attempted to resuscitate the value of their cultural capital by sacrificing their work autonomy, submitting their own labor to the norms of "productivity," captured in the "publish or perish" imperative (135–36). This has led to their imprisonment in the commodity structure discussed above. However, their ideological commitment to locating their work outside the realm of the material undermines even their efforts at such productivity. While they are increasingly pressed into both "service" duties and demands for greater scholarly productivity, they have no way of addressing the material demands such service and scholarly productivity both require. To ask for more time, for example, would be to admit that their "intellectual" work was not independent of material social conditions but the product of "labor," and so to admit to their status as laborers. But whatever intellectual autonomy they now preserve can seem precious little reward for the work time demands they are now expected to meet.

"Work" in Composition

Composition, of course, occupies a marginal position in relation to English studies, the "humanities," and the academy generally. As a consequence, its experience of and responses to the torsion between capitalization and proletarianization differ from that of faculty more comfortably ensconced within these other realms. Most obviously, composition faculty do not enjoy the same degree of work or intellectual autonomy enjoyed by these other faculty (cf. E. Watkins 138). Following Guillory's argument, this can be accounted for by the perceived greater organic significance of Composition's intellectual labor to the process of socioeconomic production. Paradoxically, if Composition were thought to matter less to that process, it would enjoy greater status and greater work and intellectual autonomy. Indeed, the public furor over the proposed first-year English course at the University of Texas, Austin, highlights above all both the perceived significance of Composition's labor to the public and the consequent lesser degree of autonomy the public is willing to grant Composition. As Pierre Bourdieu observes, "Autonomy is increasingly difficult to attain and defend the further one moves away from those fields whose autonomy is protected by both the esoteric obscurity of their products and the absence of directly social 'interest' in their stakes" ("Corporatism" 104). Thus, while the public has long treated the obscurity and politicization of MLA conference paper topics as fodder for jokes, it views what happens in composition courses as no joking matter. Indeed, particularly among conservative writers, there is the expectation, even demand, that composition courses be not simply "basic" but dull routine (see, for example, MacDonald 3–4, Traub 18; cf. Coles, "Teaching Writing, Teaching Literature" 4, 13).

Compositionists have responded to the torsion between capitalization and proletarianization of their labor primarily in one of two conflicting ways, taking the form of the by now familiar debates between practitioners and scholars, teaching and research, experience and theory. On the one hand, some have attempted to "professionalize": they seek academic disciplinary status for Composition by directing their efforts at producing knowledge about writing in general on which composition "scholars" (or "researchers") can claim professional expertise. This knowledge they produce in the commodified form of publications. However, these efforts threaten to distance Composition from its material ties to and identification with teaching. This has led, as David Bartholomae has noted, to the odd phenomenon of a "career" in Composition "that has everything to do with status and identity in English and little to do with the organization, management, and evaluation of student writing, except perhaps as an administrative problem." Thus we now have specialists "in" Composition who never teach composition ("What" 23).

Alternatively, and often in response to these efforts at professionalization, others locate themselves insistently in the composition classroom, asking of any knowledge, "How can I use this in my teaching?" These faculty define their own knowledge in terms of their experience of what "works" in the classroom, and pride themselves on their dedication to their teaching and their students. In so doing, however, they increase the marginality of their position in the academy and subject themselves to ever more degrading working conditions, since their "work" is deemed not work at all but labor exploited to produce the commodity of writing "skills" and future skilled employees.

Despite the animosity of the debate between these positions, both largely accept as a given the commodification of their work as the production of *economic* exchange value in a way that distinguishes Composition from literary study, the humanities, and the academy generally. For both represent responses to a felt lack of work and intellectual autonomy not experienced in these other spheres. The absence of any parallel debate within the realm of literary study—between, say, teachers and literary theorists—registers this difference.[6] Although debates such as the "canon wars" rage in literary study, these rarely address work practices of the profession, focusing instead primarily on methodologies of interpretation and the specific texts on which to exercise those methodologies.[7] The different position of Composition and its work in relation to the academic and the larger social realm is revealed further by the resemblance of debates in Composition, indeed their intersection, with those ongoing in the "field" of primary and secondary school education between teachers and researchers, or teachers and educational administrators, and between these educators and the public.

In short, unlike literary study, the value that counts in Compositional work is rarely imagined as value "intrinsic" to the work itself, but as the economic exchange value of the commodified literacy skills which Composition is expected to produce (just as K–12 education is expected to produce skilled citizens). For that reason, just as concrete labor in industrial production is subject to redesign to meet the needs of abstract labor, for example, via "Taylorization," the concrete labor of teaching in Composition is also always at risk of being completely redesigned by the dominant. A narrow sense of the social relations of production in Composition is thus recognized—social relations in which Composition plays a distinctly subordinate role—distinguishing the place of work in Composition from work in literary study. Work in Composition is recognized for, or defined as, the production of economic capital in the form of the commodified literacy skills to meet "society's" demands (including the "demands" of other academic disciplines). Indeed, Compositionists have sometimes exploited this recognition to make greater claims for material support from society in order to address the constant laments of a "literacy crisis" (Faigley 50, 67; Nelson and Bérubé 18–19). The bargain Composition thus makes of selling its labor to others continues to overlook the full materiality of writing as social practice rather than reified textual object or isolated skill. Moreover, it also makes explicit the material conditions of intellectual work that the academy remains loath to acknowledge. This provides yet another reason for the academy to keep Composition on the margins, and reinforces its subordination to both the academy and "society." And finally, this bargain condemns those in Composition to further relinquishing control over their labor practices: accepting the challenge to produce "outcomes" invites public scrutiny of the work of composition teachers to which college and university literature teachers have never been subjected, but with which those in K–12 education are all too familiar.

While attempts to "professionalize" Composition might seem to resist such surrender by constructing a discipline of knowledge about writing "in general," even that knowledge produced is subjected to judgment by teachers and the public for the implications it has for writing instruction in ways unimaginable for the knowledge produced in literary study. Moreover, teachers' claims to professional expertise about Composition undermine their efforts to recruit others to shoulder part of the labor of teaching composition. In my own department, at least some faculty without claims to expertise in Composition have bitterly resisted efforts in the past to require them to teach one section per year of the composition course required of all first-year students. Pointing to the reputed expertise of "the composition folk" among the faculty, they confessed their own ignorance about the subject and so their unsuitability for teaching it. Thus, defining composition as a reified "subject" rather than a labor-intensive activity (indisputably far more labor-intensive than the teaching of literature) has worked against efforts at equitable labor practices. Further, defining Composition as a body of knowledge over which professionals can claim expertise has, until recently, led to the neglect of the wide range of writing practices outside the academy, in what Anne Ruggles Gere refers to as the "extracurriculum" of Composition operating in individuals' informal writing activities, community writing groups, literary clubs, lyceums, self-help groups and guides, and the like. For recognition of this extracurriculum would place writing outside the claimed territory of the professional discipline of Composition as "author" of that subject. Hence the particular angst of the debate over professionalism within Composition, fueling charges and countercharges of self-interested careerism and betrayal, exploitation and obstructionism, elitism and anti-intellectualism (see, for example, Dobrin chapter 1; Gunner, "The Fate"; and the exchange between Rouse and Gerald Graff).

Subsequent chapters chart specific manifestations of the commodification of work in Composition. Here, however, let me outline avenues by which it has attempted to resist commodification of the work with which it is most closely identified, the teaching of writing. Commodification of teaching occurs most obviously when

Composition succumbs to the temptation to define its work in terms of "outcomes" or "results." We can see such moves not only in those arguments for pedagogies that have "practical" results evidenced in the texts students produce, their grades, or their subsequent employment, but also in those arguments for pedagogies effecting socially liberatory change. It would be futile, and wrong, to ignore the relation of work in Composition to work in and on the social. But defining our work only in terms of such outcomes overlooks the location of that work within the material social process itself—for instance, the students, class size, teaching loads, teaching facilities, ongoing history, and the host of institutional, social, and personal pressures on students—and thus the overdetermined nature of the work "accomplished" at that site.[8] While I'll have more to say about this in "Politics," here it is worth observing that such a view treats the students, their skills, or their consciousness as commodities (i.e., as Composition's "products"). Thus an emphasis on pedagogical "outcomes" or "results" abstracts the labor of composition, denying its materiality by concealing the contribution of not just teachers but students, institutions, and specific social, material, historical circumstances to its accomplishments. Just as the notion of skills requirements, as Darrah observes, "abstracts people from the specific, concrete contexts in which they work by treating the workplace as a mere backdrop to their actions" (252), so this emphasis on outcomes ignores the ways in which the mere "backdrop" of a specific site of teaching and learning in fact interacts with the imagined "outcomes" or "results" reported. Further, it ignores the various other contingencies affecting what happens to these "results"—skills, competencies, changed consciousness—as the students move to other locations. As Allan Luke points out, for example, any "cultural capital" an individual acquires through literacy education "only counts and works in combination with people's *economic capital* and *social capital*" ("Getting" 307).

This commodification of teaching as the production of results has its mirror in Composition's imaginings of pedagogy as a privileged, autonomous site of work. Tom Fox notes that regardless of any social, postmodern understandings we may favor,

> composition's focus on the classroom pulls us the other way, towards idiosyncrasy, individual students and their successes,

"good" days in single classrooms. Our experience is parceled out into 50- or 75-minute classes, and we talk about how each class differs from the others. No doubt we experience our classrooms this way because of the fact that we teach in these time periods and we grade individual students. But the institutional shape of our experience and the political theories that we admire thus may work against each other—the former towards atomistic and individualist views and the latter towards multiple, social frameworks. ("Proceeding" 569)

This institutional reification of teaching experience extends not only to thinking of individual students, class meetings, and course sections but to specific pedagogies. Often framed in terms of "what works" or "worked," we isolate specific pedagogical techniques from the immediate material circumstances of their use, locating our work (and that of our students) not in the social, historical material process but in commodifications of that work. Such commodification is manifested in the design of courses, in their public presentation, and in the neglect of specific material constraints on any pedagogy. What is concealed in such commodifications is the contradiction between the undeniable location of pedagogical work in the contingencies of material social history and the representation of that work as a commodity divorced from those contingencies and the labor involved in the work.

Increasingly, however, compositionists are beginning to re-imagine, and re-present, pedagogies as strategic responses to specific situations rather than in more commodified forms. For example, accounts of basic writing pedagogies gathered in the February 1996 issue of *College Composition and Communication* insist on locating them as strategic responses to specific institutional and historical conditions (Grego and Thompson; Soliday, "From the Margins to the Mainstream"; Anokye; Duffey; Rodby). All the writers present an institutionally designated form, "basic writing," as at best a site for strategic action—most prominently, the strategy of "mainstreaming" basic writers. But all of them also imagine any "basic writing" strategy in the context of specific historical and material pressures on those students and teachers served by it: the historical "feminization" of work in composition, especially basic writing; the absence of credit granted for students' work and tuition paid for "remedial" courses; the pervasive "down-sizing" of funding for education; the "remedial" function of composition historically. Moreover, they locate their own work in the specifics of their own institutions, rejecting the application of the pedagogies they describe universally to all institutions. Rhonda Grego and Nancy Thompson report on the strategy of a writing "studio" program they developed in response to a state-mandated elimination of credit for basic writing, but caution, "The Studio is not a destination which we urge others to pursue simply as some latest trend" (82). Mary Soliday, while describing what appears to be an effective FIPSE-funded project at the City University of New York in which basic writing students are placed in "mainstream" courses, warns that "institutional politics contextualize a main-streamed course, and once the new course is no longer protected by the prestige and funding of a special grant, politics can redefine the course's original goals"; consequently, "we have to be acutely aware of our role in a potential struggle over redefining the considerable territory which constitutes remedial education within an institution" ("From the Margins" 96). For example, Soliday notes the danger that administrators might well view mainstreaming not "as a method of enhancing instruction for open admissions students, [but] for cutting costs by eliminating remedial courses and the students these courses traditionally have served" (97). Suellynn Duffey, in her response to Grego and Thompson and to Soliday, echoes such cautions about the effects of such strategies on the material lives of students and teachers, stating "neither [article] should convince us to mainstream basic writing students at our own institutions" (104). Rather, while she sees Grego and Thompson's article illustrating that "mainstreaming can work, [it] should not be seen as evidence that mainstreaming is a desirable alternative to tracking. Instead, it describes several adaptations to enforced mainstreaming, but those adaptations argue neither for nor against it" (105). And Judith Rodby ends her response by calling for more talk and writing to each other "comparing and developing a *variety* of political strategies, private and covert, deliberate and public, to preserve the integrity of our work with students and their writing" (111, emphasis mine). Rodby's call is especially important in confirming both the value and the dynamics of such discourse: while rejecting any reified notions of basic writing, she insists on the sharing of strategies to address it precisely because it is problematic—variously constituted and reconstituted and inherently strategic—rather than a problem susceptible to merely technical solution.

While these writers all refuse the commodification of their pedagogies by insisting on locating them in specific material social circumstances, John Bell's response to the issue of *College Composition and Communication* in which their work appears indicates a continuing need to insist further on such location, and suggests how even within these writings a degree of materiality is elided. While agreeing with and admiring the programs many of these writers describe, he reminds them that the "scourge of 'productivity' is upon us" (414): at his own institution, his department is half the size it was ten years ago, teaching loads are twenty-seven hours per year, and class size is capped at thirty-two students, all as part of his department's share in "desired productivity increases" resulting from budget cuts to New York's funding for higher education (412). In light of such circumstances, he offers a single criticism of these writers and of the journal *College Composition and Communication*: namely, that they "refuse to scream . . . about the brutal everyday reality so many of us and our students live" (414). The "scourge of 'productivity'" Bell sees as upon us includes not just institutional pressures to teach more students to write "better papers" and get jobs or "better" ones with significantly "downsized" means—more and larger classes per instructor, less pay and support for instruction (restrictions on clerical staff, paper supplies, photocopying, computer facilities, library space, job security, professional training); it also includes students working more hours and taking more credits per term (to be more "cost-effective") and demanding more bang for their (higher and higher) tuition while having less time to devote to their writing (Lauter 76–79); and it includes the demand for teachers to devise and describe pedagogies in ways that "sell," that is, that meet with receptive audiences either in scholarly conferences and publications or in textbooks or in the larger public arena.

In short, for teachers like Bell, the "torsion" between the capitalization and proletarianization of Composition's intellectual labor has already been resolved in the direction of the latter: the "knowledge" represented by Composition is so devalued as to render its workers indistinguishable from wage-labor. Indeed, according to Bell, adjunct faculty at his institution (outnumbering non-adjuncts two to one, and teaching more than half the course sections) are paid "as hourly laborers, and no pay is allotted for other than classroom instruction," for example, class preparation, let alone faculty development (412). From such a perspective, debating the politics of representations of students, say, or advocating attention to students' "psychic needs" can seem like so much toying on the bridge of the Titanic. Hence Bell's question: "what does what [these writers] say, what does most of what *CCC* says, or what most of our composition scholarship says, what do these enunciations have to do, how are they connected, with the everyday realities that most of us live?" (413).

There is, of course, one strategy which remains largely unexplored within Composition to the proletarianization Bell decries: unions.[9] Primary and secondary school teachers—those with whom composition teachers are most closely associated in the eyes of the academy and the public—*have* unionized to improve their working conditions and combat and protect themselves from the "scourge of productivity" Bell laments. Historically, however, that strategy has had mixed results. Through unions following the "industrial" model, these teachers have gained in bargaining power over wages and hours, but they have also increasingly surrendered to bureaucratic rationalization of their concrete work activities, especially under pressure from an increasingly managerial model of downsizing (Carlson 91–102; A. Luke, "Getting" 310). The problem is that while unionizing does foreground the materiality of certain aspects of teaching, it leaves others unaddressed (A. Luke, "Getting" 309). Positively, unions undermine the class distinction between intellectual and non-intellectual, "manual" labor maintained through claims to "professional" expertise, claims that in fact have stood in the way of improving teachers' working conditions. As James Carey, secretary-treasurer of the Industrial Union Department of the AFL-CIO, argued in speaking to the 1962 NEA national convention,

One of the prime troubles—if not the chief curse of the teaching industry is precisely that word "profession." That term, as it is used so frequently here, implies that your craft is somewhat above this world of ours; it implies a detachment, a re-

moteness from the daily battle of the streets, in the neighborhoods and cities. . . . If the charwomen of the schools have
sense enough to band together and organize and negotiate
contracts, and the teachers do not, I wonder sometimes who
should have the degrees. (quoted in Carlson 96–97)

I have argued above that Composition has enjoyed less intellectual
and work autonomy than others in the humanities and the academy generally because of its perceived greater organic significance
to socioeconomic production, a significance it shares with primary
and secondary school education. Precisely for that reason, composition teachers would appear to have the least to lose from embracing
trade unionism, for Composition's claims to professional academic
status have done little to improve its working conditions. In Carey's
terms, the "detachment," or "remoteness," from "this world of ours
. . . the battle of the streets" inherent in such claims has served not
as a justification for greater autonomy but for neglect of those conditions. As Judith Rodby argues, the ideological nostalgia for a
utopia of good students and dedicated, "professional" teachers aid-
ing in the production of ideal texts "turns the focus from the conditions [of employment for part-time temporary faculty with minimal
job security] to their dedication to students." While deeming faculty
"saintly for their dedication as spirit guides" to students, this hides
"the reality that the conditions under which we teach, the economic
equation of no-credit for student labor, are controlled" by offices of
the administration functioning paternalistically (109; for another
account of attempts to offer saintly status as compensation for poor
working conditions, see Nelson 176, 208–9).

But historically, at least in the United States, while unions
have rejected claims of saintliness to achieve decent working conditions, they have left largely unchallenged just such paternalistic relations. The focus of collective bargaining on contracts has
increased the likelihood of top-down rationalization of concrete labor practices, as these come to be spelled out explicitly in contracts
(Carlson 98). Indeed, as Gary Rhoades has argued in his study of
faculty union contracts, faculty unions frequently hesitate to negotiate specific policies and practices to prevent faculty from being
subjected to greater managerial control and rationalization, though
management, too, sometimes uses the absence of negotiated policy

as license to exercise its discretion (14–15, 175). Unions have come primarily to engage at best in a "negative," reactive politics, resisting specific "reforms," reacting to plans already drafted by management (Carlson 99; Rhoades 261).

Rhoades' analysis of college retrenchment illustrates this negative politics. Academic managers have far greater discretion in restructuring and retrenching than is commonly recognized. Union contracts simply complicate, and thereby discourage, retrenchment by instituting elaborate procedures for order of layoff, notice, reassignment, retraining, and recall (117, chapter 3 passim). Note that this "negative" politics essentially cedes meaningful faculty participation in school decisions. For example, in those institutions Rhoades considers, decisions on whether and how to use specific instructional technology have largely been made by administrators, not faculty, including decisions to use such technology to eliminate faculty (189, 194). Professional organizations of faculty, by contrast, have often ignored material considerations altogether, relegating such matters to the unions. It is assumed, as Allan Luke observes, that "pedagogy and curriculum can be debated in intellectual and professional forums independent of debates about industrial, teaching/learning conditions in schools and classrooms, which are [believed to be] rightly the domains of collective bargaining and industrial negotiations" ("Getting" 309; cf. Rhoades 269, 271).

Debate over the "Wyoming Resolution" illustrates the limitations of this splitting of concerns.[10] For example, in a critique of the "fate" of that resolution, Jeanne Gunner notes that the original draft of the resolution emphasized unfair salaries and working conditions of postsecondary writing teachers and the ill effects of those on students, and called for establishing standards for salary and working conditions and grievance procedures. However, in the final version, "Statement of Principles and Standards for the Postsecondary Teaching of Writing," attention to such matters was replaced with an insistence on preserving the traditional privileges of tenured academics (Gunner 108–9). In Gunner's words, "instead of specific material conditions—low pay, high course load, etc.—and a particular course of action—letters of censure—the issues have become abstractions: academic freedom and job security" (112). Thus, for her, while the original Resolution is about "improving real people's working lives," the final Conference on College Composition and Communication (CCCC) document is about mandating "a rigid professional track" which implicitly excludes part-time and adjunct faculty, i.e., anyone "whose expertise [in composition] has developed outside the typical, traditional scholarly track" (117).

I address the discourse of academic professionalism more directly in chapter 5. Here, let me observe that both Gunner's position and the position of the CCCC, as she represents it, rely on and reinforce a false dichotomy between "working conditions" of "real people" and concerns of Composition as a "profession." In these arguments, one must choose to focus on either the former or the latter. Thus, academic freedom and job security, because of their identification with "professional" concerns, come to be seen as "abstractions" rather than matters of "improving real people's working lives."[11] But obscuring the materiality of such professional concerns puts at risk not just those matters but also the matters of teaching load and salary. Academic freedom without the material means to practice it means little, just as an improved salary without such freedom is both unlikely to transpire and unlikely to mean much either. The move to professionalize risks the first; the move to unionize has risked the second. While unionizing has foregrounded the material needs of teachers, it has largely assented to commodification of the labor of education, neglecting the full sense of the work of education as a complex material social process involving the specific conditions, needs, desires, and actions of students and communities. In this commodification, work comes to be seen only as labor enacted on behalf of institutions *through* teachers *on* students to the dominant's specifications, aimed at the production of abstract "skills" or "abilities." In this commodification of teaching labor, what is produced in teaching is abstracted from the contingencies of what teachers, students, and material and historical conditions contribute to that work.

This is not to condemn unionizing as a specific strategy to improve teachers' working conditions but to recognize the limitations of past such efforts so that those taking up that strategy might better address those limitations. Thus while Bell is right to remind us of the need to address "basic" working conditions, a strict focus on just those conditions, even screaming about them, would in effect do too little, for it would fail to intervene in the social relations and processes by which Composition's concrete labor is converted to abstract labor, relations and processes integral to the "scourge of productivity." Bell reminds us that, of course, that very intervention is not a matter of some teachers possessing greater intellectuality, dedication, insight, or ability: the specific programmatic interventions described by Grego and Thompson and by Soliday, though often in response to material deprivations, were also made possible by specific material support (e.g., a FIPSE grant or decent staff-to-student ratios). It is impossible to overstress the importance of such conditions as necessary to any programmatic intervention, since any neglect of the role of such conditions in producing such interventions contributes to the abstraction and commodification of the intellectual labor represented in reports of them like Soliday's, Grego and Thompson's, and countless others, that is, to the "capitalization" of that labor. We contribute to that abstraction when we fail to recognize such conditions.

But we also need to insist on locating the work of programmatic intervention in the full range of specific material social conditions to prevent the all too easy slide from a position like Bell's decrying and protesting the scourge of productivity to one of debilitating cynicism. Such a slide leads to taking the dominant's capitalization of our work as evidence of full containment by, or capitulation to, the dominant, thereby confusing the exchange value of that work for its full potential use value. Peter Vandenberg, for example, noting the irony of written critiques of the publishing system in composition studies (including his own, and applicable to the text you are now reading), argues that every such critique "is already at the point of circulation inscribed within the ideology of research . . . unavoidably yield[ing] symbolic capital for its author and invit[ing] charges of hypocrisy even as it underwrites the system." Thus, for Vandenberg, "if the working conditions of writing teachers are to change, they will change as a result of physical and symbolic action outside the order of academic publishing" ("The Work of Composition"). Of course, it would be foolish to ignore the limitations of academic publishing as an agent of change, or the subordination of the values of concrete labor to the value accrued at the point of circulation (cf. Ohmann, foreword xiv–xvi). However, to accept the values abstracted from such labor by the dominant as its *full* value is to collude with that process of abstraction. In short, to do so is to collude with what Williams identifies as the dominant's "seizure" of the social, a seizure that excludes "the full range of human practice" (*Marxism* 125). We need to bear in mind that "the social" is not fully contained by the dominant, nor by its definition of the "social." If the dominant recognizes only exchange value, manifest in circulation (what is "capitalized"), we can effect resistance only by calling attention to other values not manifest in circulation. As even Evan Watkins, one of those most responsible for bringing the term *circulation* back into consideration in English studies, observes, there is a danger in overemphasizing circulation to the neglect of production and reception (8). What is needed is not a kind of balance among consideration of each of these but intervention at the point of their interrelations: in Watkins' terms, the relative freedom granted to the concrete labor of ideological work, and the gap, or *durée*, between that work and its conversion to abstract labor (232–33). Moreover, we need not only to investigate and pursue specific ways of exploiting that freedom and those gaps, but, as it were, to "keep on keeping on," to keep up the pressure (233–34). And further, as Watkins argues, we need to resist idealizations of the "new" serving to commodify a specific practice as a technique to effect social change. As he observes, the realization of oppositional sociocultural values "never occurs immediately, . . . not as a direct consequence of classroom practices in a particular course, a letter of recommendation, a decision about a job candidate, a reading of a literary text, an explosively 'radical' theoretical essay, or indeed any concrete labor practice in and of itself" (235). We succumb to such idealizations, and thus become vulnerable to cynicism, when we expect such immediate, measurable "outcomes" of any work thus commodified, whether it be an academic scholarly essay or a pedagogical technique.

To return to the February 1996 *CCC* gathering, the writers' insistence on locating their ideas in the specific material institutional conditions and histories of their experience helps to encourage both resistance to the commodification of the practices they describe, and so to the "capitalization" of their labor, and exploration of alternative strategies, appropriate to other locations, to reach comparable goals. Further, their writings show how it is possible not simply to negotiate the terms by which we will be exploited but to counter the ways in which our work is converted to abstract labor. Most obviously, they point to the institutional mechanisms by which the work of composition teachers and students is or is not valued, through course designations, credit hours granted or denied, and so on—that is, what is and is not named work, and the valuations (or devaluations) granted it. Grego and Thompson, for example, discover through their experience with a Writing "Studio"—a workshop where small groups of writing students meet weekly with experienced teachers to work on writing for a required composition course—the ways in which Composition aims "to give an institutionally-acceptable name and place to our attention to the personal and interpersonal mental processes that compositionists . . . engage in with student writers and student-writing—and to thereby safeguard that work" (64). And Judith Rodby describes how her experience and that of her colleagues at California State University, Chico led them to abandon terms like *basic writing* and *remediation* as they came to realize "[w]e could not make crucial curricular and pedagogical changes under this rubric," for "basic writing was, more than anything else, a function of the institution, a category that worked primarily to promote other institutional functions, such as placement testing" (108). Mainstreaming all students requesting freshman writing into a one-semester writing course and using institutionally required placement tests to enroll some of these in an adjunct workshop, she reports, enabled all students to receive academic credit for their work while providing a space, in the workshop, for some of the kind of work also necessary to writing which the institution does not recognize (what Grego and Thompson note is often dismissed as the "merely personal") (Rodby 110).[12]

In pursuing such strategies, these writers attempt to intervene in the means by which the concrete labor of composition classrooms and writing workshops is abstracted into surplus value: academic credit, grades, degrees, and individual and institutional claims of "productivity." They thus negotiate simultaneously both working conditions and the meaning/valuation of the work "accomplished" within those conditions. In so doing, they challenge the distinction usually made within the academy between intellectual labor— whether conducted in the classroom or in the scholar's study—and the material conditions of that labor, and so undermine the boundaries distinguishing "one's own" work, the work of and for the institution, and the work of students. I have been arguing in this chapter that in order to address the material conditions of our labor, we must abandon such distinctions, in effect making it our work to articulate the interpenetration of all these as constitutive of our work. This will require initially foregrounding the ways in which contradictions embedded in distinctions between intellectual and non-intellectual labor and the commodification of intellectual labor play out at the site of Composition. In beginning such work in this chapter, however, I have largely neglected students, treating the work of Composition primarily as that in which only faculty engage. If in so doing I have implicitly maintained a dominant view distinguishing students from that work, the burden of the following chapter, "Students," will be to challenge precisely that distinction.

Chapter 2

STUDENTS

A student agrees with me how important it is to carefully reread a text that he is to write his paper about, but then shrugs as he explains that, since he's working full time and is often on mandatory overtime, he won't be able to do either the reading or the writing. Another, after listening quietly to my praise of her progress and my hopes for her academic career, tells me there will be no such career, because neither she nor her family can afford to pay her tuition bill.

A s many writers have noted, much of Composition's literature identifies students as the "Other," marginal in relation to teachers and to the academy generally (Heilker, "students"). This displacement of students, while in clear contradiction to their centrality to the work of composition teachers, is consonant both with identifying academic work strictly with the production of commodified texts ("our" work, with which the concrete labor of teaching interferes) and with the commodification of teaching itself. For students—as living, thinking, speaking human beings changing not just every semester but from class meeting to class meeting and often within class meetings—constitute some of the most intransigent reminders of the materiality of academic work.

Representations of students in Composition (and elsewhere) elide that materiality by locating students on maps that define levels of intellectual and cognitive development; degrees of writing experience; racial, ethnic, gender or class identity; discursive realms; an oral-literate "divide"; field-dependent and field-independent cognitive styles, or left/right brain hemisphere thinking; and so on. Both naming and fixing the salient identifying features of students, these representations aim at answering the pedagogical common sense directive to "begin where the students are" so that teachers can then turn to investigating where they should be taken, why, and how.

In *Writing Students*, an examination of representations of students in the genre of "testimonials" about teaching experiences that dominates Composition's literature, Marguerite Helmers critiques both how and why Composition has represented its students as it has. Helmers' analysis of these testimonials, like many other critiques of representations of students, reveals that students are predominantly characterized by what they lack—maturity, ability, interest, creativity, knowledge, experience, and so on. More striking, students are represented in testimonials "as if they simply *are*, and frequent appeals to shared experience with deviant students among teachers indicates a widespread assumption that there is an essential, transhistorical student" (2). In these testimonials, such an assumption extends to teachers and classrooms as well, with teachers cast in the role of "pedagogical Everyman," and classroom experience posited "as transhistorical . . . easily translatable to other classrooms" (29). Helmers links this essentializing of students with an imperialist agenda: identifying students with specific characteristics enables teachers to domesticate and govern them, as "predictable" and so susceptible to systems of correction (48–49). Moreover, this treatment of students, teachers, and classroom experiences furthers the commodification of the teaching method espoused in the testimonial. As she explains,

[W]riters of testimonials traditionally construct themselves as pedagogical heroes who enter the chaotic world of the freshman composition classroom to set things right with their methods. . . . Claims for success are enhanced when teaching techniques are played off of unresisting and mute figures, and therefore the stock character of the student is a passive entity upon whom pedagogy operates. (19)

In other words, for the commodification of the method, it is crucial in these accounts that the method be seen as easily translatable to other students, other classrooms. This is accomplished through positing students, classrooms, and ultimately the teacher herself as transhistorical, uniform, easily recognizable by readers. The popularity of these testimonials, Helmers argues, attests both to the needs of teachers looking for a quick fix to the adverse conditions in which they work (3) and to features of the testimonial itself as a commodity: it is a text relatively cheap to produce (requiring little research) and unlikely to be subject to critique, given its foundation in personal experience (4).

In these testimonials, the writing of students, significantly, is itself seen not as work but as evidence embodying the identified essential characteristics of the students: their level of ability, creativity, interest, beginner status, etc. (9). In this way, Helmers' analysis aligns with Mike Rose's earlier critique of many representations of students in terms of cognitive lack, namely those identifying students in terms of field-dependent/independent cognitive styles, brain hemisphericity, stage of cognitive development, or orality/literacy ("Narrowing the Page"). For, as Rose argues, first, such representations "lead us from a close investigation of the production of written discourse and toward general, wide-ranging processes whose link to writing has, for the most part, been *assumed rather than demonstrated*"; second, the theories "avert or narrow our gaze from the immediate social and linguistic conditions in which the student composes: the rich interplay of purpose, genre, register, textual convention, and institutional expectation" ("Narrowing" 294, 295). In other words, aside from the questionable accuracy of these representations and the ethically dubious interests they serve, they draw attention away from the actual writing in which students engage—not just their writing as textual objects, but as a material social activity, as work. Instead, that writing appears only as a trace of the writers' salient characteristics—most often, as both Helmers and Rose observe, their specific cognitive lacks.

While I would view this occlusion of the work of student writing as one of the most damaging of these representations, it is not the one on which most critiques of representation have focused. Rather, the issue of representation has been defined in terms of ethics and accuracy. Much of Rose's argument, for example, is taken up with demonstrating that compositionists attempting to understand their students in terms of concepts drawn from the fields of cognitive psychology, neuroscience, and literacy studies tend both to produce reductive characterizations of their students' cognition and to ignore the lack of consensus among the scholars in these fields about those concepts. Similarly, Helmers challenges both the accuracy of such representations of students and the interests they serve by pointing to disparities among the specific "lacks" for which students have been faulted historically, and by showing how the terms of these representations tend to correlate with the specific interests of a given historical period (e.g., in the 1960s, students were said to lack creativity; in the '90s, they are said to lack enlightenment from racism, sexism, and homophobia).

Helmers recognizes that "[i]t is quite possible . . . there may be no escape from representation" but asks that we join her in interrogating the particular purposes, uses, and interests served by the representations of students and styles of representations that we produce (149). It should be clear that I agree with Helmers on both the inescapability of representation and the value of engaging in such critiques. But efforts directed solely at challenging the accuracy and ethics of representations of students retain a view of the work of Composition as itself operating outside the material social process, and thus leave unchallenged the commodification of that work. The act of "mapping" students positions teachers, and classroom teaching, above that map. In such mapping, teachers, as professionals, are charged with identifying the problem with the students and devising and applying a remedy. Like medical patients in the traditional professional/client model of medicine, students are to be healed; or, like chess pieces, they are to be moved (according to their salient characteristics) across the board, rather than moving themselves (though it's recognized they are subject to being moved by dominant social forces, e.g. television, a culture of violence, etc.). And to be moved, they must temporarily *be removed from the map*. Teachers and teaching are themselves located not on the map but at a site outside it, acting on those brought to that site. The fixing of students in and through representations of them must, of course, be reconciled with the pedagogical method to be sold, and the aims and procedures of that method must themselves be justified. Wherever students are located, teachers must explain where they would move them (what they should become), why, and how. But the debate remains one framed in terms of accuracy, ethics, and technique.

The cultural materialist alternative for which I would argue would insist, instead, not only on the political, strategic nature of specific representations but on the necessity of their being so—that is, it would insist on both recognizing the inevitably contingent character of representations and understanding one's choice of representation in terms of the specific material contingencies of one's teaching. And these would include the agency of students, imagined not as passive bundles of fixed characteristics, varying only in the degree of pliability or resistance they offer to one's pedagogical techniques, but as participants, also subject to material contingencies, in the construction of the work conducted in the composition classroom. That is to say, I would argue for representing students as above all else workers, working on themselves, Composition, the academy, and the social generally.

That is not, of course, a dominant representation of students in Composition. Even those arguments representing students, or some students, as "working class" or in terms of students' future career aspirations, treat students' relation to work as indirect: it is something from the past affecting their behavior during their temporary stay in Composition, or something for which Composition may prepare them (or with which it interferes).[1] Students are viewed as products of the social, to be worked *on* for the social, but not, as students, already working in and with the material social process together with their teachers. As I discuss below, this elision of the material sociality of the students as students, part and parcel of the denial of the materiality of the academy generally, is perhaps best illustrated by the efforts of teachers to engage the "sociality" of students in their pedagogies, though it is also illustrated, more graphically, by the pervasive inattention in Composition to students' unmet material needs, including those signaled by and arising from the status of many of them as working adults (often employed full-time): lack of financial support, lack of access to computers or paper or printers, lack of time, lack of health and health insurance, lack of child care, lack of sleep, lack of quiet, lack of housing (see Benjamin 59; Lauter 76–79). *These* are "lacks" in students rarely addressed or even acknowledged, despite the ongoing, profound, and quite immediate effects they have on what students can accomplish in our classes.

In the attempts of Compositionists to address the sociality of students, such material aspects of their sociality remain hidden. This is in keeping, however, with a more general acceptance of limited, if dominant, conceptualizations of "the social" pervading Composition's understanding of its work. These are conceptions, first of all, from which materiality in its most basic sense has been stripped. Further, however, Composition's understanding of sociality is in accord with what Raymond Williams has observed as a tendency in analyses of culture and society to reduce the social to "fixed forms" (*Marxism* 129). In this reduction, "the social is always past, in the sense that it is always formed" (128). In Composition, the social is recognized only as something already formed, in the past, which affects what students may bring with them *to* the course (e.g., literacy skills or lacks), not as a process operating during and within the course. Williams warns, further, that if the social is represented by the fixed, explicit "known relationships, institutions, formations, positions—all that is present and moving, all that escapes or seems to escape from the fixed and the explicit and the known, is grasped and defined as the personal" (128). Applied to the anecdotes presented in the headnote to this chapter, the dominant mode for addressing the difficulties such students "present," when they are addressed at all, is in terms of "personal" problems—difficulties of the individual student beyond the realm of Composition (see Fox, *Defending* 10–17).

We see evidence of this limited conception of the social operating in Composition's representations of its students and teaching, and in its view of student work. To return again to the metaphor of mapping, students are represented not so much as moving themselves but as placed in some fixed location. This holds whether the representation characterizes students as an elite or as oppressed, as middle-class Americans or as foreigners, as skilled writers or beginners, and whether the pedagogy espoused aims at giving students the skills employers ostensibly want or at encouraging social resistance, at giving them an escape from pressure or training in how to handle it. For despite these differences, all such representations effectually occlude a full sense of the social as an *ongoing*, heterogeneous material *process* operating within as well as outside student consciousness, the site of teaching, and writing. Instead, the social is imagined in monolithic terms as something acting on, or through, students, or teaching. In short, these "reify"—treating as self-evident, independent, and stable entities or objects of study—the student, the "social," power, the classroom, even "difference." The alternative challenge Composition faces is how teachers and students can confront the ways in which each material act of writing and reading *mediates,* in the sense of actively re-forming and transforming, and is mediated by social identification, difference and power, both responding to and reconstructing or revising these.

Mapping Classrooms, Students, and the Social in Composition Pedagogy

Unable to deny the relation of its work to the "social," representations of pedagogy present the course experience as a utopian space to which to escape *from* the social or from which to act *on* the social. This is the case whether the social is defined in terms of demands for writing skills, hierarchical academic social relations, or cultural conflict. This occurs not only in accounts of "expressivist" pedagogies, often criticized for their denial of the sociality of writing, but in representations of "practical," collaborative, and contact-zone pedagogies explicitly based on theorizing writing as social. In all these, the social is imagined in dematerialized fashion: it is seen as operating *either* outside or inside the classroom, rather than being recognized as always already both within as well as outside the classroom. And it is imagined as operating uniformly—identified with the "fixed forms" of institutional demands (for conventionally correct writing, say, or for collaborative work or recognition of difference)—rather than in contradictory ways befitting the conflicted, processual nature of the social. In all these accounts, the task of the pedagogy is then to reconcile its work with, or to escape from, the social, so conceived. Similarly, Composition's representations of students locate the social not as operating within as well as outside students in contradictory ways but as operating uniformly either outside or inside student consciousness. In such accounts of pedagogy, students appear as fixed in their intentions, desires, identities, or needs, to then be reconciled with (or to) a similarly monolithic, uniform, and static conception of the social.

For example, those pedagogies touted as "practical" or "realistic" reconcile students' desires and the pressures of the "practical business" of the "real world" by equating individual student writers' desires with the demands of that world, which are themselves treated as fixed. One teacher asserts, for example, that her students "*want* to learn how to write research papers, because here . . . most upperclassmen do so every semester" (Desy 15, my emphasis; see also Campbell and Meier 30). Jeff Smith argues that college students are in college as a means to joining a social elite. Noting that admission to college itself constitutes an elite distinct from the general population, Smith argues that teachers "are ethically bound by [these] students' own aims, even if those aims seem uncomfortably close to elite values" ("Students' " 304, 317). And similarly, Lynn Z. Bloom, observing that "[l]ike it or not, . . . we are a nation of Standard English," argues we should teach it rather than arguing for the legitimacy of other forms of English, because "students themselves want and expect their work to be conducted in Standard English; their own concept of the language they should use reflects the linguistic standards of the communities in which they expect to live and work after earning their degrees" (670).

In such arguments, official consciousness is taken to represent fully what is emergent in students' practical consciousness, and institutional standards and practices are both equated with the social and imagined as fixed. Such an approach assumes a false uniformity to student consciousness: it overwrites the articulation of any emergent oppositional consciousness by tuning in only the voicing of official consciousness. This is not to deny that in some sense students do want to learn to produce what schools or society seem to demand—whether it be research papers, Edited American English, or a smiling face. But it has to be recognized that those desires are socially produced, and so neither inherent nor universal but historical. Moreover, they are not necessarily the full, uniform story—students may also, and simultaneously, want to change the demands society is placing on them, even to change who decides what is to be demanded of whom—desires which themselves also are socially produced, once one recognizes that the social is not monolithic but heterogeneous. Similarly, the fixed forms of society's "demands"—whether represented by college admissions standards, research paper assignments, or conventions of Edited American English—have also to be recognized as socially produced and therefore subject to change. Thus while it is vital to recognize current such demands and pressures on students, it is equally vital to see these, too, as not fixed but themselves subject to pressure and change.

More common are a second set of pedagogies that allow for the possibility of difference between official forms and practical consciousness yet sidestep any confrontation between these. The sidestep is typically achieved in one of two ways: either meaning is posited as existing outside a society's language practices (and thus a writer's conformity to such practices is thought to have no impact on her autonomy), or the introduction or acknowledgment of the effect of social pressures on the writer is delayed. Such pedagogies allow more room for the contradiction to play out between the imagined autonomy of the individual student and social pressures part of the "practical business" of the "real world." This contradiction appears most directly in critiques of more "practical" pedagogies. In such critiques the student is imagined both as already having achieved (autonomous) Authorship and as still emerging.

For example, in a study of teachers' responses to student writing, Nancy Sommers criticizes teachers' comments for typically distracting students from "*their own purposes in writing a particular text.* . . . appropriat[ing] the text from the student by confusing the student's purpose in writing the text with [the teacher's] own purpose in commenting" (149). Rather than "reading and responding to the meaning of a [student] text," she notes, "we correct our students' writing. We need to reverse this approach" (154). Invoking the training teachers have in reading and interpreting literary texts for meaning, she advocates that we "act upon the same set of assumptions in reading student texts" (154). That is, we need, it seems, to treat students as Authors, with autonomous intentions, separate from the demands of institutions and other representatives of the social, though to do so consistently would mean, in effect, the reduction of comments to the appreciative, and, more significantly, to denying the contract to be changed to which students' enrollment in college testifies.

This call for honoring students' "own purposes" and meaning as Authors conflicts with other advice: "Instead of finding errors or showing students how to patch up parts of their texts," Sommers goes on to say, "we need to *sabotage* our students' conviction that the drafts they have written are complete and coherent. . . . forcing students back into the chaos, back to the point where they are shaping and restructuring their meaning" (154, my emphasis). Such sabotage hardly squares with the attitudes teachers have been trained to take toward literary texts, respecting their completeness and coherence and the Authors' intentions, however inscrutable. But the contradiction here lies not so much with Sommers but between an idealized notion of autonomous authorship and the actual specific material social practice of writing—for both students and those erstwhile canonized Authors. Sommers attempts to resolve the contradiction by identifying it as "confusion of process and product: what one has to say about the process is different from what one has to say about the product" (154). But this distinction isolates a "composing process" from the larger material social process in which any textual "production" takes place. In the history of canonized works, for example, the full "composing process" includes a plethora of conflicting intentions, editions, corrections, and receptions given texts, in spite of their subsequent canonization into singular form (the product) taught as being true to what are imagined as similarly singular, original, authorial intentions (see Orgel). In the case of students, their full "composing process" would have to include the location of the students in a specific composition course, with the variety of material constraints on their writing and writing intentions that would accompany such a location, in addition to the full panoply of specific and changing material historical conditions attending individual students, such as those attested to in the anecdotes presented in the chapter headnote. These conditions contribute both to the production of student intentions and to shifts in these in response to the conditions of the specific pedagogy and teacher. But typically, "what students truly want"—that is, the student's self—is imagined as fixed, uniform, and autonomous, even when it remains inaccessible to the student, rather than being seen as socially produced, the site of struggle between official and practical consciousness played out in the material process of writing. The problem is not that it is wrong for writers either to plunge back into the "chaos" or to strive for writing that is complete, "correct," and coherent. Rather, the problem lies with the failure to recognize such desires as being socially produced. That failure can result only in doomed attempts to judge both of these desires in terms of their accord with what is imagined to be an autonomous individual desire rather than an acceptance of them as part of the struggle of writing as a material social practice.

The use of distinguishing between "process" and "product" in order to resolve the contradiction between granting student autonomy while rejecting its material enactment in "drafts" also appears in course designs that delay attention to matters of formal conventions of writing only to introduce these later in the course or the students' careers as givens to which students must then conform their thoughts. These matters are then introduced in the name of satisfying the demands of unspecified "readers" or "employers" or the academic institution itself (often in the ritual of "exit" examinations). As proponents of more "practical" "nuts and bolts" pedagogies (and their sympathizers in the public) charge, such courses can seem at best irresponsible, at worst hypocritical, in not attending to such demands from the start. Further, such courses perpetuate a conception of the individual and the social as more static and monolithic than, in fact, they are, and so contribute to students' sense of the ultimate inevitability of acceding to the demands of currently dominant elements of the social. Regardless of the intentions of the students and teachers involved, such pedagogies, as critics have argued, can thus lead ultimately to accommodating rather than altering those demands (Lu, "Conflict"; Wall and Coles).

Peter Elbow, for example, argues that he aims in his pedagogy to help students "see themselves as writers," at least in his first-year writing courses ("Being a Writer" 73). While admitting that "writers must acknowledge that in the end readers get to decide whether their words will be read or bought," he wants to devote the writing course primarily to letting students as writers "take some time for themselves" (76–77), away from the demands of readers, including teachers. As he says in distinguishing his approach from David Bartholomae's, he would "hold back much more" from critiquing students' writing, believing that "the most precious thing I can do is provide spaces where I don't also [in addition to the culture] do [students'] thinking for them" ("Response" 90, 91). Thereby, he claims, he can "cultivate in the classroom some tufts of what grows wild outside" ("Response" 90).

Like the strategy of prairie preservationists who set off and cultivate "wild" prairie vegetation and "wildlife," this strategy provides a "controlled" environment concealing the operation of that control, thus simultaneously responding to and concealing its labor and location in the material realm. We can see such denials operating in Elbow's account of how he'd respond to a student's paper. He would, he says, "try to help her make up her own mind where to take [the paper]. So if she wanted to make her paper 'perfect' [by adding detail, voice and color] . . . , I would try to help her." Not, however, wanting her to want to make her paper "perfect," he adds, in what he describes as "crucial" for him, that he would "try to remove all pressure to make papers perfect," for example, taking out the pressure of grades ("Response" 91). But that "removal" of pressure itself represents a different kind of pressuring, an effort to shape what it is the student "wants" that denies its work as social pressure. And it denies that the student's desire to make her paper "perfect," as well as her concept of what constitutes a "perfect" paper, is clearly socially produced. It is a learned desire rather than one originating with her, just as her possible decision to abandon that aim, given Elbow's removal of grading pressure, would also be socially produced rather than evidence of wild nature finally given sway.

Thus, while this strategy presents itself as opposed to those giving explicit play to social pressures, thereby avoiding contradictions between individual desires and those pressures, in fact, it exacerbates them. As Bartholomae has argued in his long debate with Elbow, expressivism is "part of a much larger project to preserve and reproduce the figure of the author [as] an independent, self-creative, self-expressive subjectivity" ("Writing" 65). The problem of the "process" or expressivist pedagogies thus lays in their denial of the material, social, and historical operating within and outside the classroom, and also, and more significantly, within as well as outside student consciousness. Instead, the classroom experience, and the teacher and writer, are redefined as free-floating, privileged sites discrete from material contingencies of the curriculum, the economy, and past, ongoing, and future history. The pedagogical commodity is touted for its "removal" of any intrusion of these into the classroom.

What makes all such courses problematic is the distinction they maintain between the individual and the social—between ideas, needs, and desires imagined as "one's own" and demands imagined to come from somewhere "outside," and between the course as a space allowing for the pursuit of individual desires, and those "outside" pressures. That distinction makes a fetish of specific textual forms, denying the possibilities both that "personal" writing is socially inscribed and that individual students may well have "personal" interests articulated in more "academic" writing. In maintaining that distinction, such courses also maintain the class distinction between the work of art, encouraged inside the course, and the work of labor, produced for others, while accepting both types of work in writing as being aimed ultimately at the production of a commodity—"personal" or "academic" writing (or its experience). In short, such pedagogies risk reifying writing, transforming it from a dynamic process of social struggle to a self-evident, fixed object. Not surprisingly, this reification is often accompanied for both teachers and students with a sense of profound alienation and bad faith (see C. Freedman 80). The work produced in the classroom comes to be seen as an artificial, and temporary, "escape" from social demands: in Bartholomae's terms, students are made "suckers" ("Reply" 128).

More recent strategies which identify the social *with* the classroom, such as collaborative and contact-zone pedagogies, despite their difference from each other and from expressivist and process pedagogies, nonetheless also imagine the classroom as utopian—not, however, as a space to escape from the social but as a privileged, dematerialized location from which to act on the social. Collaborative pedagogies, despite their breaks from expressivism in their insistence on the inherently social construction of knowledge, mirror expressivist pedagogies both in their attempts to create a zone free of power relations within the classroom and in their denial of the labor in producing such a zone. Collaborative pedagogies are aimed at fighting the academy's traditional relations of hierarchical authority by creating more democratic relations in the classroom (see Bruffee, "Collaborative Learning" 636; Trimbur, "Consensus" 605). But collaborative pedagogies differ from expressivist pedagogies in their resolute insistence on the sociality of writing (and reading).[2] Writing is likened to conversation, requiring by definition more than one party. As Bruffee, the foremost proponent of collaborative learning in Composition, puts it, "If thought is internalized conversation, then writing is internalized conversation re-externalized" ("Collaborative Learning" 641). The argument for teaching writing as collaborative is thus twofold: it will promote more egalitarian, democratic relations within the classroom, and to teach writing as other than collaborative is to give a false sense of the actual practice of writing. It thereby marries an appeal to democratic relations with an appeal to "practicality." As Bruffee puts it,

> In business and industry, . . . and in professions such as medicine, law, engineering, and architecture—where to work is to learn or fail—collaboration is the norm. All that is new in collaborative learning, it seems, is the systematic application of collaborative principles to that last bastion of hierarchy and individualism, the American college classroom. ("Collaborative Learning" 647)

In place of such hierarchy and individualism, collaborative pedagogies attempt to create a social context of "a community of status equals: peers," the kind of community in and for which, Bruffee claims, most people in business, government, and the professions mainly write ("Collaborative Learning" 642).

As critics have observed, it is precisely in this imagining of "community" that collaborative pedagogies run into trouble (see Harris, *Teaching* chapter 5; Lu, "Conflict and Struggle"; Trimbur, "Consensus"; Ede and Lunsford 112–16, 119; Gee, Hull, and Lankshear 64–65). Indeed, the "marriage" of democratic aspirations and "practicality" seals over a contradiction between the classroom as a static work space of conflict-free harmony and the actual material conditions and labor involved in the production of that classroom and in the desire for it. In terms of my argument, the community of the writing classroom is commodified, imagined as an autonomous and uniform stand-in for the entirety of the social, albeit with a conception of sociality from which heterogeneity, conflict, and struggle have been excised. From the "practical" standpoint, the contradiction between this community ideal for the writing class and existing social relations in the academy is seen not as symptomatic of the social relations outside the academy but of the failure of the academy to conform to the "real world" of business, government, and so on. Thus the pedagogy becomes one of acculturation to that larger "community." The democratic aspirations of the pedagogy end up being directed at the academy and its failure to conform to what are assumed to be the democratic relations already existing in society, in those "communities" of business, the professions, government, and so forth.

Collaborative pedagogy attempts to act on the social through the various techniques recommended for insuring the pedagogy's effectiveness. For example, Bruffee is quite aware that a democratic community cannot be established in the classroom by fiat. As he warns, unless it is organized appropriately, collaborative learning can in fact "perpetuate, perhaps even aggravate, the many possible negative efforts of peer group influence: conformity, anti-intellectualism, intimidation, and leveling-down of quality" ("Collaborative Learning" 652). This suggests an awareness that relations outside the classroom are not ideal, and the possible intrusion of these into the classroom. But the dilemma is resolved not through directly confronting such unideal relations or the heterogeneity of positions students hold as groups and as individuals but through pedagogical techniques aimed at producing a uniformity. The actual material conditions of the course, classroom, and students remain unavailable for analysis. While peers can be useful resources for each other in their mutual efforts at learning, for example, they can be so only if they become the right sort of peers engaging in the right sort of "conversation," and this requires the direct or indirect "structuring" of their conversations by the teacher ("Collaborative Learning" 644). The conditions under and for which such conversations are "right" are not critiqued; their rightness, rather, is assumed. Collaborative pedagogy thus parallels strategies in the "new" capitalism favoring flattening of hierarchy and "teamwork" to socialize people into "communities of practice." In such communities, similarly, core goals and values of work remain unavailable for the "team's" critique (Gee, Hull, and Lankshear 20–21; 64–65). As in Elbow's teacherly efforts to enable students as individuals to grow "wild," hierarchical power relations in collaborative pedagogies operate to produce a "controlled" environment for the production of a commodified egalitarianism.

This structuring of peer response rests uneasily with Bruffee's most promising argument for the socially transformative effects of his pedagogy: that collaborative learning models not only "how knowledge is established and maintained. . . . [but also] how knowledge is generated, how it changes and grows" (647). As Bruffee himself notes, this understanding of collaborative learning throws into doubt the "comfortable" view that writing collaboratively simply involves becoming acculturated into a monolithic and unchanging discourse community. For this view emphasizes the utility of "abnormal discourse," the sort that "sniffs out stale, unproductive knowledge and challenges its authority, that is, the authority of the community which that knowledge constitutes" (647, 648). To allow for the generation of new knowledge, Bruffee suggests, we need to teach the conventions of "normal" discourse as provisional, social artifacts to be set aside when necessary, to allow for the production of new knowledge (648–49).

However, the potentially radical challenge to authority that can arise from the introduction of "abnormal" discourse and from the recognition of the social construction of authority is undercut by the objectification of "collaborative learning" itself effected by the removal of the social "community" of the classroom from the material historical process. Such learning is imagined as "natural," simply "how knowledge is generated, how it changes and grows," rather than being understood as an historical product of human labor, social relations, and material conditions. This obscures the operation of the social on the classroom itself, including its construction of students as autonomous individuals who then merge to produce a uniform collectivity. Why students ought to so merge into a "community," and to what ends, remains unexamined.[3] Thus idealized and objectified, the classroom "community" as commodity is substituted for the autonomous individual author as the autonomous origin of knowledge and even the determinant of when or whether to maintain existing knowledge or to engage in "abnormal" discourse to produce new knowledge. Missing from this picture is the relation of knowledge to power and history (see Herzberg, "Michel Foucault's" 79–80; A. Luke, "Genres" 312; Trimbur, "Consensus" 603). Needs for change, for "new" knowledge, are imagined simply to arise, as the community assesses, rather than being constructed or denied, met or overlooked or neglected, by various parties in contestation.

Those pedagogies variously identified as "multicultural" or "contact zone," while sharing with collaborative pedagogies a rejection of traditional hierarchical classroom relations, aim to overcome the silencing of difference effected through the maintenance of "normal" discourse. The aim of such pedagogies is to break the homogeneity of dominant discourse through using readings representing heterogeneous positions or through encouraging students to articulate difference in their writings. In place of a utopian classroom made up of homogeneous members of a "community," such pedagogies insert the ideal of a "contact zone" where "cultures meet, clash, and grapple with each other, often in contexts of highly asymmetrical relations of power" (M. L. Pratt, "Arts" 34).

At first glance this seems clearly different from any of the pedagogies discussed above: power relations are an explicit defining element, and classroom activity appears to engage directly in the clash of culture(s). And while expressivist pedagogies, for example, claim to remove the classroom from the operation of social pressures, contact-zone pedagogies aim explicitly to identify those pressures within the classroom, re-imagined as a contact zone. Where these latter pedagogies often run into trouble, however, is in failing to recognize the contact zone itself (or multicultural education) as an historically specific strategic response, a representation of education put forth in competition with dominant representations of education as the site for (re)producing social homogeneity.[4] In commodified conceptualizations of "contact zones," not only individual students and cultures but power, difference, and the contact zone itself are essentialized, imagined as uniform entities neither produced by nor susceptible to change. Thus reappropriated, the contact zone classroom can seem at best, as Joseph Harris has complained, "a kind of multicultural bazaar, where [students] are not so much brought into conflict with opposing views as placed in a kind of harmless connection with a series of exotic others" (*Teaching* 119). The "harmless connection" or "contact" thus achieved is likely to be "superficial," for it assumes both the essential immutability of the individuals' (presumably different) cultural identities and cultural tourism as its sole motive. This is a motive, it is worth noting, consistent with the new capitalist pursuit of global marketing—that is, marketing to the globe and marketing of global difference. Harris goes on to say that what is needed instead is "how competing perspectives can be made to intersect with and inform each other . . . how (or why) individuals might decide to change or revise their own positions (rather than simply to defend them) when brought into contact with differing views" (119). Otherwise, the contact zone as a strategy for articulating oppositional or alternative discourse in order to make resistance to hegemonic discourse possible is contained, rendered into the liberal pluralist ideal of conversation: once all voices have been heard, class can be dismissed.[5]

In such a classroom, the contact zone, its claims notwithstanding, becomes bracketed from the social, material, and historical that it was intended to address and to which it constitutes a response. This bracketing is perhaps best illustrated by the reification and domestication of student "difference." As Richard Miller has observed, the type of difference for which teachers are prepared—the sort sought after, expected, and ideally produced in such classrooms—is a domesticated, socially harmless difference of politically and ethically acceptable, if varied, "perspectives." Teachers are typically not, however, prepared for the voicing of racist, sexist, or homophobic sentiments or threats, "different"— and thus in theory generative and productive—as these might be in comparison to the "normal" discourse of the classroom ("Fault" 394–95). Teachers' lack of preparation for this other sort of "difference" results from two occlusions: first, bracketing the classroom, and specifically the student, from the labor and social historical conditions in which it is located; and second, the presumption of a uniformity to student identity and consciousness. The first leads to mistaking the "normal discourse" of the classroom and the voicing of differences encouraged by the apparatuses of the classroom environment (assignments, readings, discussion questions, and the like) *for* the entirety of the social (see R. Miller, "Fault" 398–99). That is, the classroom's *production* of the voicing of domesticated differences through its pedagogical apparatuses is ignored; the classroom is imagined instead as a privileged site for the voicing of social difference thought to be already produced *elsewhere*. This is not to say that such production is entirely unwarranted but rather that these differences, like the less domesticated differences, must be seen precisely as produced. Further, such production must be understood in the larger context of global relations capitalizing on workers disposed to produce and negotiate certain types of differences (and not others) in certain ways. Thus, rather than imagining the "contact zone" as a privileged space one "enters" to act on the social, it must be seen as a type of activity in which people intend explicitly to produce and negotiate such differences and alignments to achieve specific ends, working with *and within* material social conditions, articulating an array of heterogeneous positions as strategies rather than as inherently valuable (see Harris, *Teaching* 122–23).

Teachers' responses to the intrusion of undomesticated difference into the classroom betray their presumption of a uniformity to student identity and consciousness, a presumption that further reveals their occlusion of the location and participation of the classroom in the material social process. First, the differences that tend to be recognized are those between students, not differences within them. Of course, Mary Louise Pratt's account of contact zones as places where "cultures meet, clash, and grapple with each other, often in highly asymmetrical relations of power" ("Arts" 34) does not lend itself to imagining how such clashes operate within the individual student's consciousness. But the kind of cultural tourism with which contact zone pedagogies have been charged results precisely from imagining students as uniform, fixed representatives of a specific culture rather than as themselves sites of conflict and struggle. Thus, despite the obvious genesis of such pedagogies in history, the students, as individuals, continue to be imagined transhistorically, to recall Helmers' term—as themselves unchanging, determined by (past) history but not now operating on and within *ongoing* history. In Miller's account, teachers' immediate reactions to student articulations of *uninvited* difference in such classrooms—homophobic, sexist, or racist sentiments, for example— assume just such uniformity to students' consciousness. Responding to fragments of a student paper that appeared to bash gays and the homeless, many teachers assumed the patent criminality or psychosis of the writer, rather than taking the paper as one moment in a larger, longer, overdetermined material social process of the student's negotiation of attitudes (R. Miller, "Fault" 392–93). Reactions like these conceive of written articulations of such differences as unmediated representations of that consciousness. In other words, like those who take students' writings to evince, say, their level of cognitive maturity, field-dependent cognitive style, oral cultural background, educational background, or degree of creativity, these see students' writing not as work but as a manifestation of students' essential moral or psychological character. So, if "process" pedagogies view students' written drafts as mere traces of an idealized text (a "work"), thus denying the drafts as material embodiments of a working practice, these other pedagogies, while viewing student writing as indeed a material manifestation of student's intentions, understand it only as an un-"worked" trace of the student's essence, not as material social *practice*.

Student Writing and Material Social Practice

In the pedagogies I have been describing, actual student writing is not so much looked *at* as *through*. This blindness to the work of student writing speaks to the general denigration of students necessary to maintaining hierarchical relations between students as clients of academic professionals. However, pedagogies that do attempt to focus on student writing as work tend to be limited by the dominance of understandings of what constitutes work, and academic work, generally, understandings considered in chapter 1 that guarantee the low valuation of student writing. The common reification of academic work into institutionalized forms—whether published essays, books, and papers, or credit hours, courses, and students ("full-time equivalents," or FTEs)—obscures the material practices and conditions in which these forms are produced and received. More particularly, just as teachers' work in Composition is often identified not with teaching but with published writing, so student work is identified with the production of texts, evaluated as commodities according to their exchange value, as indicated by their novelty and range of circulation. However, the institution's role in the production of student writing and the circumscriptions academic institutions typically impose on the circulation of student texts guarantee the low value of student writing in relation to other writing. In other words, student writing is evaluated as a commodity while being produced and distributed in ways that guarantee its lack of exchange value: it is clearly authored by and for institutions, not the individual writer, and has an extremely limited range of circulation. This accounts not only for the low status of those supervising its production—teachers—but also for the recalcitrance of those supervised—the students. We can see both the acceptance of dominant evaluations of writing as commodity and a recognition of the low status this guarantees Composition in laments about the "present situation" from two different periods, the 1960s and the 1990s. Back in 1969, William E. Coles Jr., complains:

> It is not difficult to see what values the student might attach to the process of Themewriting and Themerevision, particularly when he learns that all of his writing for the course is to be collected at the end of the term and burned. . . . Everyone who plays the game according to the rules is promised "a measure of ability and confidence," a share in the collective "outreachings of the mind." But for the student this is likely to mean no more than that everyone can finish work by five o'clock and go to the movies. ("Freshman" 140)

In 1998, Peter Vandenberg remarks:

> The textual work of students has the least value because it is strictly location-bound. Student writing . . . except in the rarest of circumstances follows an arc from the student, across the teacher's desk, and into the trash. . . . Student writing is value poor because it does not travel; it cannot circulate outside the narrow boundaries of its production, and therefore "works" in the least meaningful way possible. It is "practice" in the least significant sense of that term, never more than a shadowy ancestor of something yet to come.

Coles calls the kind of writing in which students thus engage "themewriting" to distinguish it from the general category of writing, and he excoriates teaching of the former for substituting "a process for an activity, perhaps a product for a process. . . . what is finally unteachable as though it were teachable," and so "non-art" for "art," with the result that "most students and most teachers of writing at the college freshman level neither like nor believe very much in what it is they are doing" (136). Thus, for Coles, writing is best understood, and approached, as an activity, a process, an "art" perhaps unteachable but something in which students and teachers could believe. The implication of Vandenberg's argument is that we need to abandon writing itself, or at least writing as the "dissemination of text," and attempt to improve Composition's status in other ways: "we cannot look to writing to restructure work-value hierarchies held in place by writing."

While there are clear differences between the two arguments, both articulate (and lament) a direct relation between existing working conditions in composition and conceptions of writing. However, and more significantly, the alternatives they posit to this state of affairs are not changes in how writing itself is conceived, taught, and practiced but removals from writing as material social practice. In place of "themewriting," Coles posits the teaching of writing as art, but he defines writing, so understood, as "unteachable," an ideal unlikely to draw material support, and one that implicitly supports a notion of writing outside material social practice. Vandenberg looks for change from "physical and symbolic action outside the order of academic publishing," preferably through unionizing, but more probably, and ominously, through public attacks on Composition and the abolition of tenure. For Coles, in other words, the alternative to the hegemonic is outside history, in the realm of the aesthetic; for Vandenberg, the alternative to existing hegemonic pressures is more pronounced hegemony, no alternative at all.

Such unpromising alternatives demonstrate the reach of what Williams terms the dominant's seizure of the ruling definition of the social. What is left, according to that definition, is absence, or mythicized as natural or "aesthetic" (*Marxism* 125, 131). Coles turns to an idealized realm of the aesthetic; Vandenberg, more grimly, sees no alternative to dominant, official meanings and practices. That reach, spanning thirty years, operates in a host of writings beyond Vandenberg and Coles, who, to be fair, in critiquing existing practices can hardly be faulted for the paucity of the alternatives offered. It attests both to the dominance of commodified notions of writing and to writing teachers' consciousness of the disparity between those dominant notions and what their practical experience of writing tells them such notions exclude. Attempts to bridge that disparity, however, all too frequently end up recapitulating dominant commodifications of student work and student writing: it is re-imagined as Authorized writing, with all the ideological baggage of Authorship this entails, or as "real world" writing, with all the ideology of the "real," set off from the "academic," that such a conception entails. I'll have more to say about the dilemma posed by such conceptualizations of writing in relation to its commodification in chapter 6. Here let me emphasize that it is within such conceptions that the term "student work," like the term "women's work," appears as oxymoron, by definition less or other than real work—than, say, the work of men.[6] And of course, these conceptions are part of a chain, or nest, of binaries derogating teaching, the academic, the feminine, the personal, and so on which distinguish labor from work, feeling from thought, experience from intellect, the personal from the social, composition from academic disciplines, and the academic from the real. Almost all the strategies Composition has adopted in attempting to combat such derogations operate within, rather than contesting, such binaries. Thus they recapitulate dominant, if varying, definitions of what constitutes "authorized" or "real" writing, and thus perpetuate the criteria according to which student writing will inevitably fall short, as at best preparatory to such work. And thus they effectively ignore or deny the materiality of student writing as student writing. Like dominant constructions of student writing, they thereby neglect the counterhegemonic potential of this site.

For example, the expressivist strategies of the late sixties and early seventies (echoes of which resonate in the statements from Coles quoted above) attempted to combat the seemingly unreal, or false, nature of the writing students have ordinarily produced for the composition classroom, often denigrated as "pseudo-writing" or "bastard discourse." Of course, as many critics have subsequently observed and as I have argued above, this strategy accepts dominant constructions of the individual in opposition to the social, perpetuating the ideology of bourgeois American individualism, and thus leading inadvertently to political quiescence. But note, too, that this strategy ends up denying the validity, or reality, of students' writing. Theme writing is seen as an effect of institutional structures or dominant ideologies operating in spite of students. In this approach, true writing (as "art"?), versus themewriting, transcends the material social realm.

The "practical" pedagogies sometimes offered in response to this strategy have students learn to produce writing that conforms to criteria ostensibly set by the corporate world or by academic disciplines. However, these also accept dominant reified definitions of what constitutes real writing, definitions by which student writing will again inevitably appear lacking. They accept a dominant conception of higher education as preparation for survival in the "real world," and equate the "real" with established textual forms. Students are treated as apprentices engaged in "practice," or training, for the real thing, identified either with writing required by other academic disciplines, or with non-academic writing. This reinforces dominant derogations of composition in relation to what are thought to be true academic disciplines, or of the academy in relation to what is called the "real world."

Such arguments are taken to their logical extreme in "new abolitionist" arguments to eliminate freshman composition on the grounds that the writing skills it teaches are irrelevant to corporate or other academic writing. In one sense, these new abolitionist arguments insist on the material historical location of composition courses. Aware of the history of the use of freshman composition to "gatekeep"—that is, to remove from college those students the dominant believes unworthy of credentialing—and of the history of using students' breaks from conventions of style to justify their removal, some argue for eliminating the course altogether. They often see the course as useless for students, failing to prepare them for the writing required in other courses and at worksites because of a disparity between, on the one hand, the thinking and writing encouraged in composition courses and, on the other, that required at these other sites. Joseph Petraglia, for example, observing that "the cognition entailed in producing GWSI [General Writing Skills Instruction] compositions is fundamentally different from that of writers who address out-of-school exigencies" (91–92), argues against expressivist-like "efforts to authenticate students' writing— within the confines of a course intended to teach writing." According to Petraglia, such efforts underestimate "the intransigence of schooling as a context" (92). Thus, since the dominant purpose of student writing in the academy, Petraglia believes, is to demonstrate "mastery over content," he argues that "adapting writing to the function of schooling will entail forsaking the teaching of writing as a productive art" (95). Rather than having teachers attempt to manufacture "authentic" purposes for their classes by, say, having them write on "real world" issues or on what they "want" to write about, composition courses can legitimately pursue at most only the unpromising alternative of "teaching a content . . . on which they may legitimately require students to write" and in terms of which their writing will be evaluated (e.g., teaching rhetorical theory or grammar *as the subject matter of the course*) (95). Charles Hill and Lauren Resnick note similarly that "[n]o matter how 'genuine' instructors try to make classroom writing, there are intractable differences between the purposes of the classroom and of the workplace [which] . . . continue to make it difficult for students to make the transition from school to work" (150). In place of classroom writing instruction, they therefore recommend the teaching of writing through apprenticeships in the "real" world:

> [r]ather than go to great lengths to bring "genuine" writing tasks into the classroom, it might make more sense to admit that this level of writing instruction can most effectively take place only once the students have begun their initial careers— that is, once they have genuine tasks to accomplish. (155)

Such writers define "genuine" or "real" writing in terms of dominant existing forms and practices, but only as they exist outside the composition classroom (for Petraglia), or outside the academy entirely (for Hill and Resnick). The specific material reality of the freshman composition course as a site for a specific type of writing is thus denied as an impediment to real writing. Thus, for Petraglia, if student writing is predominantly used (in classes outside composition) to demonstrate students' mastery of content, then the teaching of writing should conform to such practice (rather than challenging it); or if there are intractable differences between academic and workplace purposes for writing, as Hill and Resnick contend, we must forego academic purposes (merely academic) to better prepare students for uses dominant in the workplace. Similarly, even those strategies which Petraglia disparages as manufacturing a spurious authenticity, such as assigning students subjects on "topical" issues, simply substitute a different dominant definition of what constitutes the real—namely, issues the dominant has defined as "political," "public," or "social." By addressing such "real" issues, student writing is expected itself to become more "real." What none of these strategies broaches is the possibility that these dominant practices and definitions are subject to change, in flux, matters of contestation. Differences between the strategies represent only differences in the specific institutional forms and practices to which they accede: literary authorship, the academy, the corporate world, public definitions of what is "topical."

I want to be clear that I'm not repudiating teaching strategies that call attention to the conventions of corporate or academic discourse or assign topics of public interest. To not attend to these would be to ignore pressures of the dominant on our work and our sense of it and so to give sway more fully to the dominant, through retreat from engagement with it. However, I do argue that uncritical adoptions of these strategies accede to the dominant in ways that perpetuate the denigration of student writing and of compositional work generally that we need to resist. At the most general level, each risks accepting a reification of the work of writing, accepting dominant definitions of the social or the real in writing in terms of fixed forms: the fixed, commodified forms ostensibly produced and demanded by business or academic disciplines; or fixed definitions of the author or of the political or the public and its "issues." The work of writing thus comes to be located in its product, the finished text measured by its conformity to an idealized form and content. Consequently, student writing must inevitably appear lacking, as, at best, imitative of the real thing, that is, actual work in and on the actual world.

In short, these strategies ignore the location of student writing in the material social process *as* student writing. Indeed, such strategies are united in their effort to take students, teachers, and writing somehow out of their institutional location, to somehow escape the imagined confines of the composition course, or the academy, or the institutional roles of student and teacher. This symbolic escape from that location makes it impossible to address, let alone challenge, the material conditions of that institutional location, and it neglects this site's counterhegemonic potential. To put it another way, the institutional structures of composition courses are viewed in these strategies as constraints on the agency of students and teachers, constraints that operate " 'behind the backs' of the social actors who produce and reproduce them" (Giddens 71). By contrast, following Anthony Giddens' theory of structuration, we can view social institutional structures as both enabling and constraining, "both the medium and the outcome of the practices that constitute [them]" (69). This view presumes that "every competent member of every society knows a great deal about the institutions of that society" (71). This is possible when we recognize the knowledge present in what he terms "practical consciousness," embodied "in what actors 'know how to do' " (73). If institutional structures are both the medium and outcome of the practices in which actors engage, then it is through their actions that these structures are reproduced or changed.

If we see the institutional location of the composition course and its inhabitants not as autonomous constraint on actors but as a location reproduced and potentially changed by actors through their practices, then the apparent marginality of that location has potential for both hegemonic and counterhegemonic work. It is not necessary to somehow escape that location, or attempt to liberate students from it, because it is not separate from the "real" world but both constituted by and constitutive of it. Indeed, as I will argue more fully in chapters 4 and 5, precisely such a space, as marginal, can represent a site for counterhegemonic work, if only we can learn to recognize and draw on that potential. The difficulty in doing so rests with failing to resist dominant definitions of what constitutes work, and important political work at that, definitions that blind us to the possibilities of the work in which we and our students daily engage.

In this light, the much lamented positioning of students as "presexual, preeconomic, prepolitical" (S. Miller, *Textual* 87); as outside history and—while male, white, and middle-class—simultaneously classless, sexless, and drained of any color (Ohmann, *English* 145, 147); as always "emerging . . . but never as actually responsible 'authors' " (S. Miller, *Textual* 196); as beginners or foreigners but never adults belonging in the academy (see Horner, "Mapping" 31–35); as the incomplete Other justifying Composition's mission and its place (Bartholomae, "Tidy" 18) simultaneously represents the low institutional place allocated to students (and Composition), and points to the potentiality of both. Many critiques of such representations have focused on how they contribute to the low status of Composition (S. Miller, *Textual* 196). Such moves can align with theories of schooling as a site for the reproduction of systems of social inequality in terms of race, class, gender, ethnicity, and so on, accomplishing the interpellation of specific subjectivities. In other words, Composition teaching can be attacked for its complicity in reproducing an asocial, apolitical professional-managerial class subjectivity in some students and a sense in others that, as adult writers enrolled in college classes, they are, nonetheless, mere "beginners," "children" with no right to a place in the academy. In such arguments, as Paul Willis puts it, "[p]upil experience and agency become a reflex of structure. . . . Humans become dummies, dupes, or zombies" (205). However, as Willis points out, and as his study of working-class students' choice of working-class employment itself demonstrates, we should view such sites as " 'choice points' where 'structure' and 'agency' most crucially meet—not where 'structure' overpowers 'agency' " (206). Applied to the site of Composition, we can acknowledge its interpellation of students as beginners, foreigners, Others, and so forth without granting lack of agency to students, even in instances where they would appear to accept such interpellation. The much derided "themes" students have produced, for example, can demonstrate not their passive interpellation but their active participation in the work of producing just such subjectivities, wherein they present themselves in just such ways, and, more significantly, the potential for them to choose otherwise. Coles's account of his students' explicit ability to manufacture themes on command demonstrates just such active participation in "themethink," and also the potential for resistance to such discursive practices (see *Plural* 39–45). If, in other words, the most important thing a worker produces is himself in relation to a particular kind of labor (see William, *Problems* 35), then we can see in student work the potential for the students to make themselves in relation to that particular kind of labor named "student work"— not to return to an individualist expressivism, but to consider how in composition courses structure and agency meet.

The Work of Student Writing

In the remainder of this chapter, I want to consider two alternative strategies for tapping that potential: a particular tradition of looking at student writing as social negotiation, and a particular version of service learning. My aim will be to explore what it might mean to approach the work of student writing as material social practice in which structure and agency meet. The first of these strategies is a variation on what I think is a minority tradition within Composition. In that tradition, student writing is approached as the site for the negotiation of conventions of form and content, that is, as symbolic practice. The writing is viewed as social action, and the writer as social agent, in that the forms and content of her writing are seen in relation to existing, often dominant, discursive practices, as an engagement and negotiation with those practices.[7] In this tradition, negotiation is taken as a means by which the writer resituates herself in relation to those discourses, in effect re-making herself, those discourses, and her knowledge. The work the writer engages in, in this tradition, is precisely that remaking of self, language, and knowledge. Rather than revising one's text to reflect intentions, knowledge, or a self imagined as fixed, writing and revising are seen as revising those intentions, knowledge, and self.

To illustrate this strategy, I'll turn to some student writing, but before I do so, a caveat is in order that will also help explain the difficulty we have acknowledging that kind of student work. In simplest terms, the difficulty is that no student writing, in itself, can demonstrate the achievement of the kind of work that we would like to think students, and by implication our teaching, might accomplish, precisely because no student writing *exists* "in itself." As Raymond Williams reminds us, in writing (as well as in other arts) "what we permanently have are not objects but *notations.* . . . [which] have then to be interpreted in an active way" (*Problems* 47). Our practice of looking at a student text for evidence of such achievements guarantees, in fact, failure, recognized or not, insofar as we look at it as a commodity produced by either the student, ourselves as teachers, or a pedagogy, rather than as part of an ongoing practice both shaped by and shaping specific material conditions. The problem is not with looking at student writing but with *how* we look, the specific practice we engage in.

The common practice of treating student work as reified texts accounts in part, I think, for the striking absence of discourse on the pleasure of reading and working with student writing. I mean here not the pleasure of reading student writing that seems the culmination of all that we would desire, quintessentially "good" papers (often stylistically fluent). Nor am I referring to the condescending pleasure teachers sometimes take in writers' *faux pas*. I mean the experience of pleasure in working with student writing that seems intellectually important, satisfying but only in its specific material, historical context. We lack a discourse adequate to that experience—or, which is the same thing, we lack the ability to recognize, or treat as legitimate, any such discourse. As Bartholomae has recently complained, we give awards to writing we don't believe in and "turn away from the papers we do, papers most often clumsy and awkward but, as we say to each other, ambitious, interesting, a sign of a student for whom something is happening" ("What Is" 16).

I am always nervous, for example, on reading student writing that seems to me to be saying something important, or in which "something is happening." I distrust my own sense of pleasure in reading it. I wonder if it's plagiarized. Is it merely parroting back to me my own statements, by which I'm all too well disposed to be persuaded? Is it really trite, and am I losing my intellectual grip? And should I, to be safe, temper the enthusiasm of my comments to the student? What would happen to my reputation if I were to praise the writing—writing of a first-year undergraduate composition student, after all—to others, especially given its stylistic awkwardness, or its failure to contribute more than a mite, at most, to the universal fund of knowledge? I suspect, along with Bartholomae, that such nervousness is shared.[8] In my experience, composition teachers rarely have any response other than silence to the frequent, vocal complaints we hear and often make ourselves about the burden of reading student papers. Instead, in our conversations with our erstwhile colleagues, we go along, casting ourselves not as engaged in intellectual work with our students but as missionaries doing the holy work of redeeming the unwashed—work that, as holy, transcends the sullied realm of material working conditions, about which we must therefore also maintain silence to preserve our saintly status. What I am arguing is that our commodified notion of work is part of what leads to just such neglect of what seems to matter in student writing, praise for what we secretly disdain, and our own denigration, along with the working conditions that may militate against positioning ourselves in any other way. That commodified notion of work and those conditions of work lead to dismissing from consideration the use of the writing for the student, at that particular time, and to recognizing only its minimal exchange value as commodity. Thus our ways of talking about the work of student writing commonly render students "authors" in all the ways we've come to hold suspect, or define them as walking collections of deficits.

Williams has argued that to resist reification of the work of writing, we need to break away from our tendency to isolate the components of a product and learn to look instead for the nature of a practice and its conditions (*Problems* 47). What does it mean, in the context of a required composition course, for the writer of the following paper to write as he has? What practices is he engaged in? How do these interact with what specific conditions? What work is going on?

> It seems to me that Fish and Pratt are taking different paths in describing how they view the human groupings of a classroom as a whole. Fish seems to take the stand that the classroom is a homogeneous community and Pratt seems to stick with her views of the classroom as being a heterogeneous contact zone.
>
> To further explain these statements, it seems to me that the reason why Fish says the classroom is a homogeneous community, where each students is equal in their status of the classroom, and no one person can be considered different, is because, as Fish says: "It was almost as if they were following a recipe—if it's a poem do this, if it's a poem see it that way, . . ." (pg. 144)
>
> I do not want this statement to be confused with the fact that we see and interpret things based on the communities we inhabited in the past. I want this statement to point out that, that what Fish seems to be talking about here, is that students in a classroom are homogeneous because of the fact that they all behave like students are supposed to behave, meaning that when someone is raising their hand during class, it most likely means that that students either wants to voice his opinion, or is answering a question. The students are uniform during class, because they have all been taught to perform a certain way that is uniform and does not differentiate from student to student.

Pratt argues that any institution, whether a classroom, a residence hall community or even Drake University can never be homogeneous, because no matter how "trained" a community is to perform a certain way they are expected to, there can never be a uniform group, especially that of a class room. Pratt statement:

> The classroom functioned not like a homogeneous community or a horizontal alliance but like a contact zone. Every single text we read stood in specific historical relationships to the students in the class, but the range and variety of historical relationships in play were enormous,

proves the statement that no one group can ever be homogeneous.

It seems the reason why Fish is taking the particular standpoint of a classroom being a homogeneous community is that he tends to think that each student is equal and cannot be different from other students in the confines of the classroom. Pratt seems to identify the classroom as being a contact zone that is equal to some extend, as being students, but are very much different, because of their past and backgrounds. If we look at this more closely, it seems that these two statements contradict each other. Fish stated that each person is shaped and influenced by the past institutions they inhabited, yet he tends to, or a least that is how I see it, stick with the idea that a classroom is homogeneous and cannot be considered a contact zone, because students work towards a common goal in the classroom and yet they do not compete against each other. The performance of a student within a classroom does not affect the community of the classroom but solely the student himself, unlike in other institutions, which could then be described as contact zones.

If we now look at the uses of either statements of these two authors in their essays, we might, or at least I myself think that there cannot be a specific use to any one when analyzing the views of either Fish or Pratt. It does not help any one in their improvement of reading or writing by focusing on the institutions we inhabit, instead it might help people understand what standpoint one will take if he sees human groupings as either a community of a contact zone.

Fish and Pratt see the classroom as two groupings, that of a community and a contact zone. Through the eyes of an educated teacher and author as Fish, we can understand his views and also by looking at Pratt's Resume, we understand her standpoint as well. It was not able to detect any similarities in the two essays after focusing on the questions this assignment is asking. By that I mean that either Fish or Pratt say that both statements can be true. It seems to me, being s student for some twelve years and and still continuing as a students, that a classroom is both a homogeneous community and heterogeneous contact zone.

I agree with some of things both Fish and Pratt are saying, such as that we students are the same in the classroom, because we have been taught to act in a uniform manner, therefore making us appear to be equal. A good example might be a students raising his hand in class—every one knows what he is doing, meaning that every one inside a classroom thinks and acts the same—to a certain extend that is. I strongly believe that each students in a class is very different from each other, simply because every one has been inhabiting different institutions in the past. This diversity of thoughts and feelings brings different opinions and actions of each students to the attention of the teacher.

To me, Fish and Pratt are both right in their opinions, but at same time also wrong.[9]

We might say the work represented by the paper is the student's struggle to "make" himself as someone capable of adopting a stance which I would deem potentially counterhegemonic in its refusal to simplify, to give in to a dominant ideology that asserts there can be only one right answer, or to give in to the generic constraints of the comparison-contrast essay. He is trying, instead, to rework such constraints to articulate his own construction of his experience that things are more complicated. Hence his concluding statement, "To me, Fish and Pratt are both right in their opinions, but at same time also wrong." I am tempted, too, to read in the stylistic hesitations in his writing an impressive concern to explain a complicated understanding, a concern that overpowers or overrides his simultaneous desire to control his syntax. I sense such a struggle in the opening to his third paragraph, for example, in the sentences "I do not want this statement to be confused with. . . . I want this statement to point out that, that what Fish seems to be talking about here, is that . . ." and so on. Such stylistic awkwardness evokes a writer more interested in specifying his meaning than in producing conventionally good prose, though he is also trying to produce such prose. All these signal to me writing in which, indeed, something is happening worth my attention.

If we're to take Williams' advice seriously, however, we cannot simply praise this writer as someone breaking free from the dictates of conventional prose, sacrificing the demands of society to be true to the integrity of his experience. Indeed, one of the dangers of this strategy is that it risks reifying specific textual features—such as those I've been labeling "awkward"—as valuable in themselves as unconventional. This would mean forgetting that the conventionality of a textual feature is relative to the particular historical material sites of its production and reception.

A second limitation of this strategy is suggested by John Trimbur, who observes that such a strategy "by concentrating on the student writer interpreting the world at the point of production, foreshorten[s] the circuits of production, distribution, exchange, and consumption through which writing circulates as it takes on cultural value and worldly force" ("Whatever"). To begin with, this strategy, in closely reading the writing, can elide attention to its material social location. For example, by focusing on the stance of the writing, we may neglect the following: (1) this kind of stance was explicitly encouraged by the directives of the course syllabus and by my comments, class discussions, and some of the directives of the assignments; (2) the privileged space of the course afforded the writer an opportunity—both the time, physical material means and training, and luxury—to think about two perspectives on the classroom represented by Stanley Fish and Mary Louise Pratt, to adopt a stance recognizing the simultaneous validity and invalidity of both, and to present such a stance in an essay awkward in its style and confusing in its organization. As Trimbur puts it more generally, in this strategy the classroom becomes an intimate domestic space in which the student is positioned as an "active meaning-maker in [familial] relation . . . to a powerful teacher figure." The problem with such classrooms is not these relations themselves but how naturalizing them obscures attention to them as part of the circuitry of distribution and consumption. For, far from being neutral, distribution and consumption do not follow production but enter into the process of production, as elements of the conditions for it.

In looking at this paper, then, we have to look not just at the student's writing practice but at the conditions of that practice—"we" in this instance meaning everyone in the class. This means, too, that we cannot isolate features of this student's text as praiseworthy in and of themselves, but have to understand them as work, that is, as work*ing* with those conditions. For the writer to engage in this practice outside such conditions would have a very different significance, representing a very different sort of work. Thus one question we need to ask with our students is what use a piece of writing makes of such conditions: how does the writing, as work, engage such conditions, and to what ends? This involves examining the writing in relation to the conditions of time, the assignment, the positioning of the student in the "intimate domestic space" of the course, the situation of that course and its instructor within the curriculum and specific institution, and the relation of the student's writing to available technological resources for the material production of the writing—in this case, specific computer hardware and software, printers, cheap paper, and the kind of writing production these enabled.[10]

And this question needs to be asked in concert with a second: what use do our reading practices make of the writing? This question gets more specifically to the circuitry of distribution and consumption. When I had a class read copies of the paper, I found myself in the difficult position of defending it against their denunciations of its apparent contradictions, awkward style, and poor organization. In negotiating our different readings of the paper, we had to confront differences in the demands we were making of it. To do that, we had to investigate the different perspectives we were adopting, afforded or encouraged by our past histories, present institutional roles and interests, and projected futures. As teacher, I was hoping to prod students to move away from simplistic assertions and to dare to explore questions for which they had no ready answers, and I was viewing any one student paper as part of his or her "development" over the term. They as students were trained to condemn stylistic infelicities, were proud of their ability to find and criticize these, and were used to and desiring fixed answers from readings. But we then also had to confront how the mode of the paper's distribution contributed to how it worked for us, how it entered into the production of its meaning for us. As teacher I had access to other of the writer's papers and so could more readily see it as part of an ongoing process of "development." They had only the isolated, anonymous paper. It was only by exploring the interaction of our institutional and historical positionings and the different modes of the writing's distribution that we could do more than simply badger each other about whether we should condemn or praise the writer and the practice represented by his paper. This made it possible to ask how we could see ourselves as social agents who, through our reading, writing, and pedagogical practices, could reproduce or alter some of the effects of the institutional structures in which we found ourselves, and could therefore engage in resistance through changing those practices (cf. Herndl, "Teaching" 353). This would include such practices as those by which student writing was distributed to students, as well as teachers, for their consumption, and the ways they were encouraged to read such writing. More specifically, it demonstrated how the circuitry of distribution and consumption, partly embodied in our material social practices as readers, contributed to shaping the work we had wrongly been defining as an effect of the writing itself or the writer's autonomous self. And it at least raised the possibility of critiquing and considering alternatives to the structuring of our work by such institutions as grades, graduation requirements, and hiring practices, while also reminding us of the power of such institutions.

Pursuing such questions unpacks the process by which student work is commodified by revealing the nature of the practice of that work and its conditions—student work now understood to comprise not just the material production of the text but all the activities of its provocation, composition, distribution, and reception and the involvement of these with each other: work, in short, as material social practice, where agency meets structure. A very different strategy by which we may recognize the work of student writing in this way is represented by certain recent versions of the use of service learning in Composition. Of course, some uses of service learning in Composition are simply variations of student writing as apprentice work, such as those in which students work as interns producing brochures and the like for local non-profit organizations to prepare them, say, for future careers in public relations. Other variations involve students in efforts to intervene in and produce measurable effects on the school's local community, usually effects of social justice (see, for example, Eddy and Carducci). Following the arguments of the "new abolitionists" discussed above, these accept both dominant distinctions between the world of the academy and the world "outside" and dominant reifications of the work of writing. That is, they define work primarily as paid employment or in terms of its effects on and/or value in that "outside" realm.

For example, Wade Dorman and Susann Fox Dorman describe their own experiments with using service learning as aimed at moving their writing classes "closer to the messy comprehensiveness of the real world," hoping that such movement will reduce the alienation from learning which they perceive many students to experience (122). In the different versions of using service learning in composition courses they describe, students either write about their community service experiences or write for non-profit community organizations. While they see value in having their students write *about* their volunteer experiences, they conclude that such student writing was not, in fact, giving students the experience of "actually . . . being writers" (126). As they explain, the students "never faced a truly opaque audience . . . never had to meet a real deadline, only the instructor's artificial ones; never had to stay within a budget, choose an ink color or a paper stock" (126). The courses which had students write for organizations, on the other hand, are praised for enabling students to experience "real" writing. Students seemed to "own" this writing (130, 131), and one student reported valuing most "the opportunity [writing for organizations gave the student] to experience what happens in the real world; i.e., meeting deadlines, the editing process, time restraints" (quoted in Dorman and Dorman 131).

While it would be futile to deny the enthusiasm many of these students reported experiencing, it is surely worth questioning how "real-world writing" is being distinguished from student writing here. How, for example, are instructors' deadlines more "artificial" than those set by bosses? How does the experience of choosing ink and paper stock, rather than using what's supplied by the institution, make for a more real writing experience? In what sense are there no time constraints on writing assigned for courses? How are teachers not "opaque" audiences? How is writing for organizations more easily "owned"? And in what sense does "owning" writing make it more, rather than less, "real"? The assumptions governing both the teachers' and the students' perceptions of the greater reality of certain types of writing seem to rehearse dominant notions of writing as pure commodity. The material production of that commodity, or a deadline imposed by someone other than one's teacher, or time constraints arising from sources other than academic calendars, are judged as real. Anything emanating from the academy is by dominant definition less real because non-circulating, in the same way one may view private journal writing as less real than the writing of technical reports, say, or ad copy. In such versions of service learning, activities within the classroom or within the student are seen as distinct from the real and cannot in themselves have any effect on it, except negatively, as delay, or (at best) as preparation for engaging in such "real" activities. Service learning thus becomes a way to "bridge" that distinction (see, for example, Heilker, "Rhetoric"). It increases the exchange value of the writing as commodity by increasing the range of its circulation, indeed by circulating both the students and their writing outside the realm of the classroom. Simultaneously, however, it reproduces the denigration of that writing which does not so circulate, which by comparison seems somehow less "real," its audiences, deadlines, subject matter, even paper stock a pale imitation of true writing.

However, taken not as a strategy to escape the material social location of the composition classroom but to critically engage that location through their writing and reading practices, some uses of service learning may work as a means not simply to reproduce but to challenge the practices and structures that have historically denigrated students and their writing. They do this not by transforming students into real authors or the composition course into an internship service for the real world, but by redefining the meaning of being a student in a composition course, and of writing in such a course. For example, Aaron Schutz and Anne Ruggles Gere describe pedagogies in which students step outside traditional academic in-

stitutional roles to define and address an issue of concern to both
the students and local communities, such as gender equity in university athletics, or the night entrance policy at the student union
(see also Peck et al.; Wells). While these projects often lead to a
form of "public" writing, in any case they encourage students to
confront in the process "the nature of literacies and discourses as
they operate in different communities" (Schutz and Gere 145).
Service-learning projects, Schutz and Gere point out, "can encourage us to engage in dialogue [with members of local communities]
about . . . the implications of a *specific* literate activity for a *specific*
context and to the *specific* goals we intend to pursue" (146). Thus,
while those looking at student writing as the site for the negotiation of conventions of form and content risk forgetting the conditions making possible student writers' ways of negotiating various
discursive practices in their writing, attention to such conditions is
in a sense "built in" to this service-learning strategy.

For example, the "community literacy" with which Wayne Peck,
Linda Flower, and Lorraine Higgins are engaged has diverse
groups confront and negotiate differences in their home discourses
to produce a hybrid, community discourse for the purpose of addressing a specific "project": developing a new "suspension" policy
for local high schools, for example, or for handling landlord/tenant
disputes (Peck et al. 210). The "service learning" occurs in the continual re-creation of a "community" literacy forged out of conflicting
interests, literacy practices, and shared problems. Unlike those
service-learning projects that attempt to bring dominant literacy
practices to "the community," imagined as discrete from the academy, and unlike those that simply do the bidding of a "community"
organization, the literacy Peck and colleagues are advancing is one
by definition alternative to, while often drawing upon, existing
"home" discourses—whether of the academy or a specific "community." It is a literacy always in the making, in response to specific
material conditions and desires of the participants (205). It thus requires all participants—both student "mentors" from the academy
and representatives from outside the academy—not just to engage
in dialogue about the "implications of a *specific* literate activity for
a *specific* context," in pursuit of specific goals but to act on those
implications by producing a "community literacy" suited to such
specificities. In so doing, they must rewrite not just the issue ad-

dressed but their relation to others, and so their own positions as students, professors, community members. In the projects Peck and colleagues describe, "writers and mentors [are challenged] to move out of the discourses they control with comfort into hybrid discourses, creating texts in which [for example] policy recommendations coexist with rap" (212). In creating and moving into these hybrid discourses, they must redefine themselves as well.

Schutz and Gere warn that "if we are not careful [in how we use service learning], we may end up reinforcing ideologies and assumptions that we had hoped to critique" (147). Schutz and Gere are particularly concerned that service-learning projects may reinforce an ideology of "service" as a form of *noblesse oblige*, conducted in a private relationship between a selfless caregiver and a needy "other." Students, here cast outside the realm of material history, descend into it to aid others, in the role of saints themselves. To this concern I am adding that the strategy of service learning also risks reifying the work of writing, whether in terms of its immediately measurable effect on the social or in terms of its formal textual features. In such cases, using service learning to traverse the boundaries separating the academic from the public or the "community" can reinforce the academic/real world binary, leading again to the derogation of student writing as somehow less "real" than work more recognizably "public" in its form, effect, or mode of distribution.

I've suggested above that there is a risk in the tradition of approaching student writing as the site for the negotiation of conventions of form and content. For in that tradition, students may come to be defined, and understand themselves, as free agents battling material conditions in the form of academic discourse conventions, forgetting the contributions material conditions make to the production of their writing. The parallel risk taken by strategies of service learning is that of erasing the role of the writer in producing the social, and erasing the material location of the writer as student, thereby making the *enabling* conditions of that location unavailable for critique. Schutz and Gere end their essay by warning, "*How* we step outside the classroom [in service-learning projects] . . . will be crucial in determining our success" (147). I am arguing that, indeed, if we are not to fall prey to such dangers, strategies which have as part of their core stepping *outside* the classroom must also have students step back *into* the classroom to remind themselves of how their material location as students in the class-room site itself contributes to the meaning that "stepping outside" has. To return to the community literacy projects described by Peck and colleagues, we need to add to their account of such projects the ways in which the material conditions of being students, or profes-sors, or other community participants (e.g., high school students), make possible the forging of specific community literacies. To be silent about such conditions is to give sway to the sense of service learning as mere do-goodism, a matter of praiseworthy charity rather than the product of not only goodwill but material goods, and so to absolve the larger community of responsibility for the con-flicts local community literacy projects attempt to address. Conversely, an insistence on the necessity of such conditions will better position those engaged in service learning to require the larger community to live up to its responsibilities for the problems that service projects are often intended to address.

In the marginalized, if common, practices of classroom compo-sition writing, some counterhegemonic work is possible—for exam-ple, resistance to demands for the commodification of readings and writings. But this practice of resistance must be linked to the material conditions in which it occurs, which must be subjected to critique. By the same token, composition courses linked to service learning can help students and teachers critically engage the mate-rial location of the composition classroom in the process of writing and reading both within and outside that location. It thus may work as a means not simply to reproduce but to challenge the prac-tices and structures that have historically denigrated students and their writing. But it can do so not by transforming the composition course into an internship service for the "real" world but by provid-ing the occasion for reconstituting the meaning of being a student in a composition course, and the meaning student writing can have in such a course.

This chapter began with critiques of Composition's various repre-sentations of students and the effect these have of displacing stu-dents from the work of Composition, rendering them essentially marginal to it, denying the participation of students in that work.

In denying or denigrating student work, we end up denying and denigrating our own, for our own is ineluctably tied to students, who indeed constitute living reminders of the materiality of that work. As an alternative approach to overcoming the alienation felt by many in Composition, Susan Miller has argued that Composition can serve as "an already designated place for counterhegemonic intellectual politics." It can in fact undermine the standardization of writing necessary to its commodification, since it knows authoritatively and can point out, for example, that "good" writing

> is the result of established cultural privileging mechanisms, not of pure "taste." . . . that a mixture of ideas, timing, entitlements, and luck have designated some rather than others as "important" writers/thinkers. . . . [That] [t]he field's most productive methods of evaluation also judge writing by situational rather than by universal standards and thus insist on the arbitrariness of evaluations and their relativity to particular power structures. (*Textual* 187)

Miller addresses her arguments to the composition "field." I have been arguing that such counterhegemonic projects can and will have to involve as well as inform students, as the "work" of composition conducted not only in journal essays or conference talks but in the "fieldwork" of composition conducted in the daily meetings, readings, and writings of students with teachers in composition classrooms. That is to say, we need to place all our work in the material social-historical process, resisting dominant definitions of our work, our students, and ourselves. We can resist the denigrating effects of these on the field, not by promoting students' accession to an authorial status we know to be problematic, nor by consigning them and ourselves to the "low" labor assigned by the dominant to Composition, but by joining with our students to investigate writing as material social practice, confronting and revising those practices that have served to reify the activity of writing into commodified texts. In spite of the obstacles, or rather because of them, I believe that is work both students and teachers in composition can engage in with real authority.

Chapter 3

POLITICS

P olitics" in Composition carries overlapping but also conflicting meanings. From popular discourse there is the
conventional use of "politics" to designate state and civil
matters, "public affairs" and issues. This seemingly innocuous
meaning is sullied by a second sense of "politics" as the pursuit of
specific interests or agendas through planning. This usage can suggest something underhanded: private "scheming" for private (sec-
tarian, "personal") interests about what are, or should be, public
matters. We can see both of these meanings operating in the once
dominant view that politics is outside the proper sphere of women:
politics is, or was, seen as inappropriate for women both because of
its focus on public rather than private, domestic life, and because
the view of humans—i.e., men—as "political animals" pursuing
their personal interests conflicted with the self-denying, "good girl"
subjectivity expected of women.

A third sense revises these meanings by extending the reach of
the "political" to apply to all human endeavors, both those officially
designated "public" and those designated "private" or "personal" (as
in "the personal is political"). This sense also revises these meanings by its presumption of human history as one of perpetual struggle over competing interests (rather than as one of harmony
occasionally interrupted by conflict), with the proviso that these

competing interests are not those of autonomous individuals but socially produced (as in, of course, class struggle). In this third sense,
politics is an inescapable dimension of all human life, not something to regret or attempt to escape but to engage as fully as possible. So, for example, in the preface to *The Politics of Writing
Instruction: Postsecondary*, the editors assert that "the teaching of
writing is unavoidably a political act. After all, there is no such
thing as value-neutral teaching, certainly not value-neutral teaching of writing." Therefore, "a genuine force for positive change in
the ways and means by which writing is taught is possible only
when we take stock of the politics of writing instruction and begin
to enter consciously and knowledgeably into the political arena"
(Bullock, Trimbur, and Schuster xviii, xix–xx). As suggested by the
reference to values, this third view of "politics" extends the reach of
the term beyond conventional notions of governmental rule to include ideology, here understood not as something one can avoid or
escape from (as from "false consciousness") but as a matter of competing sets of values, beliefs, and ways of living.

This extension of "the political" to include "the ideological,"
however, is itself an ideology in conflict with a *prevailing* ideology.
In this prevailing ideology, the "ideological" is seen precisely as
"false consciousness"; the "political" is restricted to either statecraft
or the machinations for pursuing private interests; and ideology,
politics, and power are, if sometimes necessary, nonetheless always
dirty. Unfortunately for those adopting the (Althusserian) view of
ideology as inescapable, rather than something opposed to truth,
their ideology about "ideology" is not only not dominant; it sometimes appears to have the effect of undercutting any (ethical) foundation for pursuing their values. As Patricia Bizzell notes of those
accepting this view, "Thus enmeshed in ideologies, [they] see ethical commitments as just another ideological construct, ratified by
no transcendent authority or by no match with transcendent truth"
("Marxist" 55).

Some of the confusion in the debate on "politics" in Composition
arises from mixing these different notions of politics and ideology.
That confusion, however, insofar as it is ideological, is not readily
subject to simple resolution through a more precise definition of
terms. Some confusion, of course, does result from a mixing of different conceptualizations of the terms within the same argument.

For example, in the second statement quoted above from the preface to *Politics of Writing Instruction*, urging readers to "enter consciously and knowledgeably into the political arena," the editors at least imply a view of the "political arena" as something separate from other "arenas," something one can move into (or out of). This view of the political, however, is at odds with their more extensive sense of writing instruction as *inevitably* political. Often, however, such mixing represents not just a failure of precision but a competition between residual, alternative, and dominant understandings of "politics," "ideology," and "power." Such mixing of conflicting conceptions has come to the fore in attempts to address the dilemma of how to enact a feminist pedagogy eschewing claims of authority and power while operating from a position of institutional authority and power (as, say, a tenured professor). In an echo of Bizzell, Carmen Luke, for example, observes that "[f]eminist pedagogy, conceptualized as (maternal) nurture and distanced from claims of pedagogical authority and institutional power, leaves itself wide open to the theoretical impossibility of having a 'foundation' from which to arbitrate knowledges, student voices and experiences, and the teacher's own epistemological position" ("Feminist Pedagogy" 284). This dilemma arises at least in part from a conflict between a notion of power relations as inescapable, and hence to be engaged directly, and a view of such relations as something that can and should be escaped.[1]

Aside from the mixing of definitions of politics and the competition among these notions, a third and more significant source of confusion in debate on the politics of Composition, I would argue, is the failure to understand the "politics" of specific acts both in terms of the material conditions of their specific sites and in relation to the conditions of the larger spheres encompassing those sites. We are only beginning to question, and articulate, the political effectivity of action at one social historical site in relation to other sites. Instead, arguments about the politics of pedagogy, the profession, the academy, or "society" either treat these as discrete or, at best, assume a relation of homology between these sites. Such arguments frequently invoke a dominant, monolithic, reified notion of power, a notion that undermines, by either inflating or understating, pedagogical and "professional" politics. In place of viewing power as relational, power is imagined as a commodity, something some have or acquire and use on others, or else attempt to share with or give to others to "empower" them (see Gore 56–58; A. Luke, "Genres" 322). Accordingly, those with less power in relation to those with greater power are imagined as effectively powerless, and the giving of power becomes fraught with ethical dilemmas: the giver is ethically suspect for having power in the first place; and giving power itself is suspect for encouraging complicity with the dominant. Carmen Luke's account of the dilemma facing feminists committed to principled disregard for the institutional power that they are now authorized to wield exemplifies such dilemmas.

This same view of power in Compositional work as a discrete rather than relational force is also manifested in the perspective from which the politics of Composition has to do only with the profession and its place within the academy and society. In this perspective, the "politics" of Composition can appear to surround, and perhaps even impinge upon, without, as it were, infiltrating the site of its teaching. We can see the dominance of this perspective in the devotion of the majority of the essays in *Politics of Writing Instruction* to conflicts between various groups of its members that seem to threaten the integrity of the profession (e.g., teachers vs. researchers, those affiliated with the study of classical rhetoric vs. others, full- vs. part-timers) or to conflicts between compositionists and others (literature professors, university administrators and other departments, society at large). Alternatively, essays on the politics of pedagogy frequently ignore such issues, restricting their focus instead to relations between the instructor and students.

Schematically, we might say that the focus on the politics of the profession rehearses a conception of politics as involving strictly "public" matters, and implicitly recognizes only the exchange value of compositional work, whereas the focus on the politics of pedagogy accepts a view of politics as inherent to any activity but restricts itself to the political nature of the (relatively) private realm of the individual classroom or course, and the use value of work conducted there. My argument, however, is that we can understand the politics of either site only by locating our work with and on the "political," however conceived, in its specific material location, and by addressing the processes by which that work is converted in value from one site to the next. We need, in other words, to examine how the politics of a pedagogy intersects and interacts with the politics of the profession, and the material circumstances of teaching, teachers' professional positioning, and larger material circumstances of these, associated with the institutional and historical location of the course, teacher, and students. This requires understanding both the ways in which the "politics" of compositional work is susceptible to commodification, and the ways of resisting such commodification. I begin by examining the commodification of politics within the realm of pedagogy and the classroom, first as politics is understood as a "topic" *in* pedagogy, and secondly as it is understood as an attribute *of* pedagogy. Reviewing debate over teachers' exercise of power and authority, particularly in "critical" pedagogy, I argue that a full and differentiated sense of power as relational requires not only recognizing the different forms in which teachers exercise power and students' real, if limited, agency but also locating the teacher, students, and course—in short, the pedagogy—in relation to the larger institutional and material historical conditions of its production. This must include the means by which pedagogical work is capitalized, and the contingencies affecting its capitalization and valuation. In the final section, I examine specific ways in which the politics of pedagogy and the politics of the profession may converge, and delineate how addressing the processes of such conversion might enable us to better engage the politics of our work and the work of our politics.

"Politics" in Pedagogy

There is a seemingly innocuous place for politics *in* pedagogy as the assigned subject matter on which students are to write: abortion, pro or con; gun control, pro or con; and so forth. The theory behind this long-standing practice would seem to be that students need "lively" topics on which to write, topics that will somehow inspire them to do more than rote work. But then, typically and significantly, the point of assigning such topics is not to learn more about them, or even to learn what students' opinions are, but to produce fodder for lessons on the skills of writing formal arguments. And so long as students are judged not for what they write (or think) but how they write (with correct or incorrect spelling, say), no "political" controversy need ensue: hence the lack of public outcry over the practice. The innocuousness of such a practice derives from the commodification of both "politics" and the teaching of writing it effects. For in such uses of "politics," both the positions taken and the work of producing them are commodified, removed from the circumstances in which the actual taking of those positions and the work of adopting and advocating them have immediate use value. Instead, such pedagogies use assignments to write arguments as a means of producing the abstracted skills of argumentation (and, sometimes, research). Which of the assigned "positions" students take is a matter of indifference.

The crucial role which the commodification of "political" topics and skills in argumentation through their abstraction plays in the acceptability of such a composition pedagogy is illustrated by the counterexample of the reception given the University of Texas (UT), Austin's proposed English 306 course on "Writing about Difference." With the goading of the conservative National Association of Scholars, opponents of the course inferred from its title (or its ostensible title, many getting even that wrong [Brodkey, "Making" 248, 251]), a pedagogy of political indoctrination. The choice of subject matter on which students were assigned to write, that is, seemed to stem from the instructors' sense of what was, and was not, an issue meriting discussion, and thus was taken to be understood not in the abstract, as mere fodder, but a focal point of the course: oppression, say, or social difference. Had the "topic" of the UT Austin course been seen as clearly subordinate to a focus on acquiring abstract rhetorical skills—for example, had the title of the course been "Writing Arguments," say, rather than "Writing about Difference"—the story of English 306 may have been very different, since for mainstream culture, Composition's proper focus is precisely on such "technical" matters (see Brodkey, "Making" 247–48). Both the arguments written in such a course and the topics addressed would then be understood as of no use in themselves; rather, the value of the course would reside in the abstract skills of writing acquired and made available for exchange.

Of course, the distinction between topic and pedagogy is not so easily maintained, as Brodkey's own experience and the occasional outbursts in debate team activities and courses in argument writing demonstrate. The fragility of this distinction is also suggested when no outbursts occur. James Seitz, for example, argues that having students write on topics conventionally recognized as "political"—topics of state or civil issues of current, public debate—can in fact encourage the production of a highly restricted, conventionally "political" discourse: arrogant, repetitive, predictable, banal, and ultimately oppressively boring ("Eluding" 7–8).[2] That is, such topics have been so commodified as to seem inherently abstract to students, rather than as something that they may find use in addressing. As a response to this phenomenon, and recognizing the "ubiquity of the 'political' " ("Eluding" 8), Seitz argues that the political be taught not through invoking conventionally political discourse but through addressing the politics—which he renames the rhetoric—of all discourse:

> Since "the political," broadly conceived—in the form of assumptions, biases, selections, and repressions—runs through all writing, teachers and students must surely attend to the political influences at play in any texts examined in class. . . . The political . . . emerges along the whole spectrum of discursive practices, from diaries, letters, interviews, stories, biographies, plays, journalism, criticism, theory, and so on, as well as from essays that argue explicitly for the correctness of a certain public agenda. [Thus] [t]here is no reason to limit student writing to issues of politics in order to do justice to the political character of language. (10)

This is a very tempting argument. First, it allows teachers to claim to practice what Seitz, borrowing from Roland Barthes, terms a "discreet" politics in their teaching while offering the possibility of avoiding the fate of Brodkey, her colleagues, and English 306 (Seitz 7–8). Second, it is more consistent with the view of the "political" as indeed ubiquitous to which many of those advocating writing courses that engage the political subscribe. Third, it increases the likelihood that attention is given to issues not already demarcated by the dominant as "political" but whose political effects are often felt by the marginalized. As Carmen Luke observes, "For many women, substantive political problems often are private and not the same as those deemed as public, common interest" ("Feminist Politics" 36). The "political sphere," like the "public" sphere with which it is associated, is one defined and controlled by the dominant, and hence likely to exclude consideration of the politics of what the dominant has defined as "private." Thus, focusing on the politics in all discursive practices makes it possible to address how what is commonly defined as the "personal" is, indeed, political. Finally, pedagogically, too, this strategy may be more promising in engaging students in the politics of writing than a course devoted to the topic of social oppression, conventionally understood, since conventionally political topics may encourage a highly restricted, conventionally political discourse. Seitz reports that students taking a course about social oppression that he helped design—many of them victims of such oppression—ended up complaining about the restricted nature of that discourse, pleading, "Aren't we going to deal with anything besides *oppression*?" ("Eluding" 9). Conversely, a course addressing the politics of discursive practices conventionally defined as non-political may enable students to see the use value of their explorations of their discursive practices.

There is a danger in pursuing the "discreet" politics of this strategy, however, arising from the dilemma posed to those who do accept the ubiquity of the political. Like those who accept an Althusserian view of ideology, that view can appear to preclude teaching any particular politics or ideology, whether espoused in writing or enacted through its rhetoric. That is, the "discreet" politics of the pedagogy may remain "discreet," not something which students and teachers directly engage. Instead, those accepting this view of politics may resort to teaching and learning just politics and ideology in general rather than the discreet politics they are practicing in the discursive practices of teaching and writing. Hence that politics can become, by default, an "apolitical" politics of laissez-faire pluralism (cf. Jay and Graff 206).

Seitz's own recommended pedagogy appears to lapse into just such a politics. Seitz recommends assigning a variety of roles for students to play, "not . . . to teach a *particular* rhetorical maneuver, such as arguing for a political position, but to teach rhetorical maneuvering itself, how to shift from one discourse to another as occasion demands" ("Eluding" 11). To do this, he would assign students particular fictional roles so that they could "absorb the conventions of this particular role in order to appropriate or revise them for their own ends" (11). What those ends might be, however, appears to remain unavailable for critique. So, while in one sense this pedagogy would teach students "to locate the political even in writing that appears distant from politics" (Seitz, "Eluding" 12), it would not have students address *their* politics, or the politics of the pedagogy itself, only politics in the abstract. The use value of the work students accomplished in their writing would be made subordinate to the exchange value of the skills of learning how, and when, in the abstract (future), to take a particular stance.

One alternative to the distantiation from politics to which this pedagogy is susceptible is to insist not simply on exploring the *rhetorical* politics of adopting a particular position—for example, arrogant or not, self-effacing or not—but, as Min-Zhan Lu has argued, to insist on "the politics of assigning and assuming particular points of view and not others. . . . each individual's need and right to deliberate over decisions about where and how to position oneself in relation to diverse cultures" ("Representing" 131). Lu's is an argument for reclaiming, by redefining, "PC" pedagogy as one focused on "power and conflict, politics and commitment." Her pedagogy would thus aim at teaching not a "politically correct" position but that "no position, textual or otherwise, can be taken in isolation from the power relationships among diverse cultures with conflicting political interests" (131). Rather than *assuming* the ubiquity of the political, this strategy takes that ubiquity as its explicit focus. Further, such a focus would ground analysis of the ubiquitous political dimension of writing in the specifics of history and culture in which students and professors live, and so would avoid the abstraction of politics and the descent into laissez-faire pluralism effected by rhetorical role play.[3]

The Politics of Pedagogy: Power and Pedagogy as Commodities

In her essay, Lu is concerned with having students confront the politics they enact through the kinds of positions they take and the ways in which they take them. She is not concerned with the inflections of the specific power relations of the institutional roles of teaching and learning in the composition course, nor does she address the location of the politics students enact in the material conditions of their enactment—in, for example, a required composition course. This is in contrast to much of the debate on the politics of pedagogy, which does concern itself almost exclusively with the relations of power between teachers and students. Many of the attempts to address those relations, however, have been limited by treating power, authority and pedagogy as commodities, a treatment that undermines efforts to view teaching and learning as located in the material social process. That is, their treatment of teacher-student politics isolates these from the larger context of the courses and conditions in which they are enacted. To illustrate this phenomenon, I turn to Elizabeth Ellsworth's account of her attempt to enact critical pedagogy in a Curriculum and Instruction course ("C&I 607") on "Media and Anti-Racist Pedagogies" at the University of Wisconsin-Madison, and to debate on issues raised by that account.[4] For that debate demonstrates both the dominance of commodified notions of power and pedagogy and the need to confront the commodification of the work of composition pedagogy in our teaching and writing.

What makes Ellsworth's account troubling is the way in which she treats critical pedagogy as a commodity only to condemn it for failing to deliver as a commodity.[5] Ellsworth reports that she aimed in her course to practice key concepts of critical pedagogy—empowerment, student voice, dialogue, and so on. However, her efforts seem to have led to relations of domination the very opposite of critical pedagogy's expressed aims (298). While she expected her critical pedagogy to lead students to engage in open dialogue, establish egalitarian democratic relations, experience individual freedom, have their race, class, and gender positions affirmed, and so forth, she found that the experience of the students and herself in her course failed to conform to these abstract "myths." Consequently, she rejects critical pedagogy as "repressive," calling instead for a "pedagogy of the unknowable" (318–24).

 This account is troubling because the "failure" of the course seems simultaneously inevitable, and therefore indisputable, and yet beside the point, arising from her treatment of critical pedagogy as a commodity. Having reduced critical pedagogy to a commodity isolated from the material circumstances of its specific enactments, she then critiques it for its failure, as commodity, to address just such circumstances. That she expected critical pedagogy to operate as a commodity is apparent in the ways in which she introduced it into her teaching. For example, in her account of her teaching, she explains that when she was asked by her students what she meant by "critical" in her syllabi descriptions of the critical pedagogy of her courses, she simply "referred them to answers provided in the literature" (299), as if such a pedagogy were monolithic and fixed in meaning and effect. Noting, for example, that whereas "the literature on critical pedagogy implies that students and teachers can and should engage each other in the classroom as fully rational subjects," she complains that "students and professor entered C&I 607 with investments of privilege and struggle already made in favor of some ethical and political positions concerning racism and against other positions" (301), thus precluding the purely rationalist, analytical dialogue at which critical pedagogy aims. And she finds that "[a]cting as if our classroom were a safe space in which democratic dialogue was possible and happening did not make it so" (315). In other words, she is shocked to discover that the actual historical realities of the students, herself as professor, and C&I 607 failed to match the ideal at which critical pedagogy aims. But rather than concluding with a recognition of the need for her and her students to rework the meaning and substance of critical pedagogy anew in each historical instance of its practice, as one might expect, Ellsworth uses the inevitable gap between the aims of critical pedagogy and the lived experience of the C&I 607 course to condemn the pedagogy for its failure, by itself, to close that gap. Like an angry consumer, she rejects critical pedagogy as repressive rather than liberatory, as a commodity that does not "work" as advertised.

In keeping with this treatment of pedagogy as commodity, power and authority in her argument are treated as a single entity uniform in its essence and effects. Attributed to the pedagogy alone, power is seen not as relational but as an essentialized entity acting through the teacher on the students, its exercise always inevitably repressive. Thus she ends up rejecting the possibility of the "emancipatory authority" of the critical pedagogue as by definition a contortion of logic and rhetoric, for, by her logic, any exercise of "authority" is complicit with "authoritarianism" and so cannot be emancipatory (307). Indeed, she rejects the possibility of any ethical exercise of teacherly authority altogether: how, she asks rhetorically, "does a teacher 'make' students autonomous without directing them?" (308). In such statements, Ellsworth implies that since by definition any actual use of authority is problematic, all exercise of authority must be ruled out. The problematic of authority is grounds for its rejection (cf. McLaren 71–72).

Much of the criticism responding to Ellsworth has focused on her limited conception of classroom power relations obtaining or possible between teachers and students in their institutional roles as teachers and students. That criticism insists on a more differentiated or relational view of power that would grant, or acknowledge, a degree of agency to students and qualify the totalized understanding of the effect of power that Ellsworth seems to fear. While such criticisms complicate the picture of politics operating within the classroom, they typically do not address the relation of such politics to the larger material circumstances in which such a politics takes place.

For example, Patricia Bizzell, in a critique of Ellsworth, argues that teachers need to differentiate among the ways they can exercise power. Bizzell identifies Ellsworth's experience as exemplary of the impasse of teachers like herself who "want to serve the common good with the power we possess by virtue of our position as teachers, [but who nonetheless remain] deeply suspicious of any exercise of power in the classroom" ("Power" 54). To break through this impasse, Bizzell argues, we need a more differentiated notion of power ("Power" 54–55).

Bizzell herself differentiates three types of power: "coercion," "persuasion," and "authority" ("Power" 56–57). Where coercion involves A's exercise of power over B without the consent of B, persuasion is the exercise of power only with both parties' consent, and only in ways that change both. For Bizzell, persuasion represents the kind of power ideally exercised in dialogic or collaborative, non-hierarchical teaching. Authority, on the other hand, is exercised when A acts instrumentally over B without having to persuade B that the actions will serve B's interests; no "persuasion" is required. However, authority differs from coercion in that B must first grant A the right to exercise such power over B by being persuaded that this will be in B's best interests. Thus, in this third type of power, "once B has been persuaded to grant authority to A, their relationship changes to a less dialogic one. B empowers A to direct their course of action without A's having to exercise persuasion at every step taken" (57–58).

Bizzell accounts for the failure of Ellsworth's course as a case of her failure to differentiate between coercion and authority. Ellsworth's recognition of her own partiality incapacitates her from giving direction to the course, since it precludes the rational persuasion she sees as requisite to critical pedagogy (Bizzell, "Power" 61–63). While Bizzell sees Ellsworth's recognition of the partiality of all parties as laudable, she also sees Ellsworth's students as in desperate need of direction to bring their varied experiences of difference "around a shared project" (63). What Ellsworth dismisses from consideration as a "paternalistic" move—the teacher deciding for the students what will be necessary—Bizzell names utopian, in the positive sense of a "projected image of what we might achieve" (63). And if this seems to require the imposition of the teacher's ideology (or "politics"), then, for Bizzell, so be it. As she argues elsewhere, the eschewal of one's ethical commitments on the grounds that everything is ideological in fact "indicates a real nostalgia for the transcendent ratification that we in theory reject. For if we were utterly convinced of the inevitability of ideology, we would not feel uneasy about seeing the world through ideological interpretations" ("Marxist" 55). In other words, the disavowal of pursuing one's politics because one recognizes the ubiquity of the political represents a slide from the more extensive, Althusserian notion of ideology to the more restricted, conventional sense of ideology as "false consciousness." While recognizing one's inevitable "partiality" can affect *how* one pursues one's ethical commitments, it does not justify abjuring those commitments, which would, in effect, lead to collusion with dominant ideology—laissez-faire pluralism, again. This is not to excuse coercion in the name of one's commitment to achieving a particular utopian vision but to commit ourselves to learning to live with and confront the contradictions between our inevitable partiality and the egalitarian universals of the utopian ideals we espouse (see Bizzell, "Marxist" 64–66).

While Bizzell's differentiation of types of exercise of power offers a way of escaping the "impasse" of teachers pursuing critical pedagogy's seemingly contradictory ideals of empowering and directing students, the model she presents remains limited in its conception of power itself as an entity, to be used or distributed, in whatever different ways. In an examination of power in education, Nicholas Burbules notes this limitation in efforts to differentiate power. First, such attempts "assume that power is something an individual or group has, and uses, and that what differs is the form of exercising it"; second, such "typological" approaches tend to "hypostasize what are actually artificial points of emphasis"; finally, "the very attempt to classify discrete forms that power takes distracts from the interrelated aspect of certain elements (e.g., persuasion and manipulation), . . . and from the systemic nature of power in society as a continuous 'web' of relationships that catches up persons in a series of effects which are only partly intended" (96). We can see these limitations operating in Bizzell's formulations. These treat power as an entity individuals possess and exercise (e.g., "A" exercising power over "B," with or without B's consent), overlook the politics of categorizing power as she has, and assume a degree of autonomy among the parties involved in such exercises at odds with the Althusserian view of power and ideology that otherwise informs her arguments.

As an alternative to such approaches, Burbules, drawing from Anthony Giddens, argues for viewing power as relational (Burbules 97). Such a conception emphasizes the circumstances under which specific parties come together, and thus avoids the rationalist view of the exercise of power and the expectation of fixed outcomes from that exercise. A complex of material circumstances, as much as any uniform conscious intentions, determine, or rather, overdetermine, power relations and the effects of their operation. Further, a view of power as relational undermines the reification of power, and types of power, as always and everywhere the same entity. Rather than differentiating power in terms of the consent of those on whom it is exercised, power is differentiated according to the specifics of those circumstances. And finally, this view recognizes a degree of power in all parties rather than in just one. As Giddens observes,

> Power relations . . . are always *two-way*, even if the power of one actor or party in a social relation is minimal compared to another. Power relations are relations of autonomy and dependence, but even the most autonomous agent is in some degree dependent, and the most dependent actor or party in a relationship retains some autonomy. (93; qtd. in Burbules 97)

Applying this view of power to Ellsworth's example, we might say that her students' resistance to her efforts at achieving a "critical" pedagogical ideal represents not evidence of the failure of that pedagogy nor her failure to assume authority but students' own exercise of power in relation to Ellsworth. It was thus not something that had to interfere with the course but evidence of the potential they brought to bear on the course. From this perspective, too, Ellsworth's complaint that "there have been no sustained research attempts to explore whether or how the practices [critical pedagogy] prescribes actually alter specific power relations outside or inside schools" (301) is robbed of its force, depending as it does on a failure to recognize both the complex of power relations operating in any given historical site and the overdetermination of their effects. As Jennifer Gore argues, if power is viewed as relational, something one "exercises" rather than as an entity one has and can give to or share with others, then "we confront the unforeseeable and contradictory effects of the exercise of power and must be more humble and reflexive in our claims," recognizing that "no matter what our aims or how we go about 'empowering', our efforts will be partial and inconsistent" (62, 63). From this perspective, the indeterminate effects of Ellsworth's "pedagogy of the unknowable" are an attribute to be granted any pedagogy, given the operation of such complexes in any site. We cannot expect the exercise of power to be simply either empowering or repressive.

Critics' recognition of power as relational and of the consequent indeterminacy of its effects can thus help in resisting the commodification of pedagogy. But to further such resistance, the application of this recognition cannot be restricted to relations within the course but must also be applied to relations between the changing positionalities of students before, during, and after a course; relations between one's students and others *outside* the course; and relations between the course and the specific institutional and more general material conditions in which it is located. Ellsworth is good at differentiating among students *within* her course (by race, sex, sexual orientation, class, etc.) but fails to make differentiations diachronically and synchronically, between student positions before, during the progress of the course, and after, and between her students and others. Ellsworth does note that both she and her students experienced contradictory and shifting positionalities, a possibility she admits critical pedagogy recognizes. However, she complains about the "pain, confusion, and difficulty" this posed for herself and students (311–12). A non-commodified understanding of pedagogy would take the difficulty her students' multiple subject positions posed for their ability to "speak," however painful, as inescapable, something to be directly confronted, rather than as a justification for dismissing the pedagogy. Unlike the view of pedagogy as commodity, in which teaching and learning must be pain-free, must feel "good" to all, treating pedagogy as the site for doing work on a project would give students and teacher the perspective, context, and direction to understand and work through such difficulties (cf. Giroux, "Border" 176; hooks, *Talking Back* 52–53, 102–3; and Bizzell's discussion, "Power" 64–65). A relational view of power would aid in thinking through how to confront the different positionalities such students experience, when, and how to exercise what sort of power to help move the students as a whole towards the project of the course.

For example, Ellsworth and her students might have negotiated where and how they, in all their partialities, would direct *all* their materially limited energies to investigate and counter racist structures and practices at the University of Wisconsin–Madison (the initial topic of and impetus for the course, after all), using what expertise, authority, and resources they possessed to work toward such ends, rather than attempting the inevitably doomed project of achieving a critical utopia in classroom relations. Indeed, it appears that the students themselves came to abandon Ellsworth's commitment to achieving an ideal classroom environment when they transformed the course into what they termed "Coalition 607" (317). That is, rather than imagining the work of the course outside material exigencies, they relocated it within a particular time and place, re-oriented their efforts at achieving more reachable goals, and treated their contradictions and partialities in relation to those exigencies rather than letting them serve as obstacles to their work.

That they were successful in doing so demonstrates the need to couple attention to differences within and among students in a course over time with attention to differences between the students within a course and students and others outside the course. Ellsworth is attentive to the differences among her students, but she says little about the relation of those students to other students, to their institutional position vis-à-vis those other students, the university, herself, and the course, all of which might provide a useful perspective and context from which to understand the difficulties and successes she and they experienced. Gore, noting that many accounts of feminist and critical pedagogies "pay little attention to the location of their practices in educational institutions," argues that we need to define the contexts for such pedagogical work "historically and politically with acknowledgment of the unique struggles that characterize the exercise of power at the micro levels." Otherwise the problem of "empowerment" remains trapped in the dualisms of "power/powerlessness, and dominant/subordinate" as "purely oppositional stances," rather than being understood as a problem of "multiplicity and contradiction" (61). In the case of Ellsworth's course, differentiating between her students and others by attending to the fact that the course was a special topics, graduate education course rather than, say, a required first-year writing course would surely be significant to any understanding of the work of that course. By contrast, her failure to investigate the implications of the specific institutional, curricular location of the course and its student population for its work threatens to make her account an example in reverse of the composition testimonials which I have discussed in chapter 2, for it tends to render the course, the teacher, and the students transhistorically. Indeed, her account differs from such "testimonials" only by its use of the experience to illustrate not a pedagogy that "works," but one that doesn't. Conversely, an understanding of her students as enrolled in a graduate education program at least suggests a specific condition of power they enjoyed in relation to Ellsworth, the school, and other students that would begin to account for the particular turns and successes the course took. It would enable us to see the pedagogy as something which students, so positioned, engaged *with*, that they "worked," in particular if contradictory ways, to particular if contradictory ends, rather than treating the pedagogy as something expected to act *on* the students in predictable and uniform ways, as commodity.

In this sense, even Ellsworth's posited "unknowability" of pedagogy represents nostalgia for a transcendent master narrative that she has learned to reject, a desire for an impartial knowledge when she suspects both the impossibility of such a knowledge and the oppressiveness of claims to such knowledge. In terms of Carmen Luke's argument, the "failure" of Ellsworth's course illustrates the self-defeating self-denial to which the "good girl" myth can lead teachers. The invocation of unknowability crystallizes the limitations of a reified, totalized conception of power as uniform in its essence and effects. And finally, her call for a new pedagogy demonstrates the dilemmas on which teachers get caught when pedagogies are taken for, and judged as, commodities, for a "pedagogy of the unknowable" represents, paradoxically, the ultimate in pedagogical commodities—a pedagogy that promises, quite credibly, that it cannot *not* fail to "deliver."

Pedagogy and the Contingencies of Power

Ellsworth concludes her account by asking what it would mean to confront "unknowability," "to recognize not only that a multiplicity of knowledges are present in the classroom . . . but that these knowledges are contradictory, partial, and irreducible. . . . when even the combination of all partial knowledges in a classroom results in yet another partial knowing. . . . [when] every social, political, or educational project the class takes up locally will already, at the moment of its definition, lack knowledges necessary to answer broader questions of human survival and social justice" (321). Ellsworth's questions and my critique may be seen as implying not simply that we should expect from all pedagogies a degree of unknowability, but also that this unknowability justifies absolving ourselves of responsibility for our pedagogy, on the grounds that the effects of what we do are, after all, not strictly speaking under our control: they are "unknowable." Such a conclusion, however, would only evince nostalgia for transcendent certainty and lead effectually to giving sway to the dominant.

That nostalgia, further, again demonstrates a commodified notion of pedagogy, for it places on pedagogy a burden it cannot possibly bear alone, assigning it a task it cannot by itself perform. Indeed, we can see evidence of such a view in the exclusiveness of the concern both Ellsworth and her critics have with power in the classroom. Such a focus is suggested by Ellsworth's assertion that for her purposes in her essay, "The most important interruption of existing power relations within the university consisted of trans-forming business-as-usual—that is, prevailing social relations—in a university classroom" (299). This statement makes sense only if we accept both a unitary conception of power and a homological view of its exercise in different sites. That is, the specific relations of power occurring at a pedagogical site are seen as equivalent to relations of power at all other sites; consequently, to interrupt the business-as-usual of the university in any of its sites constitutes interruption of that business at all its other sites. Business is business.

If carried to its logical extreme, such a strategy would be a recipe for full containment of counterhegemonic efforts, since it would effectively direct such efforts to those sites the dominant has already foresworn as inconsequential. This is not to dismiss the sig-nificance of the politics of teacher-student relations but to insist that we locate those relations within their specific material sites, differentiating between the significance of power relations in spe-cific instances and locales, and considering the interaction of those relations among sites. We can account for the particularly compli-cated and angst-ridden experience of C&I 607 that Ellsworth de-scribes as in part the result of her initial failure to differentiate power in such ways.

By contrast, the "pedagogy of the unknowable" Ellsworth ends up calling for appears to require such location, for it is defined as a practice "profoundly contextual (historical) and interdependent (so-cial)" (323). While Ellsworth's invocation of a "pedagogy of the un-knowable," as I have argued above, itself suggests a lingering desire for a commodifiable pedagogy, albeit paradoxically one that fails to "deliver" a consumable product, its emphasis on the "unknowable" also hints at a recognition of the inevitable indeter-minacy of any pedagogy, critical pedagogy included, abstractly con-ceived, when put into material practice. As commodity, however, even her touted pedagogy retains crucial limitations in its concep-tion of teachers and students and does not address the relation of the politics of pedagogy to actions and social change at other sites.

To avoid succumbing to the irresponsible twins of such nostal-gia and passivity while recognizing the indeterminacy of the poli-tics enacted in pedagogy means changing the issue teachers address to themselves, as Gore puts it, from "what we can do for you" to "what can we do for you," posed as a non-rhetorical question

(62). Answering that question requires both differentiating relations of power and examining their interactions. Allan Luke, drawing on Pierre Bourdieu's differentiation of the kinds of "capital" available to humans, points to one way by which the politics of pedagogies may be so understood. Luke focuses on how the particular types of "power" of a pedagogy are "capitalized"—that is, the conditions and processes by which such power is constituted, increased, exchanged, or devalued ("Genres" 326–27). Like Ellsworth, Luke critiques versions of Freirean critical (as well as "genre") pedagogies that romanticize individual voice and student empowerment and mask the political sources of teacher authority (314). However, his critique differs from Ellsworth's by also repudiating the reification of power in such pedagogies. Describing such pedagogies as based on a "hypodermic" model of power in which the literate practices taught are imagined as directly inculcating power, he notes that this " 'pedagogy equals power equation' tends to have a one-dimensional, singular ontology of power. . . . [tending] to psychologise or textualise power, because all power is seen to be of the same logical type and empirical status" ("Genres" 315, 322–23). Power thus comes to be seen as a "possession . . . that can be transmitted (and therefore, bought, owned, rented, leased, and yes, foreclosed), something that is apparently culture-neutral and politically neutral, and something that has economic exchange value" (322).

To complicate this view of power and pedagogy, Luke uses Bourdieu's distinctions between and among cultural, economic, and social capital and his analysis of the conditions and processes by which one form of capital is converted into another. While literacy instruction can provide students with both embodied and institutional cultural capital (in the form of bodily training and practice, and credentials, respectively), whether and how such capital "counts," and for what, depends on its relation to social capital, and whether it is recognized *as* capital. For example, as John Ogbu has argued, while schools may provide blacks with cultural capital (e.g., through training in specific literacy practices), as a "caste-like" minority, blacks lack social capital (232–33). As a result, any cultural capital they acquire through schooling is less likely to be recognized *as* capital, or is likely to be devalued relative to the cultural capital others acquire through schooling, and so cannot readily be converted to economic capital. Blacks continue to be overqualified, and underpaid, for the jobs they get (Ogbu 239). Not surprisingly, this, along with blacks' ongoing history of limited access to equal education and unfair treatment in the schools, has led many blacks quite reasonably to mistrust the value of the cultural capital schools ostensibly offer as a ruse (Ogbu 238–41).[6] As Luke observes, "possession of cultural and symbolic capital is neither necessary nor sufficient for economic and social power. The cultural capital generated in literacy training can only be realised and articulated through a series of contingencies which arise in the cultural and social field" ("Genres" 330).

Recognizing the contingent nature of the cultural capital that schools generate leads Luke to call for a pedagogy that "offers social and cultural strategies for analysing and engaging with the conversion of capital in various cultural fields. . . . build[ing] for students a critical social theory of practice" ("Genres" 332). He would have us build on the strengths of "liberatory" critical and feminist pedagogies by refocusing outward from texts to "diachronic social analyses of education, text-based economies and cultures" (332, 333). Thus, his critique leads him not to disown such pedagogies but to complicate them by incorporating into them the analysis of such processes of the capitalization of knowledge. Similarly, J. Elspeth Stuckey, recognizing the ways in which "literacy" constitutes an act of violence in denying the contingent nature of the cultural capital it represents, calls for teaching those contingencies, asking that we learn to understand "the connections between literacy and economy, literacy and work, literacy and race, gender and class, literacy and English teachers" (122).

For the alternative conclusion drawn from the contingent nature of the power of literacy training—that such training is a mere ruse distracting attention from and excusing social oppression—is to accede to a more totalized conception of the hegemonic, and a more restricted notion of the political, than is justified. There is, of course, plenty of evidence to make us suspicious of the power of literacy training as either politically inconsequential or complicit with perpetuating the myth that literacy in itself justifies social relations in fact produced by classism, sexism, racism, and so on. This can especially seem the case for college level literacy instruction. As Stuckey observes, "College English teachers do not . . . teach *as a matter of course* unemployed or impoverished minority women.

They do not, *as a matter of course*, teach many or most of their children. . . . [Thus] at the precise point at which literacy becomes 'functional,' English teachers in the United States become [politically] dysfunctional" (108). Following this perspective, Jeff Smith argues that because college students constitute an aspiring elite, those teachers interested in teaching literacy as a means of combatting social injustice had best go elsewhere, where they might meet, teach, and possibly "empower" the non-elite ("Students" 302, 318). Some arguments for service learning claim similarly that because universities teach the already select, it is only by leaving the academy that pedagogy can work for social justice.

But while it is true that schooling, literacy, and the academy generally are not the driving force behind social change, they are also not powerless to effect such change.[7] There is a reversion in this reaction to a reified, monolithic notion of power: if pedagogy is less powerful than other forces, it is imagined to therefore have no power, rather than a different sort of power in relation to other contingencies. While it is well to bear in mind the limitations and indeterminate effects of the cultural capital students may acquire through literacy training, at the college or other levels, it is wrong to use those as justification for abandoning such training altogether. Indeed, to use the indeterminacy of its effects as a reason to abandon literacy training altogether betrays a familiar nostalgia for a sure thing, a simple, guaranteed cure. Of course, as those reacting in these ways suggest, we can and should grant, promote, and engage ourselves in battling injustice on other fronts, whether in our roles as academics, citizens, family members, or other capacities.[8] But our activities on such fronts need not preclude working for such goals at the site of college teaching as well.

Further, aside from the limiting nostalgia for certain cures that such reactions invoke, they also tend to essentialize the identities of students. While, unlike Ellsworth, they differentiate between students in college and those outside college, they fail to recognize the differences among those students within courses and the differences within individual students over time. While we can and should (and many have been and continue to) work to alter the gatekeeping effected through college admissions standards, it would be counterproductive to ignore, until such gatekeeping accords fully with our notions of social justice, those students presently admitted as uniformly elite. For if class and other social positions are inherently contradictory and relational, then the ostensibly "elite" students in college composition classes are themselves subject to such contradictions and so merit attention. "Class" is not a "problem" (or responsibility) exclusively of the working class, any more than race is a problem only for non-whites, or sexism just a women's concern. Further, students' social positions and self positioning can and do change over time, in response to pedagogies as well as to other forces, rather than being wholly determined.

Converging Politics of Pedagogy and the Profession

I have been arguing that the "politics" and "power" of any pedagogy must be understood not as commodities but in terms of the material, historical specificities of their enactment. Attention to such specificities requires that such "politics" be understood as acting not instrumentally but relationally. As Allan Luke suggests, the politics of pedagogy have to be recognized as socially (and historically) contingent, responding to the circumstances of the course, institution, students, and larger social historical forces.[9] I have not directly addressed the more common understanding of the "politics of Composition" having to do with the profession of Composition: its "internal" politics and its relations with English, the academy, and society generally. As I have suggested at the opening of this chapter, politics in the two spheres of the classroom and the profession are typically viewed separately; arguments for a specific pedagogy rarely address the political relations of the profession, and vice versa. In chapter 1 I address the "politics" of defining and determining the value of Composition's work, and in chapter 4 I address the politics of Composition's relations to English and other academic disciplines and programs. In chapter 5 I address the specific internal politics of efforts to "professionalize" Composition. In this final section of the present chapter, I will focus on how the politics often seen as "internal" to Composition as a profession interact with the politics "internal" to pedagogy, and on the relation of both these politics to more broadly conceived social historical contingencies.

Bourdieu has argued that "it is not . . . political stances which determine people's stances on things academic, but their positions in the academic field which inform the stances that they adopt on political issues in general as well as on academic problems" (*Homo*

Academicus xvii–xviii). Applied to composition teachers, this would mean that their institutional positions within colleges and within departments would inform their stances on politics generally as well as on "academic" issues, including pedagogy. The most obvious sense in which this is seen as true is that those teachers in more vulnerable positions—for example, those lacking tenure, in part-time or adjunct positions dependent on department chairs, deans, or provosts for their jobs—would be most pressured to adopt stances on both political and academic matters aligned, or at least not opposed, to the stances of such figures, as a means of improving their chances at job security (Faigley 66).

This is the argument made for tenure as necessary to insure academic freedom. To give this argument a more concretely materialist inflection, we can say that the working conditions of part-time and adjunct faculty increase the likelihood that their teaching will conform to dominant expectations of the academic institution and the public, whether because such conformity is written into their contracts, in the form of required texts and syllabi, or because they have neither incentive nor time to teach differently (see "Progress Report" 335). Workbooks, for example, may take less time to correct than essays. A focus on "error," whatever its "practicality" for students, may well be an eminently "practical" solution for beleaguered teachers teaching multiple sections packed with too many students, particularly those teachers trying to cobble together several "part-time" jobs and earnings to achieve full-time survival.[10] At institutions that define teachers' performance in terms of the number of students who pass required exit exams, teachers might well focus on "teaching to the test." Similarly, instructors whose job security depends on receiving favorable student course evaluations are unlikely either to be too "demanding" or to challenge the dominant ideological viewpoints of their students, another factor that may in certain instances encourage a focus on just such "practical" matters as "error" (see Janangelo).[11] Alternatively, according to this argument, tenured faculty have both the material resources and the academic "freedom" to develop and enact pedagogies in ways that run counter to the political stances of either academic administrators, their students, or the public. Their institutional position as tenured faculty authorizes them to bestow the benefits of their professional knowledge and expertise on students.

Such arguments usefully inscribe the academic within the material realm. A teacher's "politics," they suggest, have much to do with her institutional position. However, these arguments typically assume the same commodified notion of the "politics" of pedagogy critiqued above: as something to be simply read off course syllabi and teaching practices, rather than as operating in relation to social historical contingencies. While the pedagogy a teacher adopts may well be partially determined by her institutional position, the political effects of that pedagogy inhere not in the "pedagogy itself" but in the contingencies of material social history. The politics of pedagogy thus have to be understood in terms of the relations between both the pedagogy and the contingencies of its enactment.

There is an alternative view of the import of one's institutional position on the politics of one's pedagogy that nonetheless accepts this commodified view of politics. According to this view, while the material resources and job security of tenure "free" faculty to argue for, develop, and enact counterhegemonic pedagogies, that very freedom may well be earned on the backs of the adjuncts and part-timers. Who, after all, is teaching those sections from which the tenured professor is "released" to do such work? As Richard Ohmann observes of himself and the contributors to *Politics of Writing Instruction* in his foreword to that volume, "Would we have the free time to theorize the politics of writing instruction, imagine our way toward liberatory composition, and excoriate the two-class system in our field [of writing instruction] if we were in the other class [of the writing proletariat]?" (xii). Being "political" is from this perspective a luxury only those comfortably ensconced in the "professional" class of Composition can readily afford. Indulging in it may provide a demonstration of both one's membership in that class and one's moral superiority. And for those not inclined to such indulgences, their attachment to the perquisites of tenure will lead them to be less, not more, politically daring: they have more to lose. By the same token, while members of the writing "proletariat" may well feel the full brunt of pressures to teach in ways aligned to dominant ideology, it is also possible that being underpaid, overworked, and disrespected has a politicizing effect. As Mina Shaughnessy long ago reported of her fellow basic writing teachers, their shared experience of "what it means to be an outsider in academia" "radicalized" them, leading them to reject "in [their] bones the traditional meritocratic model of a college" ("Miserable Truth" 114; cf. Ohmann, foreword xi). And, given less for their work, members of such a proletariat consequently have less to lose by challenging the dominant ideology in their teaching.

I would argue, however, that such claims assume a false certainty about the politics of a pedagogy by ignoring the contingencies of the specific students, professor, institution, and historical moment involved in the enactment of "a pedagogy," let alone later consequences of that enactment. To ignore such contingencies, again, is to treat politics and pedagogy as commodities rather than strategies, oneself as idealized author, and one's students as passive recipients of, say, one's power. Moreover, the assumption of such a deterministic certainty leads to ethically noxious alternatives. Pursued to its logical extreme, it would mean promoting the abolition of tenure and the full proletarianization of composition teachers to encourage their "politicization," and excoriating all leftist political theorizing by tenured faculty as mere posturing. It is apparent (perhaps especially to those of us in tenured positions) that such arguments, out of faith in structural deterministic understandings of class identity and cultural effects, ignore historical contingencies and treat people in contradictory class positions as uniform. These same conceptual limitations obtain in arguments for insisting on staffing composition courses with tenure-line faculty. The fact is, neither the provision of tenure nor the absence of its possibility in itself confers a specific class position or politics on an individual or her teaching. Rather, it operates in contingent relation to a host of other material historical circumstances.

Efforts to understand the politics of pedagogy in relation to such contingencies have been aimed primarily at considering the interaction of specific pedagogies with specific student populations and employer demands. For example, a number of authors have explored the extent to which those pedagogies originally touted for being "liberatory," "open," "emancipatory" and so on might well effectually lead to greater control over students by virtue of the same "openness" that makes them seem so appealing (Gore 68). For example, Mary Louise Pratt notes that, as her son put it in describing his new school—one characterized by "nicer" teachers, open classrooms, flexible curricula, and a lot fewer rules—the teachers in such places are nicer "so you'll obey all the rules they don't have" ("Arts" 38). Myron Tuman has argued similarly that such pedagogies exert an invisible control more powerful because of its invisibility. Drawing on Shirley Brice Heath's ethnographic study of language practices of different communities in her *Ways with Words* and Basil Bernstein's later work on social class and pedagogy, he argues that such control favors middle-class over working-class children because of its alignment with middle-class socialization (41–48). Middle-class children, somewhat like Pratt's son, seem already to know that the absence of explicit rules, far from meaning there aren't any, means that their task is to infer and act on the inferred rules in ways to which they, but not their working-class peers, have become accustomed through prior socialization at home (44–45). A further problem with educational reforms aimed at such "openness," Tuman argues, is that the apparent achievement of greater openness and freedom provided by the adoption of such pedagogies can vitiate opposition by eliminating an obvious target for that opposition. It is all too easy, as Tuman observes, "to confuse an 'open' classroom with an open society," forgetting how "controlling institutions continue to derive much of their strength and their influence from the quiet effectiveness with which they fulfill their reproductive role" (49–50). He argues, therefore, for more traditional, explicitly "authoritarian" pedagogies, which, by making the means of their control visible, may more effectively awaken within students "both the aspirations for a better world and lingering suspicions of this one" (50).

There are limitations to Tuman's critique. First, his tendency to assume students' language practices on the basis of their class identities posits an unlikely fixity to such identities and practices, and can lead to pedagogies that accommodate, and so reproduce, the very class structures to which he is, presumably, opposed. Anthony Petrosky points to the operation of such a dynamic at work in the use of recitation and drill in poor rural Mississippi Delta public schools in order to prepare students for college admission tests and leave the Delta, the primary route to economic survival for most. Petrosky sees in that use the subversion of the call-and-response tradition of rural black culture to the language of basic skills technology, teaching students "the unspoken lesson of

the technology; [students] automatically assume a submissive position in relation to teaching and learning" (65–66). This submission
makes survival possible, but only within certain conditions. As
Petrosky puts it,

> the instructional language maintains existing class and socio-
> economic order by allowing the students who do well the op-
> portunity to leave the Delta, even though this causes them
> problems; this opportunity can be said to reinforce the values
> necessary to maintain the authority, the priorities, and the lan-
> guage that allow those values to exist in the first place. (66)

Applied to the situation of these students, Tuman's argument for
the exercise of more visible control over students because of their
greater comfort with such visible authority can seem like an argument for the maintenance of such an unjust social order. Or, worse,
his argument can easily slide into a call to encourage oppressive
practices in the hope that such oppression will provoke resistance.
Aside from the dependence of such an argument on faith in struc-
turalist determinism (like that for furthering the proletarianization
of writing instructors to provoke their resistance), the argument is
politically noxious in consigning not those making the argument
but those targeted for such oppression to greater suffering.

Nonetheless, Tuman's critique of the class basis of "open" pedagogies brings out several principles I have been arguing are crucial
to understanding the relation of politics to work in composition.
First, pedagogies touted as an escape from power relations may
well simply allow for the greater sway of dominant power relations.
Second, the politics of these and other pedagogies can be understood only in terms of the material historical contingencies of their
enactment, rather than being read off their surface. These contingencies include not just characteristics of the students but also the
specific circumstances of the economic and social pressures and
practices in which the students and teachers work. Even the politics of the pedagogy Petrosky describes cannot be understood
strictly in terms of the exercise of teacherly authority over students. As Petrosky acknowledges, since this pedagogy of recitation
and drill leads to a solution to the Delta's "most pressing problem—
getting students out of the Delta and into postsecondary education

or the military," it might well be seen not as the oppressive imposition of a restricted literacy but as evidence of "a sophisticated literacy at work *in a large social and political sense*" (65, my emphasis). Similarly, Tuman's analysis shows how pedagogical techniques of "openness" can operate to privilege middle-class students and betray working-class students. Moreover, by stressing process, individual initiative, flexibility, and interpersonal cooperation, such techniques can reinforce the ideology increasingly demanded in the workplace (Tuman 46). For example, the organizational structure of what James Paul Gee, Glynda Hull, and Colin Lankshear term the "new work order" of "fast capitalism" emphasizes egalitarianism over hierarchy and defines work in terms of projects on which people work collaboratively before moving on, as independents, to other businesses, other projects (30, 58–59). Knowledge and authority, rather than residing in one worker, are distributed, both as an efficiency measure and as a means of insuring that workers cannot take their knowledge elsewhere. Control over workers, newly "empowered," is thereby exerted, not directly but indirectly (60). Thus the very attributes and practices encouraged in some pedagogies ostensibly "emancipatory"—"empowerment," "collaboration," "teams," "self-directed learning," and so on—may well work to produce subjectivities demanded by the fast capitalists (Gee et al. 29), preparing students for lives as contingent workers engaged collaboratively in knowledge production for others.

Understanding the politics of pedagogy in terms of social contingencies involves not only exploring its relation to specific students and the demands to be made of them by specific economies, but also exploring its relation to specific teachers and the conditions of their employment as teachers. I have suggested above some of the ways in which conditions of employment may encourage a more conservative pedagogical "politics," conventionally understood. If a pedagogy encouraging empowerment, self-directed learning, teamwork, and so on can work politically to prepare students for the "new work order" of "fast" capitalism, that pedagogy may also exist in both homological and material relation to the work of the newly emerging composition teacher: the part-timer, adjunct, or "temporary full-timer" (Faigley 53). Such a teacher is typically hired on a "contingent" basis to work collaboratively with students and other faculty on term-length "projects" designed by others; he or she is "empowered" to be "independent" rather than tied down by job security to an academic institution, and is "liberated" from long-term employment and from any say in institutional governance. Indeed, many such teachers may be required to exhibit a considerable degree of "flexibility" just to get by, to be quick studies in inferring the unwritten rules of a host of institutions for which they work, sometimes simultaneously, and to be able to cooperate with all sorts of different students and faculty (see McConnel 42–48). Further, it is at least possible that in such circumstances, adopting a pedagogy that appears to be "open" and to "empower" students is preferable to insisting on an explicitly authoritative stance. The latter, after all, might provoke both student resistance and poor teaching evaluations, what people in the "flexible" institutional position of being temporary faculty lack the institutional authority to withstand very easily and have little incentive to attempt. In such ways hegemony operates to reinforce dominant ideology, making a "virtue" out of necessity for all concerned. The practicality of the "politics" of composition in this more pervasive sense makes it all the more difficult either to recognize, or to resist. For that reason, debate over the politics of Composition needs to attend especially to the ways in which the "politics" of the profession, the politics of pedagogy, and the politics of work intersect.

Attention to such intersections, while it can point to existing political dangers, should not prevent us from exploring possible alternative politics which the work of composition might also engage. First, we need to recall that the abstracted skills and practices that might be "demanded" by "fast capitalism," for example, may have very different meanings and effects in their specific concrete enactments. After all, we should not, for example, condemn all instances of cooperation simply because some version of such a "skill," understood abstractly, is hailed by fast capitalist gurus. That it may and has been used to serve fast capitalist ends does not mean it must and can serve only such ends. To recall the argument of chapter 1, we should not mistake the exchange value of our work for its full potential value. And, secondly, as Tuman's analysis hints, practices condemned or viewed with suspicion as traditional, authoritarian, or hierarchical may in fact have effects contradictory to their received meanings. Just as we are learning to see "open" classrooms, for example, as less open than they appear, so we need to reconsider the politics, broadly construed, of practices in Composition condemned for their repressiveness. This reconsideration needs to apply not only to Composition's pedagogies but to all its practices. In the following two chapters, I take up the practices of two spheres commonly viewed as counterproductive barriers to the work of Composition: what is termed the "academic" and the "traditional." Our distrust of work identified with these terms, like our trust in work that appears "progressive," may say more about the dematerialized ways in which we conceive of them than about the actual work accomplished under such rubrics.

Chapter 4

ACADEMIC

We can attribute compositionists' ambivalence toward "the academic" to the marginality of their location in academic institutions. Like their students, composition faculty seem to have no more than a slippery place in the academy, and return the ambivalence with which the academy treats them with ambivalence of their own. A contingent workforce, employers are discovering, is rarely distinguished by loyalty to its employer.

In many ways such ambivalence toward the academy is amply merited. Nonetheless, as I have suggested in concluding chapter 3, Composition's condemnation of the "academic" may also say as much about the pressure to conceive of the "academic" in dematerialized ways as it does about actual academic work. Dematerialized conceptions of the academic lead to mistaking the fixed forms in which what is "academic" is officially recognized for the full range of academic work. Attention to the fixed forms of that work elides its material location and thus its interrelation to work at other sites, and so its full participation in the ongoing material social process. Instead, all too often the work that does go on is reduced and then dismissed as "merely academic": irrelevant to real world concerns, pure ivory tower web-spinning in which students, and ourselves, get caught.

In this chapter I look at the debates within Composition over academic discourse and the academic institutional structural forms of curricula, programs, and disciplines to show the operation of such conflations and reductions. To resist these, I will argue, we need to approach the "academic" as a material site for various sorts of work practices. In both this chapter and chapter 5, however, my interest is to suggest not only how we might resist such reductions but also how we might recuperate the counterhegemonic potential of work carried on at such a site, despite its close association with the hegemonic.

Locating Academic Discourse

Confusions over the constitution of the "academic" in Composition are revealed most explicitly in the debate over academic discourse. That debate manifests a dominant ideology in which the social is identified strictly with fixed forms and an official consciousness. In that ideology, the work of academic discourse itself is imagined in dematerialized fashion, treated as a commodity divorced from the material social relations of its production. To illustrate these features of Composition's approach to academic discourse, I present both Peter Elbow's critique of it in his 1991 *College English* essay "Reflections on Academic Discourse," and a critique of the discourse Elbow enacts in his essay. Both Elbow's critique and the critique of Elbow, I argue, demonstrate this commodification of academic discourse and the limitations of such commodification.

Elbow begins his essay by claiming to "love what's *in* academic discourse" yet hate the discourse itself (135, emphasis added). What he loves is "learning, intelligence, sophistication—even mere facts and naked summaries of articles and books . . . reasoning, inference, and evidence . . . theory" (135). What he means by "academic discourse" is, he says, "ostensive," meaning "clearly or manifestly demonstrative; ostensible" (*Random House*). So, Elbow says, by academic discourse he means "the discourse that academics use when they publish for other academics" (135). As I'll show, when he goes on to tell the story of what "troubles" him about academic discourse, what he means by it quickly becomes anything but clear. But, for the moment, we can note that what troubles him about this ostensible discourse are the forms and motives underlying the use of those forms. While Elbow claims to love the content of academic discourse—what's "in" it—the forms in which that content is expressed bother him immensely. For he's convinced that those forms, particularly certain "stylistic conventions or surface features" of the discourse, serve a primarily obfuscatory function, to "avoid the everyday or common or popular in language" (145). And for Elbow, this is not simply a matter of lack of precision but of noxious social relations. First, he sees the use of academic discourse as exclusionary, a way for academics to "not invite conversation with nonprofessionals or ordinary people" (146). Second, he senses in "the stylistic and textual conventions of academic discourse a note of insecurity or anxiety" (147). Third, those same conventions, he says, often demonstrate an effect "of trying to impress or show off" (147).[1]

To critique Elbow's own discourse, I turn to Joseph Harris' well-known objections to the idea of discourse communities in the study of writing. Harris objects that the concept of discourse communities tends to be invoked to represent not actual discursive practices but discursive utopias, melding the concept of an "interpretive community" with the sociolinguistic concept of a "speech community" (99, 101).[2] While the latter refers to the speech of specific groupings of people, such as neighborhoods, the former refers not to specific groups of individuals but to a set of habits of mind. For example, in David Bartholomae's essay "Inventing the University," beginning college students are said to have to appropriate "peculiar ways of knowing, selecting, evaluating, reporting, concluding, and arguing" (134; quoted in Harris 100). The concept of a discourse community, while ostensibly defining a community in terms of its discourse, does so in reference not to spoken discourse, and often not in reference to actual instances of (linguistic) discourse of any kind, but to an undefined discourse of the sort associated with a postulated group: not the Marxist literary criticism, say, practiced by residents of a certain neighborhood in Brooklyn or Poughkeepsie in 1993, but in general. A discourse community is thus an abstraction about an abstraction. Not surprisingly, when pressed for specifics, representations about such discourse communities quickly fall apart, betraying inconsistencies and contradictions.

Elbow's depiction of academic discourse can be shown to suffer from these limitations. Most obviously, his representation of "academic discourse" appears to be an abstraction, despite his references to specific instances of discursive practice. For, as his argument proceeds, by "academic discourse" Elbow refers to all of the following:

- something used in "the papers and reports and exams [students will] have to write in their various courses throughout their college career" (135);

- "skills that teachers want: labeling and defining and so forth [in which middle-class homes ostensibly train their children]" (135);

- discourse that explains, rather than renders, experience (136–37);

- the "language of the textbook" (137);

- the "professional discourse of the field," e.g., of engineering or composition (137);

- something that doesn't exist (138);

- "giving of reasons and evidence rather than just opinions, feelings, experiences: being clear about claims and assertions rather than just implying or insinuating; getting thinking to stand on its own two feet rather than leaning on the authority of who advances it or the fit with who hears it" (140);

- a "medium whose conventions tend to imply disinterested impersonality and detachment," disguising "that discourse is coming from a subject with personal interests, concerns, and uncertainties" (141);

- discourse that "tries to be direct about the 'position'—the argument and reasons and claim . . . [yet] tends to be shy, indirect, or even evasive about the texture of feelings or attitude that lie behind that position." (145)

The manifest inconsistencies and contradictions between some of these references suggest that Elbow's representation of academic discourse does not, in fact, describe actual academic practice(s) but an abstraction about such practice. This abstract approach, we might say, prevents him from recog-

not the language academics use when publishing for other academics—textbooks are meant for students—and that neither the language found in academic publications nor the language of textbooks is the sort either commonly found in or expected of student papers, reports, and exams.

One might also account for the inconsistencies and contradictions in Elbow's depiction of academic discourse by attributing to Elbow a specific ideological position. That is, just as Elbow critiques what he calls academic discourse for the noxious social relations it ostensibly expresses, so Elbow's own discourse might be critiqued for its expression of equally noxious social relations. Linguist James Paul Gee's analysis of the ideological position expressed in the discourse used by a group of upper-class white high school students provides the basis for such a critique. In their presentation of their ranking of story characters, these students judged characters strictly in terms of whether they felt empathy toward the character or in terms of the effect the character had on their internal psychological state. They condemned certain characters, for example, because they "hit a nerve" or failed to make the students feel "comfortable," or because the students could not see the character's point of view or understand her (128–29). In this discourse, Gee observes, a "psychologized and privatized world . . . [is] carried to an absolute extreme" (129). While Gee simply names but does not explicate the basis of such a worldview in terms of the students' class and race position (and is silent on gender), it is easy enough to see how the highly privatized, privileged material social world upper-class white teenagers enjoy (private bedrooms, homes, clubs, residential communities, schools, modes of transportation, social circles, along with experiences of being paid deference by all others), and the sense of entitlement fostered by their class and race position would encourage the making of judgments about others purely on the basis of how these others make them personally feel. In such a world, it is above all their feelings that matter most. The discourse of the students seems to "speak" just such a worldview and sense of self-location.

Like the discourse of these students, Elbow's discourse offers judgments based on Elbow's personal psychological state or on the motives he attributes to others and whether he can empathize with those. For Elbow, academic discourse achieves its authority by using "a style that excludes ordinary readers and often makes us sound like an insecure or guarded person showing off" (148). But conversely, we might say the discourse of his essay achieves its authority by speaking in *place* of "ordinary people," in a style in which authority is based on who he is and what he feels, a person who already knows, because of who he is, without even having to try, what is truth. In short, Elbow's discourse can be seen as establishing a problematic set of social relations in which judgments about things like academic discourse and whether one ought to teach or engage in it are to be made on the basis of how such issues make Elbow himself feel. Indeed, the entire essay is cast strictly in terms of Elbow's feelings about academic discourse: what he "loves" and "hates," his feeling of being "troubled" (135), what "bothers" him (137), what interests him (141), what "helps [him] understand," what will make him feel "more secure" (148) or "a little better" (151). What might seem to be inconsistencies are thus resolved in terms of the uniformity of their effect on Elbow.

Within such a set of social relations, it is not surprising that, as he reports, he teaches issues of academic discourse by having his students study his own reactions to their writing, seeing himself as "the most convenient ethnographic subject" for learning about that discourse (151). Nor is his ease in asserting what indeed are the true motives behind the use of particular stylistic conventions, what ordinary people are like, what the true meanings behind (ostensibly, manifestly?) puffed-up phrases are, how a "we" talks when it's nervous, and so on. Indeed, it is this very ease that leads him into the inconsistencies noted above. From the perspective of this critique, it would have been better for him, we might speculate, had he experienced more nervousness and insecurity of the sort he condemns in academics than to indulge in proclaiming so many absurdities as if they were, in fact, unquestionable certainties. At the very least, such a critique might hold, a more scrupulously "academic" examination of his argument would have led him to eliminate such inconsistencies and hedge his proclamations that, for example, "the vernacular helps [students] talk turkey" (150); that the sole purpose of footnotes is to "take a ride on the authority of others" rather than to give credit where it's due or point readers to useful sources for further reading (148); that one can easily distinguish discourse that renders from that which explains (136–37); that students only write, and only will write, the discourse they're taught in freshman comp (136–37); that the use of the word "epistemic" means, and is intended to mean, " 'I'm not interested in talking to people who are not already part of this conversation' " (145); that academic discourse conventions disguise, rather than reveal, the writer's "personal interests, concerns, and uncertainties," and that one can know what these are (141); or more generally, the assumption governing most of his essay: that one can separate the content of academic discourse from the forms that discourse takes, and so translate it into any other discursive form (135, 137, 145, passim).

To further this critique, within the ideology of Elbow's discourse, "ideology" represents false consciousness, a distortion from the plain facts accessible through common sense (ideology), and individual consciousness is uniform. In this "common sense" ideology, style is a matter of the clarity or lack thereof with which meaning is transmitted. Elbow's condemnations of the surface features and stylistic conventions identified with academic discourse for saying less clearly, or deliberately obscuring, what could be stated more clearly in the vernacular depend on the ideological assumption that a fixed meaning exists independent of the form in which it is presented. Further, in this ideology, to understand that meaning requires only common sense, not interpretation, and thus does not require justification or explanation: let those who have ears to hear, hear. It is within such an ideology, for example, that Elbow can see no reason for changes made to his prose by the editors of academic journals except "to add a touch of distance and avoid the taint of the ordinary" (145–46). To Elbow, the inherent meanings of his phrases, their propriety as "ordinary," and the editors' uniformly low motives in changing them are all clear.

Both Elbow's critique of academic discourse and the critique of Elbow's own discourse I've presented above demonstrate the limitations of the very kind of analysis of discourse in which these critiques engage. Both critiques assume that texts in themselves "render" ideology.[3] Conversely, a view of discourse as material social practice would insist on locating meaning and ideology in the conditions and practices of textual production, distribution, and consumption. From this perspective, *pace* both Elbow and the critique of him presented above, one cannot read off, as it were, specific meanings, social relations, ideologies from specific textual features alone. Nor, from this perspective, can one assume a uniformity to the individual consciousness of either the "author" or the "reader." Instead, the consciousness of both of these would be understood as heterogeneous and subject to change. For example, while, as the analysis above suggests, it would be possible to argue that Elbow subscribes to a "commonsense" ideology, that argument depends on assuming that Elbow's consciousness, intentions, and social positioning are fixed and uniform, and that his essay can reveal only one true meaning, albeit one accessible only to those, like the presenter of the critique, with sufficient critical acumen and insight.

Eliding the act of and responsibility for interpretation in deciding the meaning of texts and discourses in such readings is of a piece with viewing writing as a commodity and the reader as consumer, just as the practice of judging writing on the basis of how it makes one feel is of a piece with the ideology of consumer capitalism. Texts are treated as commodities whose effect is seen as independent of the conditions of their production, distribution, and consumption. Discourse and its meaning are treated as fixed, hence the question becomes whether that meaning is "delivered" in a way that suits the consumer. The role of the composition course consonant with this ideology then becomes to enable students to produce such discursive commodities as will be demanded of them by others (see Elbow, "Reflections" 135–36). And what students are able to do in their writing—the skills they have—will depend entirely on what the composition course gives them (which, presumably, they've paid for). Hence Elbow's remarkable worry that unless composition teachers teach students how to "write discourse that renders" or encourage them to write notes, letters to friends and relatives, diaries, journals, stories, poems, letters to the editor, or broadsides on dormitory walls, they won't ("Reflections" 136–37). In this vision, Composition has a monopoly on writing skills; the question then becomes what writing "products" it should or shouldn't put on the market, and for whom.

The paucity of this vision of students, academic discourse, writing that might go by the name of academic, and the motives for academic work arises from mistaking the official, fixed forms and purposes for academic discourse for its entirety and full materiality: its practices, meanings, and import. Elbow's failure to recognize the role he plays as interpreter in constructing the meanings of the discourse he critiques is one example of this failure. In actual material practice, the meaning of discourse is contingent in part on how it is read and interpreted, and how it is read and interpreted is conditioned by a host of material circumstances: the occasion of reading, the past training of the reader, the genre of the discourse and the reader's familiarity with that genre, and so forth. Elbow's assumption that meanings remain unaffected by the linguistic forms used represents an idealism opposed to recognition of the historical materiality of those forms. His conflation of the discourse demanded *of* students and that used *on* students (in textbooks) and demanded of academics represents a failure to distinguish between the specific material historical locations and practices of student, textbook, and scholarly writing. His condemnation of the motives for specific stylistic conventions, such as footnotes, treats one official use of these in one setting for their full potential significance in any setting. Finally, academic discourse, however defined, is imagined as existing and operating discrete from, rather than in relationship to and with, other material social practices. These include students' (and many others') various literacy practices outside and inside school (with or without official "academic" sanction), the indirect impact of much academic discourse on non-academic life and folk and vice versa, and the constant interchanges between what might be called academic and non-academic discourses.

Locating the Academic Site

As a corrective to the fuzziness of the idea of discourse communities, Harris argues for a "specific and material view of community," for examining "the discourses of communities that are more than communities of discourse alone" (106). He would thus focus our study of academic discourse, for example, on "the everyday struggles and mishaps of the talk in our classrooms and departments" (107): in short, on discourse as practiced in colleges and universities, rather than on an abstraction about the discourse of a utopia. One of the chief advantages of attending to actual discursive practices is the greater inclusiveness that may potentially result. Rather than defining a *normative* academic discourse found, in fact, nowhere, it would include all the discourse of the everyday: student talk and writing, as well as all the discourse, formal and informal, written and spoken by academics in both their official and unofficial capacities, in a variety of contexts. The unacknowledged contradictions and inconsistencies in Elbow's depiction of academic discourse would, in this approach, be both expected and searched for. Further, attending to actual academic discursive practices would have to admit, or recognize, the interaction and overlapping of such discourse with non-academic discourse. Every utterance, after all, is inevitably subject to and exists only in its specific inflections.

Adopting this approach essentially means disowning altogether the notion of "community," with its unearned positive feelings of group membership and uniformity, and replacing it with some other conceptual image: for Harris, the city, with its collection of diverse people brought together by exigency and accident (106; cf. Faigley 232). More generally in composition studies, the notion of the discourse community has been displaced by that of the "contact zone," following Mary Louise Pratt's critique of linguistic utopias and the power relations implicit in invocations of speech "communities" ("Linguistic"; "Arts" 37–38). As I have argued in chapter 2, however, this invocation of contact zones can itself quickly degenerate into an abstract ideal removed from but mistaken for actual material practice, paralleling the problems obtaining in invocations of academic discourse communities. The notion of the classroom as community, it is worth recalling, was originally a posited ideal distinguished from actual practice, requiring specific pedagogical steps to construct (see Bruffee, "Collaborative Learning" 652). But this view of what the classroom might become quickly became an assertion of what it was. As Pratt observes, "If a classroom is analyzed as a social world unified and homogenized with respect to the teacher, whatever students do other than what the teacher specifies is invisible or anomalous to the analysis" ("Arts" 38). Elizabeth Ellsworth's surprise that "[a]cting as if our classroom were a safe space in which democratic dialogue was possible and happening did not make it so" can be seen as resulting from her assumption of the classroom as an already existing community operating in isolation from its material location (315). Similarly, the view of classrooms as "contact zones," intended initially to facilitate recognition of the heterogeneity unacknowledged in the vision of classrooms as communities, has in some instances become confused with a particular ideal for contact zones imagined as somehow already existing in classrooms. This then leaves teachers unprepared, again, for the kind of heterogeneity that in actual practice sometimes rears its ugly head. Such confusions arise from two failures: first, a failure to locate the classroom in relation to other social spheres; and second, the failure to recognize the classroom as itself producing, rather than just reflecting, specific social relations.

These failures represent manifestations of the dematerialization of the classroom as a specific site both located in and acting on the social. Such dematerializations have led to a succession of attempts either to think of the classroom as (ideally) identical to (or preparation for) the outside world, or else as entirely discrete from it. We can see an early 1970s version of the first move in the argument, caricatured at the time by William E. Coles Jr., that "the process of education, the university, can and must be made other than artificial, can and must be made in fact Real. Since you're a human being and I'm a human being, let's just be Human Beans" ("Unpetty" 378). The expressivist move to preserve the comp course for "tufts of what grows wild" represents the flip side of this: the academy, or some course within it, as retreat from the world.

However, while it's easy enough, as Coles demonstrates, to mock such moves, it is also possible, I would argue, to recuperate some value from them. If we think of the realm of the academic—or, to make this more concrete, specifically the realm of the composition classroom—as indeed in some ways distanced from the dominant, though not removed from the social, then such features of its location may make possible the use of that site for counterhegemonic work. The realm of the academic, so understood, can be approached as analogous to the realm of the aesthetic. Raymond Williams recalls that despite its limitations, historically the "definition of 'aesthetic' response is an affirmation . . . of certain human meanings and values which a dominant social system reduced and even tried to exclude. . . . a protest against the forcing of all experience into instrumentality . . . and of all things into commodities" (*Marxism* 151). Within bourgeois aesthetic theory, of course, such a definition has led to the ideological denial of the material production and reception of the "aesthetic," and a denial of the commodification of art work (152, 154). Such a denial is comparable to the denial of the materiality of academic work described in chapter 1.

Nonetheless, the alternative to this response is not simply to abandon such realms by insisting on their social "utility." As Williams warns,

> If we are asked to believe that all literature is 'ideology', in the crude sense that its dominant intention (and then our only response) is the communication or imposition of 'social' or 'political' meanings and values, we can only, in the end, turn away. If we are asked to believe that all literature is 'aesthetic', in the crude sense that its dominant intention (and then our own response) is the beauty of language or form, we may stay a little longer but will still in the end turn away. (*Marxism* 155)

Instead, we can insist on these realms neither as transparent media for the expression or operation of dominant social forces nor as opaque deflections of the social, but as specific material social realms, or sites, at which a range of work—hegemonic, counterhegemonic, alternative—might occur. The relative autonomy granted the category of the aesthetic means neither its independence from the social nor its guaranteed subservience to the dominant—which itself does not represent the entirety of the social. In the same way, the "relative autonomy" of the academic does not mean that its autonomy is spurious, any more than it is absolute, though it also does not preclude the possibility of its incorporation by the dominant. Rather, such realms are specific material sites produced by and acting on the social. Their forms and effects are thus historical and so can be engaged for counterhegemonic as well as hegemonic work.

For composition teachers and scholars, such engagement means, at the very least, recognizing and exploiting the specific material resources and conditions associated with the "academy" generally, and the composition classroom in particular: in many institutions, time, paper, library resources, the gathering for a period of several months of a relatively small number of students and faculty and the range and depth of knowledge and experience these bring to the classroom, the opportunity for frequent writing and the reading of that writing, the cultural sanctioning of "coursework," and the relative autonomy granted teaching. In addition, these resources include what, following Ken Kusterer's analysis of "unskilled" workers, he terms their "working knowledge." Kusterer found that workers so labeled possessed or developed a significant stock of knowledge unrecognized (at least officially) by management about routine procedures, materials and machinery used, and likely and useful behavior patterns (177–78). Similarly, students, in a differently "hidden" curriculum, forge knowledge out of the material circumstances of academic life that goes either wholly unrecognized or is named as "college student life," and whose value is dismissed as sentimental, nostalgic, sophomoric. Education scholars have long distinguished between an "overt" and a "hidden" curriculum, but see both of these as promoting socially dominant interests. Within this usage, as Bruce Herzberg explains, the "overt curriculum tells what is to be taught and learned; the covert curriculum insinuates values and attitudes through the structure it gives to learning" ("Composition and the Politics" 98). What I am suggesting, however, is that in addition to these curricula, we need to acknowledge as well a curriculum "hidden" from or ignored or dismissed by the dominant, one that promotes alternative or oppositional interests. While compositionists are beginning to recognize the operation of such a curriculum outside the academy, we often fail to recognize its presence within the academy, in our classrooms. In a response to Anne Ruggles Gere's argument for recognizing Composition's "extracurriculum"—represented by writing groups and literary circles unsponsored by academic institutions—Jean Carr observes that such an interest should not be "reduced to permission to leave the academic world behind as if it offered no evidence of alternative literacies, of resistant or differential uses for reading and writing, as if it were, in fact, a story already known and known fully" (96).

In addition to recognizing this extracurriculum within the academy, recuperating the academic also will involve learning to recognize the specific delimitations of such sites as specifically "academic," that is, set aside for intellectual work. Though such sites differ in important ways, most obviously from institution to institution, their official designation as sites for ("advanced") learning and, for some, producing knowledge both shapes and constrains the work done there. Recognizing the delimitations on that work can provide a useful directing of our, and our students', inherently limited energies. I have in mind here the way in which such delimitations can direct us away from attempting to use our classrooms either as sites for engaging in forms of political action, conventionally understood, or as sites for engaging in the pursuit of pleasure, also as conventionally understood. Such delimitations keep me from using my job of teaching a first-year "seminar in reading and writing" to have students write letters to the government protesting U.S. military policies or "English Only" legislation, unless I can justify such assignments in terms of an educational enterprise. Similarly, they keep me from having my students simply write in whatever ways they believe will give them pleasure. Instead, I have to attempt to involve my students in activities recognizable as contributing primarily to learning, at least theirs, ideally my own as well. This does not mean that pleasure or work having social impact is proscribed from the composition classroom, nor that the pleasure and social impact achieved are somehow less real, nor that one precludes the other. Instead, it means only that the pleasure and social impact are specific types taking specifically academic forms. The pleasure students experience, for example, is likely to be intellectual, and so not readily recognized *as* pleasure (indeed, intellectual pleasure is commonly viewed as oxymoronic). Similarly the social impact of the activities in which we engage is, however real, not officially recognized, and likely to be attenuated and indeterminate. But that is to say simply that the work done, insofar as it is "academic," is likely to be less readily susceptible to commodification.

Giddens suggests this in a defense of the "utility" of sociological language. Giddens observes that there is a "two-way relation involved between lay language and the language of social science, because any of the concepts introduced by sociological observers can in principle be appropriated by lay actors themselves, and applied as part of 'ordinary language' discourse [and vice versa]" (248). The appropriation of such concepts—for example, the adaptation of "economic" from lay discourse by technical specialists—involves the addition of new meanings which then return to lay discourse (248). Comparable lay appropriations of terms from the academic fields of Composition, education, literary criticism, and social theory, as well as appropriations among these and other academic fields, are frequent (I'm thinking here, for example, of pervasive references in current mass media journalism to different "cultures," "literacies," "ideologies"). Whatever objections academics may make to the new meanings these terms acquire in lay discourse as simplifications, misconceptions, or perversions of the terms' supposedly "original" (academic) meanings, such uses of the terms demonstrate the full appropriation of the "knowledge" ostensibly embedded in the terms and the reality of the social impact, however "attenuated," of academic work, as well as the location of that work in the full social process. As Jean Carr observes, "The academic and the extracurricular can never fully be quarantined from each other. Each extends its influence to the other, although in differing degrees and through different mechanisms of power and transmission" (95). The fact that some of what I have been terming "lay appropriation" of academic knowledge in fact represents its commodification does not mean that all lay appropriation of such knowledge is tantamount to commodification, nor even that commodified "lay" versions of such knowledge drain it of any subsequent potential use value.

The official unrecognizability, invisibility, or indeterminacy of much academic work does not preclude or excuse from consideration conscious efforts at making productive, directed use of the academic character of the classroom site. While I have said more in chapters 2 and 3 about specific work composition students and teachers might accomplish, let me suggest here how a course might attend productively to academic discourse itself. I ended chapter 2 by suggesting that Susan Miller's call for Composition to turn its knowledge of the situatedness of the evaluation of writing to counterhegemonic ends ought to include students as well. Now if, as is sometimes claimed, one of the official purposes of composition courses is to teach students something called "academic discourse," then we might use the occasion of such courses to involve students in investigating the implications of the material location, production, distribution, and circulation of specific forms of academic writing in order to both critique and revise their and others' practices with it. Such investigations would examine not only official representations of academic discourse (like Elbow's, as dematerialized, depersonalized texts, say) and the contradictions in any such representations. They would also examine all the writing that might reasonably be associated with academic sites, student writing included; the different uses as well as failed opportunities evinced by such writing; and how the material conditions and practices of its production and circulation delimit the work of such writing. Such a course would be "academic" but in neither a matter-of-fact nor dismissive sense. It would make use of the academic site to investigate and potentially revise, exploit, or work against that site's constraints and possibilities. Such a course would not ignore or deny official, dominant definitions of and practices with "academic discourse," such as the use of the "bastard" discourse of examination writing for social credentialing. But it would contextualize these as historical, and so subject to change, and therefore as not representing the full, or fully possible, range of academic discourse. Further, in locating academic discursive practices at the site of the academic, it would demonstrate and explore the politics of the operation of such practices in various relation to discourse at other sites. It would thus work to show the variety of discourse possible at the site of the academic, the availability of alternative sites for carrying out different sorts of projects, and the politics of which projects to attempt, in what ways.

For, again, one of the debilitating effects of viewing the academic in dematerialized fashion is that we forget the practical use of seeing the material limitations of what we can do at that site: "practical" not in the sense of deferring to imposed restrictions but in the sense of recognizing how best to marshal and direct which energies where, when, and by whom. Imagining the academic as the only site for all work that might be socially useful can lead to despair at how little, in comparison, can and does seem to get done at that site (and restricts our vision of what does get done to official renderings, blinding us to the social impact of what seems purely "academic" work). By failing to locate the academic in relation to other sites, we forget the potential of other sites, and more specifically and damagingly, the capabilities of students. It is only from such a seemingly idealized but actually myopic vision of the academic, for example, that one could worry that if we fail to teach students to write notes, or broadsides on dormitory walls, or in ways that render rather than explain experience, they won't. Like the canon debate, which, Katha Pollitt has observed, depends for its energy on the assumption that students will read or encounter only what they're assigned in school, this vision of the academic achieves an inflated sense of the importance of that site only through denigrating work accomplished elsewhere, under less "official" guises (Pollitt, "Why"). And again, blindness to such work shows the dominant tendency to mistake official, fixed forms for the totality of the social. Writing, reading, and learning outside the academy is ignored, dismissed, or discounted as somehow less real because less official.

Locating Academic Institutional Structures

Mistaking fixed, official forms and effects of academic discourse for its totality has its counterpart in mistaking the dominant or official origins, features, or effects of institutional structures of the academy for their full potentiality. Composition's resistance to the academic is often manifested in its opposition to such institutional structural forms—composition courses, curricula, or programs, and established disciplines—condemned as hierarchical, patriarchal, rigid, oppressive. This resistance appears in debates about "mainstreaming" Basic Writing, the abolition of freshman composition, and the place of Composition in relation to English departments and cultural studies programs. Those arguing for *abandoning* such institutional forms point either to the history of their oppressive effects or their "function" in reproducing unjust social relations, or they slide from noting such effects to asserting these as their social function. Those arguing for *adopting* particular academic institutional forms point similarly to official purposes, origins, features, or effects as evidence of the (desired) functionality of those forms. But in so doing, all these arguments ignore the contingencies of material history, mistaking the dominant or "official" origins, features, purposes, or effects of academic institutional forms for their full potentiality, realized or no, admirable or disgraceful. Selecting a version of the history of a given institutional form, such "functionalist" arguments remove that form from its historical location, treating its given historical effect as an essential, timeless characteristic, or "function," of that form. Where, historically, given forms might seem to have had unintended or unacknowledged effects or consequences, in functionalist arguments these are explained away as functioning to fulfill the "needs" of society, just or unjust.

For example, in a critique of Basic Writing programs, Ira Shor sees

> the BW/comp story as part of a long history of curricula for containment and control, part of the system of school tracking to divide and deter non-elite students in school and college. The students themselves are tested and declared deficient by the system, which blames the apparently illiterate and cultureless victim, stigmatizing the individual as the problem while requiring BW/comp as the remedy. The structure now in place helps maintain the inequality built over the last century or two, tilting resources to elite students and lush campuses, rewarding those who speak and look like those already in power. This arrangement is undemocratic and immoral. ("Our Apartheid" 98)

In Shor's argument, the "system," however unjust, has its needs. Basic Writing is identified as a program functioning to fulfill such needs, here the reproduction of unequal social relations. As in other functionalist arguments, there is a slippage here between effects and function. Various forms of tracking have indeed historically had the effects, intended or not, acknowledged or not, of reproducing unequal social relations. But in renaming these as functions rather than effects, Shor appears to be offering an explanation when he is not. To the question of why these forms continue to exist, given these unintended effects, he answers that that is their unacknowledged function. But, as Giddens observes, in a critique of functionalist arguments generally, "Not even the most deeply sedimented institutional features of societies come about because those societies need them to do so. They come about *historically*, as a result of concrete conditions that have in every case to be directly analysed; the same holds for their persistence" (113).

The alternative to functionalist explanations is to locate instances of the unexpected or unacknowledged effects of given institutional structural forms in the contingencies of history rather than to abstract those forms from history. Functionalism, by contrast, attempts to explain the unintended consequences of actions by renaming those consequences as fulfilling the needs of social systems, imputing a teleology to those systems, which are imagined as operating behind the backs of social actors (Giddens 7, 112). Aside from the noxious view of social actors as dupes in such arguments, they are limited in assuming a cohesive relation between part and whole (Giddens 110–12). Like the assumption of homogeneity in discourse communities, functionalist arguments assume a condition of systemic homeostasis and an (often) organic or homological relation between the system as a whole and elements within it. Thus contradictory and contingent effects are rendered invisible or subsumed within systemic "functionality," and historical specificity and change are effaced. Shor, for example, treats tracking, freshman comp, and BW as essentially synonymous and uniform in their origin and social function. "BW," he claims, "has functioned inside the larger saga of American society; it has been part of the undemocratic tracking system pervading American mass education, an added layer of linguistic control to help manage some disturbing economic and political conditions on campus and off" ("Our Apartheid" 93). This functionalist approach is also manifested in Shor's failure to differentiate between basic writing at CUNY (his institution), specific aspects of some basic writing programs (such as placement and exit exams), and other basic writing programs. This is in contradiction to the fact that, as Terence Collins observes in a response to Shor, "there has never been a homogeneous Basic Writing entity which ought now to be 'mainstreamed'" (98).

The difficulty in resisting such functionalist arguments is how to acknowledge the historical veracity of many of the effects of an institutional form while also acknowledging the partiality of the functionalist representations of that history so that one can reject the labeling of those effects as fulfilling a social function. We can see Collins negotiating just such difficulties in stating:

> Shor is surely right that there is a history of exclusionist practice in higher education . . . and some practices in writing instruction and tracking are undoubtedly tied to this history. [Nonetheless] it is an unfair corollary that there is a Basic Writing industry acting out a cynical apartheid agenda. Rather, there are any number of situated, institutionally constrained iterations of things like "Basic Writing," some more fortunately located than others, some more successful in

resisting pariah status than others, some formed with more authentic educational purposes than others. (99)

So, for example, programs of testing may and have in certain instances had the effects Shor observes of transferring power "from classrooms, teachers, and students at the bottom to administrators at the top" ("Our Apartheid" 96), but may also have had contrary and other effects. Similarly, while specific Basic Writing courses may have shunted some students from education, as Shor claims, and others have sheltered students, as Karen Greenberg argues (see Shor, "Our Apartheid" 96), one cannot then assume that Basic Writing "functions" always in either of these two ways for every student. Further, one cannot assume that eliminating Basic Writing programs would inevitably result either in "freeing" all students from "apartheid" or perpetuating their denigration and abandonment, though one can predict such effects in specific cases.

An examination of recent events at CUNY may help to illustrate the difference between recognizing the historical effects of institutional procedures and forms and construing from the history of those effects a social function attributed to those procedures and forms. In her response to Shor, Greenberg warned that if Shor's vision came to pass,

at least half of the students now entering the university where Shor and I teach (CUNY) would be barred. The University, far trimmed down in size, would probably return to the elite institution it was before 1970, when open admissions began. Of course, there are reactionary political forces currently trying to achieve precisely this barring of access and precisely this reduction in size in colleges across the country. Eliminating testing would, in fact, justify the curtailment and the consequent reduction or elimination of basic skills programs. . . . No one should make the mistake of believing that the current atmosphere of draconian cutbacks would not operate in this way if opponents of basic skills courses are successful in their goal. (94)

A few months after the publication of Greenberg's response to Shor, Greenberg reported on the Conference on Basic Writing listserv that CUNY did in fact effectively end open admissions, with one CUNY trustee apparently even citing Shor's article as justification for doing so. CUNY's Office of Institutional Research reported its prediction that this will result in far fewer African-American, Hispanic, and Asian students being able to enroll in CUNY senior colleges (Greenberg, "The End"). But while we can assume this predicted effect to be entirely likely, it does not follow from this effect that eliminating basic writing programs will and always will have the effect of excluding such students—that that is the *function* of eliminating basic writing programs. To make such a claim would be, again, to elide the differences among specific basic writing programs, institutions in which they are housed, and their student populations—to remove a specific historical action from history and apply it transhistorically to all such programs, and to impute a purpose to historical causal relations. While this distinction is no comfort to those suffering specific effects like those predicted for CUNY, it is crucial for thinking about Composition's resistance to academic institutional forms. For it precludes the easy abstraction from specific historical effects of instances of institutional forms to arguments about their inevitable, intended functions, and letting these "functions" dictate how we explore and bring about actual effects. The fact is we cannot read off the significance of such forms outside the specificity of their material instantiation, any more than we can read off the significance of "academic" discursive forms outside their material instantiation. What we can do is examine the specific ways in which an institutional form has led to certain effects: to see, in other words, how such forms, in specific instances, have worked strategically.

This is, I think, in keeping with David Bartholomae's critique of the tendency to see Basic Writing as "something naturally, inevitably, transparently there in the curriculum" ("Tidy House" 8). Bartholomae's critique is commonly read as calling for the abolition of Basic Writing courses (e.g., Collins 98), in spite of his statement, "Would I advocate the elimination of courses titled 'basic writing' for all postsecondary curricula beginning next fall? No. I fear what would happen to the students who are protected, served in its name" ("Tidy" 20). Such readings themselves betray a kind of functionalism, mistaking statements about the historical effects of a program for statements about its "functionality." But in fact,

Bartholomae calls for recuperating the *"strategic* function" of basic writing as a name for "a contested area in the university community, a contact zone, a place of competing positions and interests" (21, my emphasis). It is only when we understand programs like basic writing in dehistoricized terms that their strategic value, and strategic limitations, are mistaken for their functionality as, in effect, commodities.

The same confusion obtains in debate over the abolition of freshman composition. The arguments for abolishing freshman composition typically attribute to the course the performance of some function, whether praised or condemned, in relation either to non-academic social needs or other academic work. But in these arguments, either the composition course itself or the demands of the world outside that course—in other academic disciplines or outside academia altogether—are posited as static, both transhistorical and uniform. Sharon Crowley, for example, argues that the "heart" of the problems of "Freshman English" arises from its "unusual origin" "as a response to perceived deficiencies in students' literate skills, rather than as an arena in which to study a body of received knowledge." Thus, "the course has never appropriated an area of study for itself that would bring order to its teaching" ("Perilous" 11). In other words, the ostensible purpose behind the historical introduction of a freshman composition course is taken as indelibly marking and guaranteeing the function of freshman composition courses since that introduction. For Crowley, that origin accounts for Freshman English being "plagued throughout its history by recurring tension between English teachers' desire to make the course teachable and respectable by grounding it in some discipline, on the one hand, and their attempts to fulfill their supposed responsibility to the culture at large by improving the level of students' literacy, on the other" (11). Put thus, the choice is between pursuing academic disciplinary respectability, and the order it brings, and carrying out a debased and debasing task. In this argument, "Freshman English" remains a monolith defined by and largely unchanged in purpose and effect since its "origins." Further, while Crowley rejects the latter task of teaching a "mechanical literacy" as both demeaning and impossible to achieve, given what we know about the production and correction of "error," the former goal remains unchallenged. That is, the institution of academic disciplinarity is treated with what Giddens terms a "normative functionalism," in which an institution, and elements of it, are imagined as fulfilling the needs of an unquestioned, rather than unjust, social order in its totality (see Giddens 110–11). For Crowley, academic disciplinarity is functional, freshman comp, dysfunctional.

Some of the arguments presented in *Reconceiving Writing*, a recent collection of "new abolitionist" arguments against the institution of freshman composition (dubbed "General Writing Skills Instruction," or "GWSI") ascribe a similarly fixed identity to college composition courses and a similarly normative function to academic disciplines or to the workplace, with troubling results. David Russell, for example, argues that unlike GWSI courses,

> in courses designed to teach activities other than composition, students have more opportunity to learn who the participants in an activity system are, what they do, and how and why they do it—and thus what, how, and why they write the ways they do. . . .
>
> [G]eneral chemistry or psychology leads on to the activity systems of the disciplines and professions of chemistry or psychology, within and outside academia. ("Activity" 64, 65)

On the one hand, Russell evinces a concern aligned to the argument I make above of the need to attend to academic discourse(s) in terms of their material social specificity. As he observes, rather than thinking of academic discourse in general,

> academic discourse consists of the dynamic aggregate of all the many specialized discourses of all the activity systems (disciplines and departments) that make up academia. The protean tool called writing is appropriated and transformed by each activity system according to its object(ive)s and the material conditions of its work to evolve myriad genres within academia. (60)

On the other hand, he neglects this interest in material specificity when he decries GWSI courses on the basis of their ostensible, rather than actual, failure to acknowledge or address such material differences, and he seems to slide at times into accepting at face value the normative claims for the discursive practices of these other disciplines, treating these as "functional" in opposition to the putative dysfunctionality of GWSI. While not completely uncritical of these, he is primarily concerned with attacking the institution of GWSI for perpetuating the myth of an "autonomous literacy" and "universal educated discourse" that GWSI is supposed to give students. This myth enables the blame for student difficulties in mastering specific disciplinary work to be placed on the students for being generally poor writers lacking universal educated discourse, not on those disciplines for failing to assist students in mastering their specific discourses (65–67). But while this is a sharp criticism of the effects a "GWSI" course can have, it does not follow that this is how fresman composition does/will function. To assume that it does is, again, to slide from recognizing the historical effects of an institutional form to assuming those effects to be the form's inevitable function.

In the same volume, Aviva Freedman moves similarly between ascribing a normative function to disciplinary courses outside freshman composition and a dysfunctionality to freshman composition. Freedman argues that whereas the "discursive context" for student writing in disciplinary courses is "rich—coming as it does after so many lecture hours, so much common reading, and often so many carefully orchestrated seminar groups,"

> The composition class seems bare and spare by contrast. There is simply nothing of the same shaping and enabling from the environment. The context is barren, and consequently must be invented by the student, or rather, must be imported from the larger cultural context. (137)

While careful to qualify her argument with an acknowledgement that "the disciplinary class is [not] a kind of shangri-la" (139), she does not provide corresponding acknowledgement of the kind of potential in courses masked under the GWSI label. Instead, like Russell, she accepts at face value the "generality"—and thus the inauthenticity—of the writing skills ostensibly taught there.

Cheryl Geisler, while viewing courses in other disciplines differently than Russell or Freedman, nonetheless also grants some legitimacy to rejecting freshman composition for its disjunction from such coursework. Observing that the job of students in most disciplines' coursework is "learning extant knowledge" and that "writing is a fairly poor tool for this purpose" (102), she argues,

> In general . . . students and teachers in academic settings appear to be justified in not using very much extended analytic writing. In fact, this kind of writing seems to distract students from learning the broad range of content required by the tests they take. (112)

Geisler ultimately concludes by calling for an alternative to existing academic practices by reinventing general education so that student writing is taught not as consumption of knowledge but as epistemic. She sees, however, that this alternative is "by far the most difficult" (118). The more likely alternative would appear to be to abandon the teaching of analytic writing because it interferes with existing pedagogical aims and test practices of the disciplines outside Composition. Here, Composition's emphasis on analytical writing is dysfunctional in relation to these other pedagogies, however problematic.

Just as many of these arguments tend to treat academic disciplinary work outside Composition as normative, so they tend to treat non-academic writing as functioning normatively. For example, Joseph Petraglia, quoting Jeff Smith, claims that, unlike writing in composition courses, " '[i]n the real world, writing's motives are clear. [People write because they want to accomplish something that requires communicating; they] already feel the force of an issue and sense ignorance or error in their would-be audience' " (91–92, quoting Smith, "Against" 206). Given this ostensible difference between academic and "real world" writing, the cognitive abilities taught in freshman composition are inappropriate, since "the problem solving entailed in writing for real audience, with real purposes, using situationally appropriate information differs significantly from cognition devoted to *appearing* to address an audience, *looking like* you have a purpose, and *pretending* to be knowledgeable" (Petraglia 92). Similarly, Charles Hill and Lauren Resnick argue that students in writing courses cannot "learn in the classroom much of what they need to know to write in professional contexts" because true writing instruction is a "process of socialization, of induction into a community of readers and writers working within particular contexts" (146). Of course, it may well be true that there is a difference between the socialization involved in writing in the classroom and writing on the job, and between the problem-solving skills involved in writing for a fictional audience for an imaginary purpose and those tapped in writing for an actual audience for a real purpose. But it is not at all clear that workplace writing represents the normative site where the only "real" writing occurs. We need to question the normative function of workplace writing and the need for composition courses to accommodate it. Further, we need to recall that, as discussed in chapter 2, composition courses do in themselves have particular contexts in which student writers and readers work.[4]

The problem with these abolitionist arguments is that their focus on the dominant or "official" origins, features, purposes, or effects of academic institutional forms blinds them to aspects and effects of such forms outside the ken of such "norms." So, for example, while many freshman composition courses have historically been viewed officially as the site for "General Writing Skills Instruction," the actual work accomplished at that site may well differ significantly from that official purpose. As Charles Bazerman observes in a critique of some of the abolitionist arguments described above, "Just because we have been funded with a reductionist notion of our task has not meant that we have been bound to follow through in a reductionist way" (252). By the same token, the normative ostensible "functionality" of professional workplace writing and academic disciplinary work may say more about its official claims than its actual ongoing historical practices and effects. It may well be the case, for example, *pace* Petraglia, that not only writing inside the academy and inside freshman composition courses, but also much writing *outside* the academy, as well as outside freshman composition courses, involves "cognition devoted to *appearing* to address an audience, *looking like* you have a purpose, and *pretending* to be knowledgeable." More pertinently to the concerns of this chapter, the reality of "academic" concerns and writings is not so easily dismissed. Bazerman reminds us that indeed, for students, "the literature essay and the chemistry lab report due next week are about as real as you can get. . . . [And] [i]f we start analyzing the first-year writing course we find it is a very real place" (254). As I discussed in chapter 2 in addressing service-learning pedagogies, we should not let our recognition of the materiality of non-academic writing blind us to the materiality of academic writing. It will not do, then, to dismiss student work for its academic location. Nor, further, will it do to identify that work strictly in terms of whatever are claimed to be its official academic purposes. For example, we need to recall that the postsecondary school experience is in practice associated not only with training in preprofessional or official disciplinary discourse but also with "personal, developmental, educational, reflective, philosophical, cultural" discourse (Bazerman 256). That is to say, in addition to the officially sanctioned knowledge and skills the academy is charged with producing and distributing, students (and others) also produce what Kusterer terms "working knowledge" in that more positive curriculum "hidden" from official academic view but nonetheless forged out of the material conditions of academic life.

We can understand how the structure of freshman composition as a universally required first-year course could help students to engage in such work by recognizing what Giddens terms the "duality of structure." The view that institutional structures "function" as barriers to individual agency ignores the duality of structure, that is, the mutual dependence of structure and agency, and thus the role structure plays in the production of action (69, 70). If, as Giddens argues, "all social actors, no matter how lowly, have some degree of penetration of the social forms which oppress them," and if the commitment of most to dominant ideologies is overstated, then their practical consciousness of those forms can be elicited to draw them into critique, to act otherwise, and so to enact different structures (see Giddens 72, 148–49).

Kusterer argues similarly that while traditional Marxist theory rightly identifies the source of alienation in the social structure of capitalism, it tends to exaggerate the power of that structure and neglect workers' struggles against its alienating effects (148, 149). Based on his study of "unskilled" workers, Kusterer finds that in fact these workers developed communal networks and a "working knowledge" about the routines, machinery, and use value of their work to "invest their own work activity with meaning," devoting "a lot of energy in de-alienating themselves, in learning the working knowledge and building the work relationships that add to their own control over work processes, decreases [sic] their social isolation, and make their work meaningful" (153–54, 161). This working knowledge typically goes unrecognized by management and workers alike. However, because managers, in their concern only with increasing exchange value, do not recognize that knowledge, their actions frequently can render "whole subjects of working knowledge obsolete, disrupt communal networks, and thus undermine or eliminate entirely the resources that the workers have used to render their jobs meaningful and to turn their work activity into life activity" (158). Applied to Composition, those "abolitionist" arguments concerned with increasing the exchange value of Composition, a concern evidenced by what Bazerman notes as their tendency to "dissolve [higher education] simply into preprofessionalism" (255), may well pose a similar threat to the "working knowledge" of composition teachers and students, since they do not in fact recognize such knowledge, despite its actual significance to academic life and the life of the academy. In Giddens' terms, like the "normative functionalists," the abolitionists are blind to social agents' "understanding, practical and discursive, of the conditions of their action" (Giddens 112). And just as the workers Kusterer observed who resisted such changes were viewed as "anti-progressive, anti-technology, anti-change," so composition students and teachers who resist significant programmatic changes to their existing academic practices, such as the abolition of freshman composition or basic writing, are liable to be charged with being obstructionist, hidebound traditionalists, and the like.

Alternatively, to push these arguments further, the specific structure of the freshman composition course may provide an academic institutional framework that can be used to mobilize students' "working knowledge" and practical consciousness of that and other institutional structures. In this sense, the academy as an institution is in a position to enable students to make active use of their working knowledge. There is a danger, of course, that recognition of working knowledge may take the form of its appropriation and commodification. In that sense, its very unrecognizability by some may have a strategic value, something that cannot be bargained away because not recognized in the "contract" between student and teacher, or between teacher and institution. Kusterer observes that "to note that working knowledge is a source of worker's control is to raise the possibility and plausibility of institutionalizing that control, of creating real worker self-management," but he is quick to caution that this "is not to suggest that workers' emancipation has already somehow secretly occurred" (185). In other words, to recognize their working knowledge is not tantamount to supporting it. And resistance should not be confused with emancipation. To draw any such conclusion would be to forget that it is not the workers alone who are engaged in structuration, hence their resort to strategies of resistance. Worker control operates in conflict with attempts at appropriation. To apply this insight to the situation of the academy, the "working knowledge" of academic ways that students develop and possess, so long as it remains at the level of practical consciousness, unarticulated, may help individuals survive and even exert a degree of control over their day-to-day encounters with the academy. Nonetheless, so long as it remains unarticulated to the students, it cannot lead to control over the academy as a whole. In unarticulated form, we can say of their working knowledge what Kusterer observes of the workers he studied: their working knowledge and communal relations remain "fragile social constructions, dependent for their existence on conditions in the work environment over which management retains ultimate control" (183). Using the freshman composition course, or other courses or academic forums, to support and sustain students' working knowledge is one way of strengthening it and increasing its potential for radically transforming the "normative functions" promoted in and outside the academy, and thus, the academy itself. But we need to avoid slipping from a recognition of the potential of such an institutional form to a belief that it inevitably functions to realize such potential.

Relocating Academic Disciplinary Work

If critiques of the institution of the freshman composition course mistake its official function with its actual practices and effects, Composition's debates over its relation to "English," the discipline in which most such courses continue to be "housed," or to other academic disciplines or programs, such as rhetoric or cultural studies, reveal a similar tendency to mistake the overt claims and forms in which these are typically recognized for much of the work accomplished under their rubrics. There is an unrecognized gap, in other words, between the official, dominant ideology of these, on the one hand, and, on the other hand, the actual views and practices of those working in them.

In a critique of professional discourse on how to "connect" the various elements comprising "English studies," James Slevin points to this tendency to ignore such gaps ("Connecting"). Within that discourse, the trope of synecdoche in particular posits literature as central and composition as marginal and reinforces a particular sense of each of these. In social practice, Slevin observes, synecdochic representation "reifies a single part *as* the whole, making it . . . equal to the whole; and . . . shifts attention away from other parts, subordinating or even concealing them" ("Connecting" 546). It is through synecdochic representation that "English" is taken to mean only literary study despite the devotion of many of those working in English to practices more closely associated with composition. Indeed, synecdochic representations of "English studies" tend to conceal composition from view altogether. Similarly, "composition," Slevin observes,

> gets used so that all sorts of important practices are equated with teaching undergraduates to write, only *one* of the range of projects that make up this "cluster" . . . that so-called "composition" people undertake. . . . As a result, the activities that are in fact undertaken within composition—activities that include significant research in a wide variety of areas, very sophisticated teaching at all levels, and complicated departmental and university administration—all these activities remain suppressed by the figurative device that identifies them with "freshman comp." They are thereby named as basic, introductory, elementary, usually remedial, and generally any other sort of thing that someone with any self-respect would want to avoid. (546–47)

By means of the same trope, while compositionists are associated with the status of the eighteen-year-olds in freshman composition courses, "a writer of an obscure article on some obscure poet is named by his or her association with Chaucer, Shakespeare, and Milton" (547).

Slevin's analysis is aimed primarily at showing how dominant discourse perpetuates the denigration of composition in relation to literary study and at combating efforts to achieve a "global" unity by suppressing differences within what, for lack of a better term, I will continue to call "English studies." In place of such assertions of homogeneous community, he calls for finding "local" connections, such as an interest in the sociality of the production of writing that might, for example, bring together some of the work in composition studies and work on Renaissance authorship (548–50).[5] We can further such an analysis by recognizing the full range of beliefs and activities that goes on under cover of the name of English literary study, or that of other disciplines. Synecdochic representations of English collapse that range by highlighting certain beliefs, practices, and institutions in English and throwing into the shadow more common beliefs, practices, and institutions, and by mistaking official representations of individual English workers' beliefs and practices for those enacted. As I will show, arguments against Composition's ties to English, and arguments for linking Composition to programs like cultural studies or rhetoric, typically identify English, cultural studies, or rhetoric with synecdochic representations of their work. They thus fail to consider both their material strengths and limitations, historical and potential.

In chapter 1 I have already discussed the ways in which "work" in the academy is associated almost exclusively with the production of scholarly texts, rather than with teaching, despite the preoccupation of the vast majority of college faculty with teaching (as well as other non-publication related matters, such as administration and committee work) (cf. Nelson and Bérubé 12; Oakley 275). Much of Evan Watkins' study calls attention to the unrecognized predominance of this other work in English. By extension, it is the association of "composition" with teaching that in part accounts for its invisibility in official representations of English despite its predominance in the work, or labor, of most English teachers. Indeed, as a number of compositionists have observed, even scholarly critiques of "English studies," such as those by Gerald Graff and Evan Watkins, typically take "English studies" to mean almost exclusively the study and teaching of literature, despite the fact that the bulk of the work performed in English departments remains the teaching of composition (Berlin, *Rhetorics* xiii–xiv; Friend; R. Miller, "Composing"; Slevin, "Depoliticizing" 4–10).

By means of the same trope, work in English at research universities (or rather, some of that work) comes to be taken as representative of English in all postsecondary institutions. As in many mass media accounts of higher education, such representations obscure the range of postsecondary educational institutions—community colleges, private and public four-year colleges, mid-sized universities, as well as large private and public research universities, in addition to such institutions as libraries and less formal gatherings—and the very different material conditions and concerns shaping the work done across that range. One effect of this trope is that graduate education in English often fails to prepare teachers for the work they are later hired to do. It may well be that much graduate training emphasizes fluency in the discourse of theory and promotes research and publication in specialized areas of literary study (broadly construed) and teaching in such areas, often to undergraduate students from privileged backgrounds. However, once hired, faculty in many postsecondary institutions find their work consists primarily of teaching undergraduates composition and other "general education" and "generalist" literature courses, it emphasizes teaching and service far more than research and publication, and it serves student populations very different from those encountered in graduate school training (see Final Report 23–25; Day 35–37, and responses by Atkins 40–41, and Knapp; Gadzinski; Gardner; Jones; Mauzerall; Slevin, "Disciplining" 163–65).

Beyond these specific disparities between types of postsecondary institutions and between training and work, there is a disparity between what we might term the ostensible dominant professed ideology of English and both the practiced beliefs and work practices of its workers. Compositionists who question the link between Composition and English typically address what they perceive to be the dominant ideology of English rather than the actual beliefs and practices of their erstwhile colleagues. For example, in her 1985 Conference on College Composition and Communication chair's address calling on Composition to break its "bonds" with English studies, Maxine Hairston clearly means by English studies the study of literature, and by the study of literature she means literary criticism, or contemporary literary theory, which she characterizes as "a commitment to criticism for its own sake" ("Breaking" 273–75). In her subsequent 1992 essay decrying what she perceives as the growing tendency of compositionists to think of their work in politicized terms, she accounts for that politicization by describing it as "what happens when we allow writing programs to be run by English departments" ("Diversity" 183). More specifically, she means "critical literary theories of deconstruction, poststructuralism . . . , and Marxist critical theory," which she sees as trickling down from "upstairs" to the "lower floors of English departments where freshman English dwells" ("Diversity" 183). From an entirely different perspective, William Lalicker also argues that Composition should break with English. He does so, however, because he thinks English is too *un*theoretical. Instead, he urges Composition to link up with Cultural Studies, arguing that while "theory" is *not* taught in most literature departments, Composition and Cultural Studies share a "rhetorical epistemology" encouraging interdisciplinarity and valuing pedagogy.

Despite their differences, Hairston and Lalicker share a common strategy of identifying English (as well as, for Lalicker and others, Cultural Studies) strictly in terms of its ostensible history or dominant ideology. They can both call for leaving English while pursuing opposed ends because they happen to adopt different but equally reductive definitions of the history and ideology of English. For Hairston, English has been taken over by theorists and leftist ideologues; for Lalicker, English remains dominated by the epistemology of antitheoretical Cold War liberalism. Arguments for linking Composition to the fields of Cultural Studies, or to Rhetoric, evince a similar tendency to define these strictly in terms of official representations of their ideology and work, located in published texts: with Cultural Studies rather than cultural studies, Rhetoric, not rhetoric, *PMLA*, not colleagues.

In their analysis of different approaches to understanding relations between composition and theory, Patricia Donahue and Ellen Quandahl term this type of identification "affiliative." Such an approach

> attempts to make composition less peripheral by aligning it, or claiming a *filial* relationship, with the body of work that carries the most weight in English departments these days. The

argument is that composition resembles and even mirrors theory because it shares its beliefs in the epistemology of process, the function of textuality, and the significance of writing. In fact, some affiliative studies go so far as to say that composition was ahead of its time. (5–6)

We can see such attempts at "affiliation" in Lalicker's claim that by joining with Cultural Studies on the basis of a common epistemology, Composition can increase its "market value" and gain materially, since, while the cultural capital of canonical literary study is being devalued, the demand for rhetorical techniques of cultural interpretation is increasing. And James Berlin, while careful not to proclaim Cultural Studies as the knight that will save Composition, also sees the two as "compatible," for Berlin because of the similarities in their research activities and rhetoric ("Composition Studies" 100, 101). That similarity leads Berlin to claim that "since its formation in college English departments a hundred years ago, [composition studies] has in many of its manifestations attempted to become a variety of cultural studies" ("Composition Studies" 102), and that many of Composition's recent pedagogy and research projects signal the "emergence of a social epistemic rhetoric" aligned to cultural studies in its focus on "signifying practices in relation to the ideological formation of the self within a context of economics, politics, and power" (109).

In a critique of neoclassical histories of composition that assert composition's intellectual continuity with ancient rhetoric, Susan Miller warns,

> Focusing on a limited "intellectual" history of composition to the exclusion of its material circumstances implicitly places composition in academic "Big" history, where it will accrue entitlements from "authority and the ancients." But this tactic also sustains the hierarchies and privileging mechanisms that those in the field complain of so often. ("Feminization" 50)

The attempts to link composition with "theory" or with "cultural studies" employ a similar strategy, with similar results. In a manner all too stereotypically "academic," theory and "cultural studies," like "English," are imagined in dematerialized fashion, the full range of their institutional work practices identified strictly with one, official, ideal aspect of published work, located in a Platonic field—their professed politics, theory of the subject and textuality, epistemology, "rhetoric" (cf. R. Miller, " 'A Moment' " 417). This is not to deny that affinities (or significant differences) exist between composition and perspectives presented in the published work or political tendencies found in work associated with cultural studies, rhetoric, "theory," or English. Nor is it to deny the potential in exploring such affinities and differences. However, we need to understand each and all of these in terms of their material institutional locations if indeed they are to be of use. Berlin, drawing on Stuart Hall, himself warns that "the institutional position of any academically situated project must never be ignored in assessing its potential for creating change" (*Rhetorics* xvi–xvii). And to recall Bourdieu, "it is not . . . political stances which determine people's stances on things academic, but their positions in the academic field which inform the stances that they adopt on political issues in general as well as on academic problems" (*Homo Academicus* xvii–xviii). While these statements can be read as setting up the "academic" purely as barrier, as the "institution" blocking change and determining politics, my argument is that it is only through thinking of the "academic" fields of English, Cultural Studies, or Rhetoric in such material ways that composition programs can make productive use of the specific institutional locations of these fields and their identifications with and disparities from such fields.

In practice, this means attending to the processes by which the concrete labor of our work within the academy gets capitalized, refigured as exchange value, in particular instances, and how to negotiate such processes. Applied to the situation of Composition, what is needed is not efforts to increase Composition's exchange value or cultural capital by claiming it has, all along, been carrying out "Cultural Studies," or can trace its lineage to the hoary tradition of Rhetoric, or to whatever passes for the official work of English these days, theoretical or not. Nor does it need to distance itself from these. Rather, it needs an institutional framework for supporting and sustaining the as yet unrecognized working knowledge and communal relations that have so far kept work in Composition, as well as work in these other "fields," as meaningful as it often is, in particular material circumstances. Rather than attempting to refute the charge that much of that work is merely "academic," we can insist on it, and on preserving it as such. So long as we attempt to "affiliate" with disciplines to acquire greater exchange value, we subject ourselves to the commodification of our work. And at any rate, as Allan Luke warns, "capital is only capital if it is recognised as such; that is, if it is granted legitimacy, symbolic capital, within a larger social and cultural field" ("Genres" 329). Or as Bourdieu explains, "the conversion or transformation of capital is mediated by one's position within the relations of power and knowledge in a social field" (*In Other Words* 231, quoted in Luke, "Genres" 327). Indeed, if, as Berlin claims, Composition has been practicing "Cultural Studies" for a hundred years, that history suggests that future attempts to capitalize on its affiliation with Cultural Studies (and its "cultural" capital) are unlikely to be effective: its affiliation has yet to be recognized, and by itself Composition, as Composition rather than Cultural Studies, lacks the social capital that would encourage such recognition. "Big" history is not only no help; it hurts. Instead of pursuing greater cultural capital, we need to find institutional frameworks that can sustain and support the use value of our labor and resist those processes of its commodification that would undermine such frameworks.[6]

Refocusing attention from the official, synecdochic representations of disciplines toward their material institutional instantiations means attending to such distinctively academic institutional forms as courses or curricula, departments or programs, in their interrelations, and exploring how to use or alter these to recognize and support the full range of concrete work carried out at and through these sites. As a precaution against allowing superficial "connections" between fields to blind us to differences, in carrying out such explorations we should insist first of all on defining these in terms of their specific historic, institutional, material distinctiveness. Otherwise, in our search for affiliations and alliances, we risk perpetuating the denigration of the working knowledge in all these fields and, more particularly, the denigration of Composition as a lesser form of some other field, a means or prelude or precursor to (or less positively, a bastardized form of) some legitimate activity: English literary study, Cultural Studies, Rhetoric, writing in other disciplines or the professions. Further, as a precaution against the seductions of synecdoche, we should define both the distinctiveness of Composition and its relation to other fields not in terms of a canon of texts, journals, techniques, or official ideology but in terms of the activities in which we engage. These activities include, certainly, for many in Composition the reading of certain texts and journals and participating in scholarly debate over technique and ideology, but not only these activities, or even primarily these. Or rather, these activities themselves must be understood as material social practices rather than markers of individual "scholarly" merit (cf. Trimbur, "Writing Instruction" 141–42).

To illustrate the ways in which academic institutional locations might work for or against preserving, recuperating, or promoting the concrete labor practices of composition, I turn to four locations at which the "comp" course intersects with other institutionally designated sites: its relation to other writing courses; its relation to literature courses; its relation to WAC programs; and its relation to service learning. The official name given "freshman comp" courses, going under such uninviting titles as Seminar in Reading and Writing (at my home institution), "General Writing," or more commonly English 101, speaks to its seemingly generic character. This has been taken to signify its alliance with the worst or most limited understanding of writing, as in "General Writing Skills Instruction." At my own institution, faculty have now addressed this by re-naming what was English 1 as a "First-Year Seminar," each section of which carries a distinctive title: "Media Magic/Media Critique," "Beasts, Blood Brothers & Blondes: Fairy Tales."[7] Versions of these first-year seminars are taught by faculty outside as well as inside English.

As these section titles suggest, the effect of this resituating of English 1 has been to eliminate its identification as a course on writing (of any kind), to emphasize its value as commodity (advertised through such titles), and to devalue the concrete work practices carried out in the course (on which such titles are silent). Because all first-year students are required to take one of these seminars, the practice of advertising individual versions through such titles has the effect of further degrading even their exchange value: How compelling, after all, can courses be that students are required to take, if faculty must advertise them? Further, because the titles locate the value of these seminars in their topics, any writing done in these seminars is valued only as a means toward understanding those topics, topics whose own value has already been made suspect. This is not to condemn the concrete work accomplished in such courses but to highlight how the institutional framing of that work delegitimizes it in relation to its official, already degraded exchange value as the fulfilling of a requirement in which not even the institution seems to believe.

By contrast, the more generic identifications of freshman comp courses—Rhetoric and Composition, General Writing, and so on—like the generic identification of many other courses—Music Theory 1, Biology 1, Organic Chemistry, Literary Study—both imply and raise as a question the significance of the work to be accomplished. This is not to claim that work carried out under such titles is in all or even most instances unimpeachable, only that the framing of a course in such ways *can* raise productive questions among students and faculty, ideally within the course, about the value of the concrete work accomplished there. Students may well ask what such courses are "about" or "for," if not to advisors or faculty, then to each other; I doubt they would ever ask such questions to anyone about a required first-year seminar on beasts, blood brothers, and blondes, except to register surprise at its being offered at all.

The offering of multiple sections of composition courses carrying generic titles can provoke similar productive questioning among those faculty teaching the course and students within different sections of the course. Giving individual titles to sections of a course effectively renders those sections separate courses, with their own numbers (the first-year seminars at Drake in fact are identified by different course numbers), thus encouraging both faculty and students to treat them as discrete entities bearing no necessary relation to others. The kind of "working knowledge" acquired and maintained through a body of faculty and students teaching and students enrolled in multiple sections of a generically designated course has much less chance of developing in discretely identified courses. I'll have more to say about the potential of such an institutional framing in chapter 5. Here, however, let me note that while such working knowledge at least has the potential to develop in the more common generic frame, that knowledge is likely to remain largely unrecognized and delegitimized. One of the distinctive virtues of composition studies is its efforts at legitimizing the working knowledge of teachers through the scholarly attention it gives to teaching. This is not the occasion to critique the limitations of those efforts. But such efforts might well be furthered at the local institutional level through designating the unofficial practice and exchange of "lore" as "faculty seminars," preferably funded through grants to bring in specialist faculty (from within or outside the institution) as seminar leaders and to give release time to all other participants. Similarly, the cross-comparisons of course sections in which students already engage unofficially might be given official recognition and made the occasion for academic learning, to raise explicitly questions about the nature, purpose, and material historicity of the work carried out in individual sections. This would require offering the time and occasion for such reflection, in forums on the courses, so that what might be taken for Platonic ideas—Composition, General Writing, Rhetoric—can be understood as socially constructed, and so liable to change. Giving official sanction and an institutional location for such cross-comparisons would both recognize the knowledge-making in which students already engage but also direct them away from the likely ordinary degeneration of that knowledge-making into debate over the personalities of faculty members or students and one's luck (or ill-luck) at being in one section versus another. In other words, it would provide for making such reflection "academic" in the most positive sense.

The structuring of the relationship of this generic comp course to other courses in writing in ways that would support students' and teachers' "working knowledge" is more complicated. If we rule out the structuring of these courses according to some imaginary developmental sequence, from basic through advanced, how then might they be structured? What writing courses, if any, ought to be offered in addition to General Writing, which by its title appears to address all writing? Does Composition constitute an academic "discipline" itself comparable to other disciplines, meriting a curricular structure comparable to that of other disciplines? Pursuing such questions, James Seitz has argued that Composition define itself as a subject, "writing," rather than just an occasion for refining a practice ("The Rhetoric of Curriculum"). Arguing that Composition will continue to be denigrated so long as it focuses its energies on improving the writing of beginning college students, Seitz calls for a four-year curriculum in writing that takes writing as its subject, or object, of study. That study would involve students in both examining the writing of others as well as engaging in the production of writing—for example, a course on satire in which students read examples of and commentaries on satire and write their own.

Seitz insists that only by identifying writing as a subject/object of study can Composition improve its disciplinary status and, hence, material situation in the academy. To see writing courses only as an occasion for "practice," he contends, implies a curricular structure based on levels of proficiency, from basic to advanced and preprofessional. While he does not abjure courses aimed at providing such practice, he insists that a writing curriculum needs to consist primarily of courses on the history, theory, and politics of writing in all its various permutations. To those objecting to the breadth of "territory" such a curriculum would cover, he notes that other disciplines offer a similar breadth: think of the range of phenomena subject to anthropological study, for example, or history, or physics. And to those concerned about such a definition impinging on the turf of literature or rhetoric, he argues that Composition needs to define itself on its own terms rather than in terms of the leftovers from these other fields: if Composition, so defined, subsumes literary study, for example (as it would appear to do), so be it. What would result would be, in effect, a curriculum that would prepare its "majors" for graduate study in Composition, just as other disciplines do, so that graduate programs in rhetoric and composition would no longer need to subsist on converts from literary study. Further, the breadth of its definition would ensure that Composition would retain its vaunted interdisciplinary ties to other fields, but, importantly, "from a less subservient form. . . . When Composition eventually teaches something other (or at least more) than preparation for study in other disciplines, the field's relationship with these disciplines will undergo significant change." Finally, drawing from Slevin, he argues that combining the practice of writing with study of the history of and theories about writing should make students more critically reflective about their writing, rather than simply more fluent in reproducing dominant practices.

In many ways, Seitz's argument is compelling one. It promises to improve the status of Composition within the academy, offers an array of possible course offerings attractive to those of us used to teaching composition as a single course, and inverts the relation of composition to literary study by subsuming the latter within Composition, a prospect that, aside from its logic, is especially tantalizing to those of us feeling institutionally subsumed by literature departments. Further, it is sensitive to the effects on Composition of the restrictions its most common institutional location at the beginning of postsecondary curricula imposes on its status as, at best, preparatory. Despite these advantages, his argument is silent on significant dangers to which any attempts at implementing such a curriculum would be subject.

Seitz offers his curriculum as admittedly speculative, something we might "imagine." In keeping with speculative projects, he understandably does not address the material constraints that might shape implementation of such projects or, for that matter, the material barriers that have prevented the development of such curricula already. What has stood in Composition's way, in his argument, is its lack of a subject. So, for example, while past considerations of Composition's disciplinary status imagined Composition allying itself with up-and-coming interdisciplinary fields such as African-American studies, women's studies, film studies, and critical theory, Seitz explains that such alliances have failed to form because, unlike Composition, each of these "has a *subject*, a body of material and a set of questions that scholars, teachers, and students in the field are expected to investigate."

This argument, however, takes the official representations of these fields, and the official purposes ascribed to Composition, for their full significance. Most obviously, these "fields" are identified with a reified subject "matter." Less obviously, the disinterest, and sometimes outright disdain and hostility, which these (and many other) fields have exhibited and continue to exhibit toward Composition are understood in the terms in which that disinterest, disdain, and hostility are expressed: Composition's lack of "subject." And so, in response, Seitz offers up what's officially demanded. While I'd be willing to hope that establishing a subject for Composition would improve its academic standing, I also believe that Composition's peculiar existing status and role in the academy and the historical conditions of English faculty pose significant obstacles to such an establishment, and that the full attraction and academic use of Composition would likely be lost on the way.

Given Composition's lack of *any* capital—whether economic, cultural, social, symbolic—it is in fact not surprising that fields attempting to improve their own positions would hold Composition at bay. Within the realm of the academy, they would have everything to lose and nothing to gain by allying themselves with Composition. By the same token, Composition's own purported "subject" or "object" of study could continue to be devalued. Capital, to recall Luke and Bourdieu, "is only capital if it is recognised as such; that is, if it is granted legitimacy, symbolic capital, within a larger social and cultural field" (Luke, "Genres" 329); and "the conversion or transformation of capital is mediated by one's position within the relations of power and knowledge in a social field" (Bourdieu, *In Other Words* 231, quoted in Luke, "Genres" 327). While Composition may claim disciplinary status, and think of itself as a discipline, others may refuse to recognize it as such, given its position in relations of power and knowledge in the social field of academic institutions.

But Composition's lack of status accounts only in part for its lack of allies. After all, in a significantly shorter time, other fields, like the "studies" programs mentioned above, have improved their academic standings and, further, have formed alliances with each other, all the while continuing to disdain Composition, despite the scholarly efforts of Compositionists to construct a "subject" of their own and to form alliances with these other fields. We can better account for Composition's continued lack of academic status, I believe, as a response to the threat it poses to the status of all academic fields. The composition course identifies academic work as a material social practice. Even in its most debased, skills and drills forms, it takes as its primary focus the materiality of the writing that constitutes the bulk of academic work. In focusing on the materiality of academic "discourse," of whatever stripe, it threatens continually to reveal the location of academic disciplinary work in the material realm. That is to say, Composition reveals what most disciplines deny: the contradiction between the apparent stability of their disciplinary subject as an abstract, reified entity, and the necessity for its continual, material reproduction through pedagogy generally and writing in particular. Academic disciplines both need and resent their need for Composition, hence the close parallel between the attitude taken toward Composition and the attitudes often taken toward the auto mechanic, plumber, or electrician, and toward women in general in their "mothering" function (Tuell 131–35).[8] Unlike the threat posed to established disciplines by programs like cultural studies or women's studies, which seem to undermine the epistemological foundations of those disciplines, Composition, to revive an old Marxist concept, threatens to expose their material base.

Of course, in one sense, such an exposure itself constitutes the undermining of a dominant epistemology. But the material form of Composition's challenge differs significantly from that presented by these other programs. A threat to the epistemological foundations of a discipline, so long as it takes the material form of scholarly theorizing about that discipline, far from posing such a threat, simply provides fodder for the production of additional critical texts and courses. Hence, *pace* New Right conservatives' fears, the academy's invasion by cultural studies, women's studies, African-American studies, queer studies has led not to the demise of humanities but to increases in interest and enrollments, and in humanities scholarship to a feverish increase in activity (see Oakley 279–81). In my own department, a revamping of the undergraduate curriculum in light of a growing acceptance of a "social-epistemic" rhetoric associated with cultural studies has resulted in more, not less, literature and literature-based courses generally, more courses in British literature, and an increase from one course in Shakespeare to three (and counting). "Literature" has in effect been expanded, as has "Shakespeare." The generic composition course ("English 1"), on the other hand, has been abolished, replaced by topical, college-taught "first-year seminars." For the composition course calls attention to the material location and production—the labor—of academic work that academics are at pains to deny.

Recent developments in my department point to the role of material history and circumstance in altering the pursuit of speculations like Seitz's about what a composition curriculum might look like, or what relations might be established between its courses and others within or outside English. As speculative, Seitz's imagined subsuming of literary study under the aegis of composition, however tantalizing, understandably does not address how one moves from present conditions to such a subsumption, thereby ignoring the obstacles to it posed by the historical training of those "in" literature, the cultural capital of literary study and Composition's lack of capital, and the material demands of the teaching of writing. The history of my own department's revision of its curriculum illustrates the operation of just such obstacles.

From one perspective, Drake's new curriculum can be seen as dislodging the binary of literature/composition altogether, subsuming both under the generic "English" rubric. The department has described its new curriculum to undergraduates as follows:

> The Department of English is engaged in the study of the power of language to mediate relations between people and the world around them. Courses in the department provide students ongoing opportunities to rethink their understanding and critical practice of reading and writing; to develop critical awareness of the implications of language use; to assess and develop their own ideas and to understand better the constraints that competing discourses might place upon those ideas; to explore the wide range of texts and topics that currently constitute the subject of English studies; to engage with a variety of theoretical and critical perspectives on, about and within English studies; to situate English studies in relation to intellectual work in other disciplines. (*Drake University Catalog* 67)

Absent from this description is any reference to either "literature" or "composition." There are only the relatively value-neutral terms "language," "reading and writing," "language use," "competing discourses," "texts and topics." By this representation, English at Drake might well be mistaken for the epitome of the type of English studies curriculum Seitz recommends, in which literature constitutes only one subspecialty, and in accordance with the tenets of the social-epistemic rhetoric James Berlin advocates. Berlin argues that social-epistemic rhetoric can provide a basis on which to refigure English studies (*Rhetorics* 84–88). Social-epistemic rhetoric undermines the poetic/rhetoric binary by refusing the distinction between representational and creative texts, since it holds that "language in all its uses structures, rather than simply records, experience" (*Rhetorics* 86). Thus, within social-epistemic rhetoric,

> Producing and consuming [texts] are both interpretations (as all language is interpretive), requiring a knowledge of semiotic

codes in which versions of economic, social, and political predispositions are inscribed. . . . These codes are never simply in
the writer, in the text, or in the reader. They always involve a
dialectical relation of the three, a rhetorical exchange in which
writer, reader, text, and material conditions simultaneously
interact with each other through the medium of semiotic
codes. This encounter in language is never totally free, since
semiotic codes are themselves already interpretations. Thus,
the signifying practices of a poetic or rhetoric are always historically conditioned, always responses to the material and social formations of a particular moment. (*Rhetorics* 86–87)

In theory, this is a promising basis for refiguring English studies and addressing the inequities visited upon Composition by its location within English, since it eliminates the distinctions usually
invoked to justify those inequities. There is a gap here, however, between the theory espoused and the argument presented. If indeed,
as Berlin warns, "the signifying practices of a poetic or rhetoric are
always historically conditioned, always responses to the material
and social formations of a particular moment," then the signifying
practices of an English curriculum are also "historically conditioned,
always responses to the material and social formations of a particular moment." In other words, so long as Berlin's analysis operates in
the realm of the aesthetic/academic (conventionally understood), his
refiguration works, presenting an intriguing, utopian totality (see
Berlin, *Rhetorics* 74). When viewed in terms of its material implementation, inevitably, limitations appear.[9]

In the specific history of the Drake English department, several
factors in particular have conditioned the "signifying practices" of
its curriculum. First, the primary training and commitment of the
majority of the faculty were in the interpretation of texts. This was
no less true of those committed to cultural, women's, multicultural,
and American studies than of those committed to literary study as
traditionally understood. Second, experience had impressed upon
all faculty the fact that writing courses were more labor intensive
than other courses while carrying no more credit (for either faculty
and students) than these other courses. Third (and relatedly), while
all faculty were committed to teaching, they also felt increasing
institutional pressure to publish. And fourth, at Drake, caps on

course enrollments were tied to whether the courses were designated writing intensive or not.

Given these conditions, "dislodging" the binaries of lit/comp,
reading/writing by claiming that "[p]roducing and consuming
[texts] are both interpretations (as all language is interpretive)"
could be used to justify treating courses which focused primarily on
the interpretation of texts as courses not simply in "reading" but in
"writing," for by this claim, writing is reading is writing. One could
teach a course in reading (for which one's past training may best
have prepared one), claim it as a *writing*/reading course, and
thereby be rewarded with a lower class size without having to suffer the greater labor-intensity of a traditional writing course. Thus,
in response to demands from other Drake colleges that English provide writing courses for their students, the English department,
having dislodged the reading/writing binary, declared that all of its
lower-level courses *were* writing courses, whatever their title or
topic, and so could be used to fulfill the writing requirements these
other colleges made on their students. Insofar as these courses
were thus of "service" to these other colleges, the department had
found an ideal way to provide service with a smile.

Ironically, the dislodging of these binaries, and indeed the revision of the English curriculum as a whole, had begun in a revision
of the (then) required English composition course (subsequently
abolished), evidenced in its published catalogue description:

> A course in writing and reading as *interdependent* activities
> stimulating intellectual inquiry and growth. Emphasis on in-
> tensive *critical engagement with texts through writing* will en-
> courage students to *interact with ideas in the texts*, to develop
> their own interpretations, and to become aware of how lan-
> guage use in different discourses shapes and constrains mean-
> ing. (*Drake University Catalog* 180, my emphasis)

Thus, while the revision of Drake's English curriculum would seem,
in theory, to promise either Seitz's subsumption of English literature under Composition, or Berlin's ideal of dislodging the lit/comp
binary through affiliation with a social-epistemic rhetoric, the material social conditions in which that revision was enacted led not to
Composition's ascendance to its rightful place subsuming Liter-

ature, nor to a happy utopia free of binaries, but the practical reinforcement of those binaries, which, no longer codified impositions, were now more free to operate as (unmentioned) historical and material givens. Reading and writing, literature and composition, were equalized, but history and material conditions led some to being more equal than others. The explosion of new course offerings under the new "English" curriculum did not include a greater number of courses in writing, which both faculty and students rightly perceived to require more labor, but to more reading/writing courses, with little question as to which, in practice, was to be the governing term.

This is not to say that the use of writing in these latter courses somehow does not count, that learning may not be enhanced through the inclusion of writing in such courses, as in some WAC (writing across the curriculum) programs. But we should not confuse the practices undertaken in these courses with writing courses, any more than we would confuse a novelist with an individual who claims to have a novel "up here, in my head." The effacement of the material differences between the practices of reading and writing through these theoretical dislodgements enables those differences to operate all the more powerfully. The threat writing courses pose to revealing the material base of disciplinary work becomes contained, as the material practice of writing is idealized into, subsumed within, and contained by "reading."

The history of recent changes in writing instruction at the State University of New York at Albany reveals a similar containment of Composition's threat (or, from my perspective, potential) in WAC programs. Responding to the view of other colleagues that the purpose of the freshman composition course was to "fix" students' writing errors, and in order to end these colleagues' habit of blaming English faculty for the errors found in student writing, SUNY Albany's compositionists abolished the university's freshman composition course in the mid-1980s, introducing in its stead a writing across the curriculum program.[10] As Lil Brannon explains the argument for doing so,

> We thought, naively, that we could change the faculty's minds
> if they had to struggle with the teaching of writing them
> selves. . . . that they would learn as we had learned, . . . that

writing could be more effectively taught within the boundaries of disciplined inquiry. . . . that students would learn facility with language best as they were learning the concepts of the discipline. They could use their writing to learn a field of study because they would be engaged with practitioners of the field. Their writing in the disciplines could serve the making of knowledge needed in today's world. ("Confronting")

Concomitantly, in a move akin to those promoted by Seitz and Berlin, composition teachers attempted to "work with [their] colleagues in English to refigure English studies; that is, to interrelate writing, teaching, criticism, and theory," ultimately creating a sequence of courses for English majors that would "[blur] the boundaries between rhetoric and poetics" ("Confronting"). However, what they failed to anticipate, Brannon warns, was that "[b]y supporting writing across the curriculum and focusing our intellectual work within the English department, we were simultaneously limiting the purposes of writing instruction to the project of assimilating students into practices of academic discourse (not asking them to question those practices) and we were bracketing off the larger public purposes that writing can serve for thousands of undergraduates" ("Confronting"). What freshman composition had provided, and what its abolition and the introduction of a WAC program prevented, was "an ongoing university-wide conversation about the purposes for teaching writing" ("Confronting").

In terms of the argument I have been making, the "naiveté" of Brannon and her colleagues lay in their failure to take into account the material interests and historical conditions in which they instituted WAC and abolished freshman composition. In an earlier essay justifying these changes, Brannon hints at some very basic material obstacles to achieving the goals of these programs. She points to "persistently insoluble problems [such] as class size, teacher workload, classroom materials, access to technology, funding of the Writing Center, the education of faculty and tutors" ("(Dis)Missing" 247–48). And she warns that what, finally, is needed is "systemic change, an imaginative restructuring of the current practices of schools in the context of a reexamination of the realities of U.S. life" (248). But of course, the realities of U.S. life include the basic material obstacles to the achievement of SUNY's initial goals for its WAC program. More disturbingly, any re-examination of such realities in the direction of imaginatively re-structuring "current practices of schools" would itself constitute a material practice for which existing structures provided little context or support. Instead, existing structures subsumed any radical potential of Composition by relegating its teaching to a service position in relation to these other disciplines.

This is not to say that institutional structures themselves determine effects. WAC programs, for example, have potentially both radical and conservative effects. At the same time, however, within certain institutional contexts, certain structures may more readily lend themselves to explicit critique. Again, as Myron Tuman has warned, "[c]ontrolling institutions continue to derive much of their strength and their influence from the quiet effectiveness with which they fulfill their reproductive role" (50). Individual disciplines may contain WAC's potentially radical challenge to them through subsuming them within the institutional structure of individual disciplines. In his critique of U.S. WAC programs, Daniel Mahala sees their radical potential residing in the forum they might provide for addressing conflict between disciplines and between the academic and the non-academic (786, 787). However, the "horizontal," segmented institutional structure of many colleges and universities provides no space for such a forum, containing conflicts within the boundaries of individual colleges, disciplines, courses, and course sections. While students may well, on their own, consider the conflicting relations between their experiences in such courses, and faculty too may unofficially compare notes, the structure often does not provide a site that would support such work. Conversely, if, as Tuman argues, more explicitly "authoritarian" pedagogies may awaken opposition by the very visibility of their control (50), so more seemingly authoritarian institutional structures may better occasion challenges to the authorization of those structures. In this sense, as I have suggested above, the required freshman composition course may provide a better forum for investigation and revision of the "academic" sphere than writing centers, writing courses linked to specific disciplines, or courses in established disciplines designated "writing-intensive." Brannon ends up arguing as much, calling for first-year writing courses that situate students "within and against academic discourse . . . to help students position their [home] knowledge in relation to disciplined knowledge" to prepare students to become what Gramsci terms the "new intellectuals," those positioned to speak across the boundaries of public discourse and disciplined academic inquiry" ("Confronting").

It may appear at this point that I have made arguments for two contradictory, functionalist proposals: to find institutional frameworks that would sustain and support the working knowledge of students, and to insist on retaining those institutional frameworks that are most likely to provoke explicit dissent. My use of specific institutional histories, too, might be seen as demonstrating that specific structures, such as WAC programs or the presence or absence of required first-year composition courses, function in specific ways. These interpretations, however, remove such structures from their material location and dependence on specific actors, rendering them into commodities. That is, the unintended consequences of specific actions, like those detailed in the (inevitably partial) histories of Drake and SUNY Albany presented above, argued here to be the *effects* of specific structures, are taken as evidence of their *function*, whereas they illustrate at most the *mutual* dependence of agency and structure. By contrast, what we need to search for, and the most we can hope to find, are the ways in which an institutional framework, or structure, might be put to specific uses. Thus Brannon's call for first-year writing courses as the avenue to the production of Gramscian new intellectuals is not an argument that this is what first-year writing courses do; it is an argument for how they might be used, an argument congruent with my own.

In this light, to return to the question of what other courses a composition curriculum might offer in addition to first-year writing courses, let me sketch a speculative vision of my own. In addition to any WAC-like courses, reading/writing courses within English departments, or preprofessional writing courses such as Writing Business Reports or even Writing the Short Story, all of which may potentially be put to radical use, Composition might offer continuing cross-college writing courses for students in each of the subsequent years of their college careers. While such courses could well be used for gatekeeping or be seen as occasions for "brushing up" or "polishing" students' fluency in a purported academic discourse, or "GWSI," I am suggesting that such courses also could be used to continue and further students' critique of the academic in light of their continuing experience with it in their lives, and for the revision of their earlier critiques. The point would not be to offer senior, junior, or even sophomore "capstone" experiences, which are usually understood as discipline-specific. Rather, they could be used as occasions for students to apply their increasing experience of work in a variety of disciplines (as well as their increasing experience generally) to rearticulate that experience and their prospects, to redefine for themselves the significance of their "academic" experiences. These would, ideally, engage in explicit critique of the material production of those experiences, including questions about the different levels of intensity and kinds of student and faculty labor expended in the work of different courses and types of courses, particularly writing courses. If universally required, these courses would appear less as occasions for remediation, and would make possible the exchange of a greater diversity of perspectives on academic life. Further, students' increasing experience in the academy would presumably give them greater authority to challenge abstracted claims about it (like those found in department, college, and university "mission" statements), an authority that first-year students by definition lack. And ideally (to continue in this speculative vein), such courses would provide forums for both sharing and supporting the working knowledge students would have been developing. Kusterer found that the working knowledge of the "unskilled" workers he studied, if recognized, had the potential to improve work generally, both in terms of efficiency and usefulness of the product (though this was often at odds with management's pursuit of increasing exchange value) (132–33). The increasing seniority of students would presumably signal their increasing possession of such working knowledge of the academy and so, too, their potential to be effective "change agents" of its structures, able both to work and rework those to better ends.

As preceding discussions show, and to return from speculation, significant obstacles stand in the way of getting from existing conditions to such a curriculum. In this light, the gap between official claims for and practical effects of programs might be exploited. In a response to Mahala's critique of the formalist and conservative tendencies of WAC programs, Patricia Dunn, while agreeing with Mahala's critique, notes that "those working to establish such [WAC] programs do not have the luxury of critiquing from the outside and must do the best they can within their particular circumstances," and that "to confront [her] already arguing committee [charged with establishing a WAC program] with [issues Mahala addresses] at this time would be disastrous" (732, 731). Instead, Dunn suggests that while "a cooperative approach that appeals to a common ground may, indeed, be a compromise of sorts. . . . having such a committee intact provides what was not there before—a forum in which such important philosophical dialogues may eventually take place" (732). Thus, what matters materially at such moments is not an official statement of uniform commitment to a specific philosophy of writing but the establishment of a communal network for thinking about and working through how to implement any such philosophy. The account by Francis Sullivan, Arabella Lyon, Dennis Lebofsky, Susan Wells, and Eli Goldblatt of the transformation of the writing program at Temple University suggests, in fact, that official discourse about writing and students in the name of which writing programs are maintained and transformed can be reworked rather than rejected. So, for example, in the process of reforming their program, Sullivan and colleagues found that the "appeal to skills that [Temple] students lacked," however noxious to many in Composition for its apparent denigration of students and composition teachers, led to "considerable support from the faculty at large," especially when the language of "needs" was reinterpreted from "student deficits to a way of talking about desires" (376, 379). Such reworking of the terms of our work, however, means defining these—needs, skills, standards, even "writing"—not abstractly but in relation to specific material practices, as Sullivan et al. attempted in asking their faculty colleagues about the specific desires and writing practices they wanted for student writing.

I have argued above that the radical challenge Composition poses to the academy is its threat to reveal the material base of academic knowledge. That WAC programs pose a similar threat can account for efforts at domesticating them into exercises in mastering abstracted formalist principles of disciplinary writing. In our critiques, we should not confuse domestications of such programs, or of required first-year composition courses, with their full potential or actual effects. Service learning poses a somewhat different threat to traditional notions of academic knowledge by calling explicit attention to the learning achieved in non-academic settings. Granting academic credit to the learning achieved in non-academic settings legitimates that learning and the knowledge produced in those settings, hence the debates over how to evaluate service learning within academic terms (Adler-Kassner et al. 6–7, 13; Bacon 48–52). Moreover, if only by implication, it calls into question the status of the knowledge produced in academic settings and the validity of those settings as a site for learning and knowledge production. At a "basic" level, if one can best learn needed skills "on the job," as it were, through a service-learning experience in, say, the writing and production of brochures, of what use is academic learning?

Rather than taking this question as rhetorical, I think we can pursue it as a real question, not simply by and for ourselves but as an explicit issue for our courses. In chapter 2 I suggested that the value of service learning for Composition lay not in the résumé-building opportunities it can give students, nor in the ostensibly greater "reality" of non-academic writing, but in the ways in which such experiences can enable students to confront the materiality of all writing, as they compare the conditions of writing outside the academy with those inside. It is in this sense that, like composition generally, service learning can reinforce the materiality of academic work and lead us and our students to better understand the specific uses and limitations of the types of learning practiced and possible in the academy and elsewhere. While for some, the challenge service learning poses to the validity of academic learning might be a good reason to condemn service learning, I would argue that such a response betrays a kind of academic bad faith, an underestimation of the value of work made possible by at least some of the specific material conditions of academic sites.

Several writers have pointed to some of the specific disparities in material conditions of traditional academic and community service writing and learning. Nora Bacon, for example, observes that some of these disparities make it a struggle for teachers to find points of intersection between their composition teaching and service learning. As she notes, "Our customary lessons about the processes and the formal features of writing are often irrelevant to nonacademic writing, and we are confronted with the fact that as long as we design our courses around personal and literary essays, we are teaching a tiny corner of the world of discourse" (52). And there are more concrete disparities which those involved in service learning have encountered as they attempt to work out the logistics and administration of programs linking courses, and their students and teachers, with community organizations (Adler-Kassner et al. 1).

One response to such struggles, of course, is to adapt academic ways to the non-academic. If, for example, community service writing emphasizes such issues as document design, then, by this argument, composition courses ought to address such issues (Bacon 51). Alternatively, composition (and other) courses may keep the service-learning experience at arm's length, using that experience at most as grist for reflection on a particular subject (e.g., literacy, homelessness), or as providing a seemingly more "authentic" motivation for attention to that subject (Adler-Kassner et al. 2–3). In such approaches, the service-learning experience plays a role something like "fieldwork," ideally providing "hands-on" knowledge of the subject about which students may then write. This would be especially true of those service-learning experiences involving students primarily in tasks other than writing, such as tutoring or preparing food at homeless shelters. Here too, however, struggles for intersections between academic and non-academic work arise. This is perhaps made most immediately evident as teachers confront the task of coordinating academic and non-academic schedules and demands (Adler-Kassner et al. 11–12). But it also arises as teachers discover the lack of fit between the disciplinary boundaries of a specific course and the highly interdisciplinary knowledge demands of community service work (Adler-Kassner et al. 12–13).

But rather than either attempting to adapt academic courses entirely to the demands of non-academic work encountered through service learning, or abandoning or keeping on separate tracks the disparities between the structures and demands of academic and community-service experience and work, I would argue that productive academic use be made of those differences to support and increase students' working knowledge of both spheres. As Bacon has argued, "A course that sets academic writing side by side with nonacademic writing invites comparative analysis; it doesn't guarantee critical distance from academic writing"—or non-academic writing, I would add—"but it offers the possibility" (43). Reflecting on academic writing in the light of non-academic writing, she argues, can help students "interrogate" the relationship between the composition classroom as a context for writing and the type of writing conducted there, as well as the form and function of writing in other courses and in non-academic settings (43).

Of course, the distancing that results from comparative analysis does not and should not preclude the possibility of any accommodation of non-academic work or deny the value of maintaining some independence for pursuing the contradictory goals of the different realms, but it allows for such accommodations and contradictions to become explicit focuses of service-learning courses. So, for example, while it seems highly appropriate for Composition to learn from students' experience in community-service writing about the need for teachers to attend to issues of document design, attending to such issues can and should include investigating the apparent indifference of academics traditionally to document design (and I suspect it's an indifference that masks its importance, like the studiously casual attitude many academics stereotypically take toward dress). Similarly, the lack of fit between academic calendars and work in community organizations, and between academic disciplinary structures and the knowledge demands of community-service work, can and should lead both to the possibility of modifying academic calendars and the boundaries of coursework and to investigating the material conditions of possibility for those structures.

Proponents of service learning have justified it not simply as a means of providing more, and grittier, grist for coursework, nor as an extended internship program, but for its potential to challenge the traditional divorce between the academy and the community, both as these are understood abstractly—the "ivory tower" versus "society's needs"—and concretely, in terms of specific town/gown relations. Both of the alternatives I've described above point to ways in which either of these threatens to subsume the other: the academy as vocational training, subsumed by a community's officially understood needs, or the community as archaeological "dig" site for academics, a living lab. Of course, often enough these are the terms by which such programs are officially advertised, along with the goals of citizenship education and doing social good (Bridwell-Bowles, "Service-Learning" 21, 24, 25). Without denying

that service-learning programs may be put to such uses or the validity of such justifications for service learning, we need to be wary
of the reductive view of both the "academy" and the "community"
in such representations: the academy as either servant to the business world or ivory tower, the community as either the fallow territory of unexplored, percolating "experience," or a swamp of
unmet needs—and both as discrete entities.

For the obvious disparities between academic and community-
service work may blind us to significant intersections between
them and lead to mistaking official representations of each of
these for their full significance. The potential of service learning
to bridge the academy and the community is usually described
in terms of making learning "authentic" (Adler-Kassner 2–3;
Bridwell-Bowles, "Service-Learning" 21). What makes arguments
for service learning that invoke authenticity problematic is their
tendency to associate authenticity (sometimes, "reality") with the
realm of the community, as if all community-service work was inherently authentic, and academic work inauthentic, "merely" academic in the worst sense.

Without questioning the validity of the experience of authenticity in such accounts, I would identify that experience not with the
specific type of work performed but with the relationship established between the worker and the work. In a critique of Harry
Braverman's landmark analysis (in Braverman's *Labor and
Monopoly Capital*) of the degradation of work through its increasing routinization under monopoly capital, Kusterer argues that
"unskilled" work remains "a unity of concrete and abstract labor, of
use value and exchange value production, of real public utility and
merely private profit." The continuing presence in work of the former aspects enables workers to achieve in the labor process a sense
of "satisfaction and self-respect that comes from learning, growing,
and making a useful contribution to society" despite those aspects
of the work that would alienate them from it (192).

Following Kusterer's argument, the degree to which work, either academic or community-related, seems either authentic or not
would depend not on the sphere of its location or even its ostensible, official purpose but whether the worker is able to learn to use
the occasion of the work to learn, grow, and contribute to society, or
at least to see herself as doing so.[11] There are several ways of ac-

counting for the apparent meaninglessness or inauthenticity of students' academic experience. First, only its exchange and not its use value may be recognized. Students readily understand the "exchange" value of the credits accumulated, requirements fulfilled, grade transcripts compiled by means of work with no readily apparent use value. This is exacerbated by the emphasis given this exchange value in dominant culture and by the schools themselves (see L. R. Pratt 38–39).[12] Official claims about the "use" of academic knowledge often call attention not to its use value but its exchange value, as when students are told that they should learn abstract writing skills because such skills will make the students themselves hot commodities on the job market. Second, the attenuated character of the use value of much academic knowledge-making, already commented upon, makes it less immediately visible. Finally, much of the working knowledge in students' academic work that might and does contribute to a dis-alienating experience goes unrecognized or is dismissed under the general term of the "college experience," something for which contributing parents and alumni may be encouraged to feel nostalgia but which is otherwise ignored, and which may be undermined by specific institutional practices weakening the development of communal social relations among students and faculty.

Conversely, community-service work, insofar as it seems to be "voluntary" and to serve the "community," may be recognized officially primarily for its use value as work, however lowly and routine (e.g., stuffing envelopes), that contributes to the betterment of society, often in seemingly concrete ways: the construction of affordable housing or playgrounds, feeding hungry mouths. While students may also acquire marketable skills and build up their résumés through community work, the "exchange value" thus acquired may be attributable to their status as students rather than to the work itself. Less apparent is the degree to which much community-service work itself constitutes a significant sector of employment for non-students—labor for pay—and a means of acquiring cultural capital for its workers. Both 1998 candidates for Lieutenant Governor of Iowa, for example, listed their community-service work as providing them with appropriate job training.

Alternatively, the view of academic work as removed from the "real" world of social action in comparison to community-service work ignores the close association of much academic work with service to the "community." Much postsecondary education can be, and has been, seen as having a "service" mission to the community (Deans 31), most obviously in the stated purposes of land-grant universities, though such missions are often seen as something to which academics give mere lip service. Aside from its contributions of technical expertise, the academy "serves" the community by providing jobs training and community "enrichment" through arts events and humanities education, and has had the effect, if not the purpose, of lowering the ranks of the unemployed. There is a sense, that is, in which education *is* an answer to unemployment—not, as politicians like to claim, by providing would-be workers with skills employers desire but by putting the unemployed to work in courses, as students, just as government programs in human services can help to eliminate unemployment and the social ills attending unemployment by employing people to work in those programs.

I do not mean this cynically as an aspersion on either education or government programs but positively. Such observations are seen as cynical only if we accept a degraded notion of work as the production of exchange value, blind to its value as an activity enabling people to re-create themselves in relation to each other and the natural world. By the same token, the "extracurriculum" of composition to which Anne Ruggles Gere has pointed that obtains in non-academic, largely free and voluntary writing workshops should be recognized not only in these non-academic sites but also hidden within the academic site of the composition classroom. Pointing to the Tenderloin Women's Writing Workshop or the Lansing, Iowa Writer's Workshop as contemporary examples and to literary societies in the past, Gere defines this extracurriculum of composition as "constructed by desire, by the aspirations and imaginations of its participants. . . . [positing] writing as an action undertaken by motivated individuals who frequently see it as having social and economic consequences, including transformations in personal relationships" (80). But recognizing this extracurriculum outside the academy should not blind us to its operation within the academy. Not only non-academic writing but also students' (and faculty's) academic writing may be shaped by their aspirations and imaginations, have social and economic consequences, and transform personal relationships. That official representations of academic writing do not highlight these aspects does not mean they do not obtain or do not contribute to those aspects of academic work that do receive official recognition (cf. Carr 95–97).

Structurally, of course, such aspects receive attention only in CSL (community service-learning) programs, where they are *supposed* to obtain. In that sense, despite the overlap between academic and service-learning work to which I have been pointing, CSL programs constitute an important structural space for maintaining such aspects, just as basic writing, required freshman composition courses, and WAC programs can provide institutional space for work and people that go unrecognized and unrewarded elsewhere in the academy (Deans 30). Such structure as these programs enjoy remains fragile. Indeed, Tom Deans, drawing on David Russell's study of WAC programs, argues that both WAC and CSL programs work against the grain of the modern university structure (Deans 30–33). As Deans observes, both "require a significant departure from traditional teaching and learning in college courses," both are more labor-intensive, both "can prompt faculty to adopt new perspectives on the values and conventions of their home disciplines," and both lack the academic prestige of specialized scholarly activity (29–30). Further, as "interdepartmental" programs, both typically exist outside the disciplines and are "claimed by administrative structures in Student Affairs, where they remain largely disconnected from the academic curriculum" and thus "end up in an 'institutional no-man's land' " (Deans 31).

Barring any radical overhaul of the existing academic institutional structures, such programs have attempted instead to redefine work within them (Deans 32). As Russell observes of WAC movements, they "work through the disciplines to transform not only student writing but also the ways disciplines conceive of writing and its teaching" (*Writing* 299; quoted in Deans 32). There is a danger in this strategy, Deans warns, of accommodating institutional structures at the expense of sacrificing the "progressive vision of teaching and learning" that informs both WAC and CSL programs (33). In response to such dangers, Deans advocates increasing the academic cultural capital of CSL programs by a commitment to research on CSL, tailoring CSL programs to individual institutional contexts, building "grassroots" support by encouraging faculty's own experiments on the value of incorporating

CSL programs into their work, and allying with comparable programs, most obviously WAC (33–34). In short, he advocates strategies of building up professional status and disciplinary knowledge through research, finding institutional allies, and affiliating especially with those who already have status.

As the discussion in this chapter suggests, these are all strategies that Composition has pursued in attempts to improve its own institutional position within the academy. Without denying a degree of utility to such strategies, I have been arguing, however, that the radical challenge to the academy posed by composition as well as by CSL and WAC programs can be strengthened most by tapping within the structured realm of the "academic" itself the working knowledge to effect that challenge. However, to tap that potential will require revising our notions of the "academic" to recognize the full material social process of work hidden within the forms by which it is officially represented as precisely "academic." In chapter 5, I explore the barriers to recognizing such work, and the avenues by which it may be recuperated, both of which take the guise of "traditions."

Chapter 5

TRADITIONAL

We should not cede tradition to the conservatives!

—Anthony Giddens, *Central Problems* 7

I n debate on the disciplinary status of Composition, "tradition" and the "traditional" are almost always terms of derogation. This is perhaps most evident in the use of the term "current-traditional" to designate those theories and practices against which compositionists must define themselves if they are to reclaim pedagogy as a site for Composition theory and research. But it is also evident in the difficulties encountered in attempts to defend traditions or the traditional in Composition. To designate a practice or theory "traditional" is to call forth a more powerful opposition to it, whatever one's own professed alignments.

But the derogatory connotations of tradition in Composition, like those associated with the "academic" discussed in chapter 4, may speak to limitations not of tradition and the traditional, but in how these are conceived. Raymond Williams has warned that "[m]ost versions of 'tradition' can be quickly shown to be radically selective," emphasizing certain meanings and practices while neglecting or excluding others (*Marxism* 115). Conceptions of "tradition" dominant in Composition exemplify this selectivity, overlooking what may be counter or alternative to the hegemonic within tradition. In these conceptions, a focus on elements of the residual incorporated into dominant culture leads to ignoring those residual "experiences, meanings and values which cannot be expressed or substantially verified in terms of the dominant culture" and which "may have an alternative or even oppositional relation to the dominant culture" (Williams, *Marxism* 122).

These conceptions make it difficult for those attempting to reclaim the category of "tradition" for Composition as an active, activating process and force for counterhegemonic work, since the very terms *tradition* and *traditional* operate in dominant discourse in Composition to name that against which compositionists have defined their projects. More specifically, as I will argue, to reclaim the category of tradition requires contesting a dominant ideology within Composition that conflates knowledge with writing, both understood in terms of professional disciplinary writing practices. This conflation denies or denigrates the validity and utility of actors' practical consciousness and nondiscursive knowledge, which are lumped under the category of the traditional. To illustrate what reclaiming tradition might involve, I turn to Robin Varnum's account of a thirty-year tradition of teaching English 1–2 at Amherst College during the mid-twentieth century (*Fencing*). That tradition, I argue, exhibits traces of alternative practices drawing from residual elements of dominant culture that, until recently, have remained largely hidden under blanket assumptions about the hegemony of "current-traditional" practice. I examine the writings of two compositionists who extend this tradition, William E. Coles Jr. and David Bartholomae, and the relationship between them to illustrate how dominant conceptions of tradition also blind us to traditions in Composition understood, and practiced, differently.

Looking to traditions hidden *within* the dominant can complement recent efforts to recover composition practices marked as *outside* the dominant, such as Anne Ruggles Gere's investigations of the "extracurriculum" of Composition located in non-academic writing circles and clubs. Gere uses her investigations of Composition's extracurriculum both to challenge the "uncritical narrative of professionalization" dominating histories of the field and to foreground "the importance of learning from amateurs" (86, 88). Recognizing this extracurriculum, Gere argues, both requires and leads historians to "uncouple composition and schooling" (80), and to turn to materials and sites beyond the school to understand past and ongoing traditions of reading and writing. As Jean Carr observes,

> [Gere] challenges histories of literacy instruction that have traced too neat a tradition from old world rhetorics to 19th-century elite universities to the current field of composition . . . urg[ing] us to . . . recognize how many other "traditions" could be located, how many other routes of influence and instruction need to be explored. (94)

In using Composition's extracurriculum to expose these other traditions, however, there is a danger, Carr warns, in assuming that the academic world itself is "a story already known and known fully" (96); the danger, that is, I have argued against in chapter 4 of mistaking official representations of the academic for its "full story." To avoid this danger means that we need to not only "open up for scrutiny the rich and boundless cultural materials Gere suggests," but also "return to material we thought closed, or empty, to texts we have dismissed as simple" (Carr 97). Further, Carr warns, "We need to rethink the notion that influence and tradition are produced in straight lines, that theories are uttered and then get 'implemented' somehow and the influence spreads down and out until it is diffused in the hinterlands" (97). It means, in short, that we need to rethink what constitutes traditions in Composition.

Tradition, Academic Professionalism, and Composition "Lore"

The terms *tradition* and *traditional* carry a variety of different meanings, admittedly not all derogatory. Most innocuously, *tradition* is sometimes used in Composition historiography (and elsewhere) to name a theory, school of thought, or intellectual practice without necessarily signaling any negative (or positive) view of these. A more strongly evaluative meaning for *tradition* begins to obtain in references to practices deemed common or ordinary. The derogatory connotations of such usages arise from the sense that such practices are carried on as unconscious habit, informed at best by mere "common sense" or a "false consciousness" that remains uncritiqued, even unexamined, as in the common complaint Sharon Crowley observes of "the presence in Freshman English of a few pieces of discursive and pedagogical dogma, none of which seem to be organized according to any perceptible fashion, unless it is the order dictated by tradition" ("Perilous" 12). Such derogatory connotations become fully manifest in references to practices or theories as "tradition*al*," in which the term specifies the identification of what the term modifies with the past and presumes that it must be less informed than the present, or at least the writer's present state of knowledge. For example, the seemingly oxymoronic usage "current-traditional" refers to those theories and practices of the past (i.e., "traditional") that continue to exist ("current") without benefit of the enlightenment afforded by present thought.

The linking of the traditional with the unenlightened can be accounted for by the association of the traditional with the oral and, by implication, the circumstantial, shared, common, and immediate. For "tradition" refers also to the medium by which a practice or theory is transmitted (*OED*). If traditional knowledge is oral, then the chances of its practitioners subjecting it to studious critique are presumed to be less likely. It is only with the advent of writing, we writing teachers like to tell ourselves, that the claims of tradition can be examined critically, compared with competing claims for inconsistencies, and judged objectively (Goody and Watt 13–17). The teaching of writing itself is thus intimately invested in critiques of, and breaks from, tradition, at least as "tradition" and "writing" are now commonly conceived. I refer here not merely to the utility of the medium of writing in formulating critiques, and so to specific uses for writing that might be taught, but also to the interest writing teachers have in claiming professional expertise and membership in an academic discipline worthy of respect. For it is through subjecting traditional knowledge and practices to written critique that such status is thought to be acquired. Thus in Robert Connors' examination of the history of composition instructors' focus on "mechanical correctness," he describes studies that question that focus as an indication that "composition studies are finally coming to constitute a genuine discipline and are no longer a mere purblind drifting on the current of unexamined tradition" ("Mechanical" 71).

Written critiques of (oral) tradition, however, confront a dilemma: it is only through writing that what is named "traditional" is rendered inert and subject to critique. For in traditional—that is, oral, non-literate—societies, the "content" of what is "transmitted" *as* tradition is always subject to transformation through the process *of* tradition, always mediated by present social concerns, never inert (Goody and Watt 6–7). The seeming unconscious "inertness" of traditional knowledge is not inherent in the practice of tradition. It arises from the removal of that knowledge from tradition as it is transformed into writing. Within the practice of oral tradition, mediation of the "content" of knowledge occurs "silently" so that its authority *as* "tradition" remains intact (see Clanchy 152; Ong 46–49).

Failure to recognize this mediation represents another instance of what Anthony Giddens has termed the "derogation of the lay actor." Such derogation results when theorists fail to recognize that knowledge resides not only in discursive consciousness but also in practical consciousness. That knowledge is embodied "in what actors 'know how to do,'" not just in "what actors are able to 'talk about' and in what manner or guise they are able to talk about it" (73). In the case of oral as well as other traditions, avoiding such derogation means recognizing the operation of practical consciousness, of unarticulated knowledge, in actors' "silent" work. We can see the operation of such practical consciousness in the "unskilled" workers' production of "working knowledge" that, Kusterer observed, often goes unrecognized by either management or the workers themselves. To fail to recognize workers' understanding is to treat lay actors as "cultural dopes or mere 'bearers of a mode of production'" (71). This tendency mistakes official renderings of actors' thinking with their practical thought. It thereby exaggerates the commitment of the dominated to dominant ideologies and neglects the degree to which all social actors "have some degree of penetration of the social forms which oppress them" (71–72).[1]

While Giddens points to the need for theorists to recognize lay actors' practical consciousness, bell hooks takes such a move further, insisting that the practical experience of marginalization by the dominant offers the potential for producing counterhegemonic discourse ("marginality" 341). Recalling her own experience of living on the margins of a small, racially segregated Kentucky town,

hooks argues that this marginality, while certainly a site of deprivation, served also as a site of resistance, for it gave her and other
blacks "a particular way of seeing reality. . . . both from the outside
in and from the inside out. . . . remind[ing] us of the existence of a
whole universe, a main body made up of both margin and center"
("marginality" 341). She thus argues for the need to "struggle to
maintain that marginality even as one works, produces, lives, if you
will, at the center" ("marginality" 341). Her aim is not to romanticize the oppressed or the experience of oppression but to tap the potential for the marginalized to use that experience as a site of
resistance rather than defining it strictly as a site of deprivation
("marginality" 341–42).[2]

Furthermore, hooks locates the counterhegemonic discourse of
the margins "not just . . . in words but in habits of being and the
way one lives" ("marginality" 341). But identifying counterhegemonic discourse in this way poses a difficulty. The challenge for a
discourse that speaks in more than, or ways other than, words is
that it is often not only not recognized by the dominant but displaced by the discourse of the latter. What often happens, hooks
warns, is that speech from the margins is displaced by speech *about*
the margins: "We are re-written. We are 'other.' " She therefore insists on attending to not only "what we speak about but [also] how
and why we speak," and who is speaking to whom ("marginality"
343). For, as Jacqueline Jones Royster has warned, interpretations
from outside a marginalized community "tend to have considerable
consequence in the lives of the targeted group, people . . . whose
own voices and perspectives remain still largely *under* considered
and *un*credited" ("When" 32, emphasis added).

The displacement these writers warn against points to the difficulty dominant discourse has in grasping the traditional knowledge of lay peoples, a difficulty that renders traditional knowledge
simultaneously both vulnerable and impervious to criticism.
Following Giddens, Kusterer, hooks, and Royster, traditional
knowledge as I have been framing it is located not simply in words
spoken but also in the concrete, materially situated practices with
that language, with ways of being in relation to language. Of
course, dominant discourse may displace the traditional knowledge
of marginalized peoples altogether, as when the intellectual tradition of black women writers is simply denied in order to dismiss

the capacities of its practitioners, as Royster has argued ("Perspectives" 105, passim). But alternatively, dominant discourse may simply rewrite and thereby reify such traditions by removing them from the immediate circumstances of their use. Through this strategy, critics of traditional knowledge can easily find its limitations—most frequently, its lack of general value or validity as commodity. By so removing it, however, that which the critic faults can be rejected as, in fact, not representative of the tradition but separate—by being separated—from it as part of an ongoing material social process. The practical, non-discursive knowledge tied to the circumstances of its use gets "written," or "rewritten," transformed into something other. And there can appear to be no acceptable alternative, only silence, to embracing the official forms for "rendering," or rewriting, that knowledge.

The debate over "current-traditional" rhetoric exemplifies this dilemma. Current-traditional rhetoric has been critiqued in terms of its epistemology, deemed intellectually bankrupt, and its ideology, thought to be consonant with conservative politics (see Crowley, "Perilous" 11–12; "Around" 66; "Composition's Ethic" 231). These are inferred primarily on the basis of textbooks and textbook sales (see Crowley, "Around" 64–65, "Perilous" 11; Connors, "Textbooks"; Faigley chapter 5; Herzberg, "Composition and the Politics" 110; Varnum 14). Arguments in response claim Composition's pedagogies and epistemologies inhere not in the textbooks so derided but in practices with them. Susan Miller, for example, argues that in the composition class, it is inappropriate "to believe in the coherent stability of a textbook apart from its reader's situational, purposeful, constructive *use* of it" (" 'Is There' " 22). Histories of composition teaching based on the publishing history of its textbooks, she claims, "inadvertently imply that composition pedagogy, classroom practices and methods, and writing courses in general have slavishly followed textbooks and that the way to change the teaching and learning of composition necessarily depends on changes in composition textbooks" (22). In Giddens' terms, her argument thus charges critics with derogating lay actors, overestimating their commitment to dominant ideologies and imagining institutions operating behind actors' backs to constrain them. As an alternative, Miller argues that we need to examine "how students have learned to write. . . . assum[ing] that popular classroom practices . . . have depended not on massively adopted textbooks, but on the prior or tacit knowledge and opinions of teachers interacting with students" (23; see also North 73–74; Brereton, *Origins* xiv). Composition's traditions are thus here linked with its daily practices and "tacit," non-discursive knowledge. Examining traditions so defined would of necessity be far more complicated than researching textbooks, for teachers' interactions with students, especially those in the past, are not readily accessible. That is, we would need both to subject to scrutiny a far wider array of cultural materials and to understand all materials, conventional or not, differently, considering the different uses to which these materials, textbooks included, might be put.

But there is more at issue here than questions of the comprehensiveness and feasibility of competing historiographical methodologies. There is the inevitability of "rewriting" those traditions in the process of naming and examining them. Any invocation of "tradition," the present one included, represents part of a "struggle for and against selective traditions" (Williams, *Marxism* 117). The identification of some practices as "traditional," for example, furthers a particular ideal of what ought, and ought not, to constitute the work of Composition. By this I refer not simply to my own interest here in reclaiming certain aspects of tradition. Rather, I refer to the desire to legitimize the work of Composition. Enacted within the discourse of professionalism, this desire has come to be expressed in terms of making Composition a professional academic discipline.[3] In this discourse, tradition is defined narrowly as something to work against, and theory and practice, scholarship and teaching are set in opposition. In its attempts to establish itself as a professional academic discipline, Composition has distanced itself from what is identified as its "traditional" concern with the immediate demands of teaching, for within the discourse of professionalism, such concerns are thought to interfere with its efforts to establish an explicated body of knowledge about writing (in general) which compositionists can claim as the subject of their professional expertise, knowledge which they can acquire, add to (produce), and distribute. As Martin Nystrand and colleagues observe approvingly, "Composition studies . . . emerged as a discipline as its focus began to transcend traditional problems of effective pedagogy. During the 1970s, in addition to writing teachers wondering how to teach writing better, researchers began to investigate what sort of phenomenon they were dealing with" (272; see also Crowley, "Around" 72–73, "Composition's Ethic" 229–30; Brereton, *Origins* 22).

In chapter 1, I have described the danger of commodifying the work of Composition posed by both its pursuit of academic professional status and the alternative of proletarianization. The discourse of academic professionalism limits how we think of the work of Composition, defining legitimate work as the acquisition, production, and distribution of print-codified knowledge about writing: the production and reception of (scholarly) texts. In this discourse, the "work" associated with such activities as teaching is deemed "labor," the implementation of the work of professional knowledge, and thus susceptible to proletarianization. For the purposes of this chapter, it is the conception of knowledge in this discourse that is significant. For in academic professional discourse, knowledge is recognized only as it appears in commodified textual form as explicitly theorized. Concomitant with this view of knowledge, the discourse of professionalism assumes a particular work path as one of progress and elevation for both individual professionals and their disciplines, their success measured in terms of the specialized knowledge acquired, produced, and distributed. The greater the amount of knowledge produced, and the further removed this knowledge appears to be from lay knowledge, the more "advanced" is the stature of the individual professional or discipline. Within this discourse, then, "tacit" knowledge is no knowledge at all, nor is "common knowledge" of the sort shared by the (lay) public. Professional knowledge is reified: knowing becomes the known, removed from immediate social, material contingencies through a discursive rendering that is then identified as and with knowledge and owned by the specialist, the writer, who is thought to have "produced" it.

Professionalism, so understood, can effectively contain, even end, social debate. In Burton Bledstein's account of the historical role of American universities in the development of the "culture of professionalism," universities "quietly took divisive issues such as race, capitalism, labor, and deviant behavior out of the public domain and isolated these problems within the sphere of professionals" (327). Thus isolated, these ideas "could be managed in functional terms rather than radicalized in a socially demanding

ideology" (329). Controversial social issues were contained by academic professionals by reducing the problems "to scientific and
even technical terms" (327).

As several writers have noted, identifying the work of Composition with such a professional "disinterested" pursuit of knowledge removed from direct engagement with students, history, the
social is striking for being in contradiction with many Composition
professionals' professed allegiance to a "radical" politics (see, for
example, Crowley, "A Personal Essay" 165–70; Gere 87–88). The
process of professionalization requires the containment of any "radical" political impulses, if by "radical" is meant efforts to fight for
democratic control of social and economic goods. For it excludes
laity from a voice in addressing social problems (see Zeichner 367;
Gere 87).

The antidemocratic effect of professionals redefining social
problems as susceptible to strictly technical solutions is exacerbated by the use of professional identity to establish and reinforce
the superiority of professionals' class position. First, claims to professional identity arrogate to the professionals a special status of
authority and responsibility for determining the nature and outcomes of work performed. It is Composition's failure to achieve such
arrogation that Crowley appears to lament when she complains
that in the infamous debate over freshman composition at UT
Austin, "persons who literally had no *professional* or financial stake
in the design of the course [at UT Austin, such as non-English faculty and members of the press] felt entitled to criticize a syllabus
developed by the people put in charge of it by the university, people
who are *professionally identified* with rhetoric/composition studies"
("Personal" 159, my emphases; see also Bleich 136, quoted in
Crowley, "Composition's Ethic" 232; Gere 87). The stake of the
Composition "profession" is here set in opposition to the "common
sense" of the laity, which threatens the intellectual "property"
rights of Composition professionals over the composition course by
treating it as in fact "common" property in which all have a stake
(see Crowley, "Personal" 159, "Composition's Ethic" 231–32).

Secondly, as I have argued about the position of academics generally in chapter 1, the class status of the "professionals" is maintained through denying the materiality of their work, material in
the sense of work as both physical manipulation of a medium and

part of a fully material social historical process. We can see Composition's participation in such attempts at maintaining class status in its professionals' common derogation of any training in or demand for those aspects of writing tellingly named "mechanical" or for teaching the "instrumental" uses of writing, and their almost complete silence on the physical demands of writing (for physical materials and technologies, environment, time, writers' bodies). These betray an interest in distinguishing the subject of writing, "our" field, from manual work and the low, ordinary business of everyday life (see Williams, *Marxism* 160). This distinction has been furthered by the tendency, observed by many critics, in much of the early research establishing Composition as a discipline to ignore altogether the location of the "writing process" in the social.

In calling Composition out for the classist implications of its complicity in the discourse of academic professionalism, I don't mean to ignore the real insights Composition research by those deemed "professional" has yielded to understanding and teaching writing. In rejecting particular uses to which writing research may be put, we need to guard against rejecting the project of researching writing. Indeed, some of that research has contributed precisely to fuller recognition of writing's ineluctable social materiality (see, for example, Brandt; Fox, *Social Uses*; Heath; Hull et al.; Lu, "Redefining"; *Politics of Writing*; Scribner; Scribner and Cole; Stuckey). Nor do I mean to give succor to the *faux* populists of the New Right engineering attacks like those on UT Austin's proposed composition course. Rather, I mean to highlight how an allegiance to professionalism can undermine compositionists' best efforts to make composition courses accomplish politically liberatory work. If we take class to represent a process engaging individuals (see Resnick and Wolff 20–21), then we should be wary of attempting to engage that process simultaneously to further and fight oppression. Instead, we will need to learn how to take seriously (which does not mean uncritically) and engage public demands and interest in our work, whether expressed as a demand for teaching "the basics" of writing or as a seemingly nostalgic quest for "traditional" Freshman English (see Crowley, "Personal" 156; Mortensen).[4] We should not, Giddens warns, cede tradition to the conservatives. To avoid doing so, however, will require rethinking the meaning of what "traditional" English might be.

At first glance, what is "traditional" in composition teaching seems an unlikely counter site from which to fight class (and other) oppressions. Most obviously, knowledge deemed "traditional" often does not enjoy the kind of authority that dominant discourse accords professional academic knowledge. Rethinking the traditional thus requires overcoming these dominant perspectives on what constitutes knowledge, knowing, and academic work. The difficulty of this task is perhaps best illustrated in Composition by attempts to recuperate "lore." This is the term Stephen North uses for the knowledge and practices of those he terms "Practitioners," those in composition not identifying themselves as scholars or researchers, and closely associated with the "traditional" in Composition (*Making*). Whatever the ethical merit of these attempts, their foundation in the discourse of academic disciplinary professionalism leads them to eviscerate the substance of that which they would recuperate.

North introduces the term "lore" to name that knowledge Practitioners produce and draw on in responding to the daily exigencies of their teaching. He does so in making an argument to counter what he sees as the discipline of (upper-case) "Composition's" derogation of Practitioners and their knowledge. He traces that derogation to the fact that lore does not appear to be "acceptable, formal, academic inquiry," and he dates the birth of Composition by the emergence of efforts to "replace practice as the field's dominant mode of inquiry" (15). However, in his attempts to recuperate lore and practitioner practice, he applies to it criteria for achieving academic disciplinary status for Composition as a profession—criteria by which, alas, Practitioners and lore are doomed to measure poorly. Try as he might to dress up Practitioners and their lore as academically respectable, their "low" background shows through.

North argues that Practitioners engage in a "mode of inquiry" involving a series of steps that contribute to a field of knowledge (*Making* chapter 2). According to North, at least some of the time, Practitioners follow a regular procedure in order to discover knowledge that can then be put to immediate practical use, and so can be said to engage in the professionally respectable disciplinary practice of knowledge production. Unfortunately, the knowledge constituting lore doesn't stand up to the usual criteria for achieving status as disciplinary knowledge. As North admits, much of it is contradictory, and Practitioners have, or employ, no mechanism for evaluating competing claims. Thus, "While anything can become a part of lore, nothing can ever be dropped from it, either" (24). As a result, as North admits further, "judged against non-lore standards, Practitioners are bound to seem consistently undiscriminating, illogical, and sloppy" (27). To address these defects, North suggests that Practitioners will have to "make the same efforts as other communities to become methodologically aware," or may be "enfranchised by being trained to make knowledge other than lore" (372). In the end, in other words, it seems the lore produced by Practitioner Inquiry just won't cut it as knowledge, and so they had better retrain.

I would argue, however, that North's difficulties in recuperating Practitioner Inquiry arise from applying the template of how professional knowledge of academic disciplines is understood, constituted, and used to a practice to which such a template is inimical: the engagement in residual experiences, meanings, and practices unverifiable in terms of dominant culture, the "practical" knowledge of ways of being and living. First, North assumes the production of a reified knowledge as the practitioners' goal. But while this is a goal legitimated within academic disciplines, it differs from the understanding of traditional knowledge, which is never imagined outside the context of its immediate use. The need to produce a knowledge, or retain it as a body, even in the form of North's rambling house of lore, which is then applied to specific cases, is counter to the disposition of knowledge in tradition, in which knowledge exists only in its practice rather than representing a storehouse of tools on which to draw. The impossibility North confronts of evaluating knowledge claims and eliminating those deemed unsatisfactory can be understood as a problem only in terms of the criteria of academic disciplinary views of knowledge. "Traditional" practice, rather than contesting the validity or usefulness of knowledge directly, mediates it silently. In this sense, the contradictions with which lore is rife are present only when it is approached "untraditionally," as constituting universally valid claims. North thus ends up writing lore out of the work of Composition in the very attempt to legitimize it, because the terms he applies for the legitimation of work are drawn from the discourse of academic professionalism.

This same dilemma to which North's arguments lead him in defending lore appears in Patricia Harkin's efforts to defend lore as "postdisciplinary." Like North, Harkin hopes to find ways of "getting the academy to change its understanding of knowledge production" (135). Thus she attempts to demonstrate that Mina Shaughnessy has indeed "produced knowledge" in *Errors and Expectations* (134), and she defends teaching generally as the site where knowledge is produced, however secretly (138). But her proposals, aimed at improving the status of Practitioner lore, eviscerate the silent mediation of knowledge in the practice of tradition. She notes that teachers tend to "think of teaching as a site or moment when we are free, behind closed classroom doors, to be eclectic, to ignore recognized procedures, to do what needs to be done. . . . to escape the panoptic gaze of the disciplines for a silent, secret moment of postdisciplinary knowledge." But she then calls, ironically, for subjecting those moments to just such a gaze: "We should do all we can," she concludes, "to bring lore to light" (138).

Presumably, efforts like these to redefine Practitioner lore as academic disciplinary knowledge are intended in part to improve the working conditions of Practitioners. The assumption behind this strategy is that improvement in those conditions can result only as a consequence *following* the achievement of academic disciplinary status. Unimaginable in this discourse is the possibility of justifying improvement in Practitioners' working conditions according to criteria coming from non-"academic" spheres. It is noteworthy, for example, that Composition has largely ignored the history of primary and secondary school teachers' efforts to improve their working conditions, despite the close relations between their work and that of Composition. But to admit those relations would risk Composition's further marginalization from the "academy"—that is, "higher" education—hence these are denied. Instead, efforts are directed at proving the validity of the knowledge, and so the higher academic disciplinary status, of Composition. If it can be demonstrated to the academy that Practitioners produce knowledge according to professional disciplinary criteria, then, it is assumed, they will be judged to deserve, and will receive, merit as members of a professional academic discipline.

However, like the attempts described in chapter 4 to increase Composition's cultural capital by "affiliating" Composition with fields like critical theory, rhetoric, or cultural studies, such efforts ignore the dependence of the value of one's cultural capital on one's social capital (which Composition distinctly lacks), a dependence demonstrated by the long history of the refusal of other academic fields to recognize any "cultural" capital, in the form of knowledge, that Composition's Practitioners have purportedly been producing all along. And in the unlikely event that this strategy were to succeed in improving Composition's professional status, it would mean that the work of Composition would change, becoming more typically "disciplinary" in its pursuit of "disinterested" knowledge. As James Slevin explains, because teaching is peripheral in current dominant understandings of academic disciplines, in attempts to imagine Composition as a discipline, "We . . . buy into a conceptual framework that makes every effort to change things—even just to see things clearly—impossible. . . . plac[ing] those of us interested in teaching at a serious disadvantage" ("Disciplining" 158). Efforts to define Composition in terms of its disciplinarity are either doomed to failure, given Composition's identification with teaching, or they will transform Composition into something unrecognizable, a discipline in which teaching is peripheral, not central.

That compositionists should continue to pursue professional academic disciplinary status despite the history of its failure to improve their working conditions and despite the dilemmas to which it leads attests both to the hegemonic force of professionalism and to the apparent paucity of alternatives to embracing it. For the only alternative to achieving professional academic disciplinary status by producing commodified knowledge seems to be full submission to the dictates of the labor "marketplace" and complete, concomitant alienation from one's work: the proletarianization of teaching, on a stereotypical model of industrial unionism, in which, through collective bargaining, teachers surrender to bureaucratic rationalization of their work in return for the right to a chance at better pay (Carlson 91–102).

The Amherst "Tradition"

In chapter 1 I have addressed the specific prospects and limitations of faculty unions as a response to the increasing commodification and proletarianization of work in Composition. Here I will argue that at least some work deemed "traditional" could pose alternatives to the alienation of both professionalism and proletarianization because of the particular relationship to knowledge its practices enact, a relationship that effectively counters its reification. Further, these practices allow for carrying out, rather than simply subscribing to, a view of knowledge as contingent, and a radical politics of inclusiveness in teaching, to both of which many in Composition have testified their commitment. These practices do so by transgressing the limits of formal representations of knowledge, rejecting the claims and class status of professional expertise, and sharing responsibility for any work accomplished as widely as possible, including with students and the public.

Fencing with Words, Robin Varnum's account of the almost thirty years of Amherst College's English 1–2 course (1938 to 1966), suggests one version both of what such practices might look like and the conditions for their enactment. I pose this course, it should be understood, not as a fully realized example of counterhegemonic practices but as pointing in idealized form to the counterhegemonic potential in work practices blanketed by the term *current-traditional*. Those practices at Amherst I highlight include teachers' principled resistance to published accounts of their work, a view of their teaching as an ongoing activity rather than transmission of a codified philosophy, explicit disavowals of any professional expertise on the teaching of writing, and a treatment of the work of the course as a "common" activity shaped by the collective efforts of the teaching staff and students.

I approach this ideal of Amherst's English 1–2 practices not simply in terms of the immediate institutional and larger social and historical conditions in which they were enacted nor just the teachers' ostensible allegiance to a specific epistemology but in terms of how these practices produced, reproduced, and changed these, establishing a tradition on the margins of the academy. In naming this course a tradition, however, and so linking it to what is deemed marginal, a caveat is in order. Of any seemingly "marginal" tradition we need to ask what it is marginal to, to what effect, in what social historical circumstances, according to whom. We cannot simply label cultural practices marginal or central, dominant or residual, outside history and circumstance. For example, in *Yearning*, hooks recalls her illiterate grandmother's practice of insisting that her children and grandchildren tell the "particulars" of their names and kinship relations when entering her home. In many ways this was a "dominant" part of hooks' lived experience of her home culture, something that, as a child, she experienced as "frightening," an "interrogation" (116). Yet, within the dominated culture of African-Americans, this dominant tradition had counter-hegemonic force, enabling the participants to recall and maintain their history in the face of dominant U.S. culture's efforts to deny and erase that history. Conversely, the tradition on which the Amherst course draws was a residual element of dominant culture (an element valuing independence, spontaneity, individuality, anti-commercialism). As residual, however, it may still be effectively alternative or oppositional in its relation to the dominant—say, for example, the dominant's insistence on planning, uniformity, and the interchangeability of both parts and people.

Clearly those associated with the Amherst course were not "on the margins" in the sense that, say, hooks and her family were "marginal" (or marginalized) in Kentucky. They were part of a socially dominant male, white, upper-class elite. Any understanding of the course as part of an alter- or counterhegemonic tradition on the periphery must confront this. Rather than being marginalized, they used the freedom granted to them by virtue of their dominant social position to practice a type of marginality (Varnum 140). hooks argues for a marginality delegitimized by the center that can be "a site one stays in, clings to even," struggles to maintain "even as one works, produces, lives, if you will, at the center" ("marginality" 341). By contrast, those at Amherst sought out, or produced, their marginality from a position legitimized but not dominant within the center, an established tradition residual within the dominant, operating in a relative isolation made possible by its location within the dominant. It would thus be a gross distortion to equate the two marginalities, like confusing pleasure camping with the makeshift arrangements of the homeless. Nor is there any hint that the specific marginality achieved at Amherst represented an attempt to "stand with" the marginalized. If it distinguished itself from the dominant, it was a distinction that set it "above" rather than "below" the dominant, risking preciosity, as its critics have suggested. At the same time, the marginality enacted suggests the potential of tradition as a site for counterhegemonic pressure, realized or not. Composition is learning to draw on the strengths of oppositional traditions of the dominated. It can now learn to draw as well on alternative practices blanketed under the notion of dominant traditions, not ceding tradition to the conservatives. If hooks illuminates the potential of margins as the site of resistance, her work also poses the challenge of looking to alternatives *within* the dominant.

Of course, however one links Amherst practices with tradition, they clearly, also, are part of a literate rather than an oral culture. We can nonetheless identify their practices as traditional in the ways in which they practiced literacy. As critics of the literate/oral distinction have observed, claims made on behalf of either literacy or orality have tended to confuse a particular practice with writing or speech with the medium as a whole (H. Graff; Scribner and Cole; Tannen; R. Williams, *Marxism* 159–60). The Amherst tradition does not abjure writing. Rather, it represents a different literate practice for students, teachers, and those who would know about the course that resists dominant beliefs about the uses for writing.

Those practices associated with the Amherst course that have proved most troubling to historians illustrate the specific form such resistance took. Perhaps the most obvious difficulty the course has posed to Composition historians is the paucity of any formal discursive representations of the course. I refer here not only to the almost complete absence (until Varnum's study) of any published account of the course, its methods, or any "theory" behind those methods but also to the studied indifference of those associated with the course to attempts to make such representations. The almost complete absence of first-hand accounts of the course, Varnum notes, meant that in studying the course, she "had no choice but to adopt the *annales*-style of historical scholarship" (11–12, 6–7). While Theodore Baird, the director of the course, has published a few descriptions of it, they appear in such obscure, local venues as the *Amherst Alumni News* and the *Amherst Graduates' Quarterly* (see Gibson 152, 137).

While this lack of publications can be explained partly as the result of the absence of pressure on the teachers to publish, or the lack of time they had for writing, given the demands of teaching the course, it can also be seen as principled resistance. Walker Gibson, who taught the course for several years, suggests as much, observing that according to the "Amherst position," "the course is an ongoing activity . . . not a body of knowledge to be readily laid out on paper. It is an action" (137). Skeptical of formal representations of the course, the teachers associated with it, dubbed the "Amherst Mafia" by Ann Berthoff, have resisted any efforts to codify their teaching in terms of a philosophy, "school" of thought, or "following." James Broderick, in one of the few published studies of the course, echoes Gibson, reporting that its "originators and practitioners . . . disclaim any philosophy; for them the course just happened, it evolved, it is their changing ways of handling certain problems in class. They are firm in their insistence that the course is not the reflection of any philosophy they know of" (44–45). Baird himself has claimed, "I don't think I ever had a clearer motive [for English 1–2] than the determination not to be bored and everything as far as I was concerned followed from that" (quoted in Gibson 137). And in an interview with Varnum, Baird dismissed the linking of the course with any particular philosophy, insisting the course "was homemade; that's the truth of the matter, and it was no better, no worse than we could make it at home" (quoted in Varnum 49). Richard Poirier describes his identification with other figures associated with the course as merely "temperamental" (22). And Varnum writes that in her interviews with several of these figures, they "displayed what I took to be a desire to disabuse me of any notion I might have had that they were acolytes of Baird," reporting that William E. Coles Jr. informed her "Baird had made it impossible for others to imitate him" (Varnum 224).

This resistance to codification has not, of course, prevented others from attempting to represent the course in just such ways, as the "Amherst Mafia" epithet itself suggests. The course has been linked, for example, to the ideas of such thinkers as Alfred Korzybski, Wittgenstein, Henry Adams, Percy Bridgman, I. A. Richards, and Robert Frost, among others (see Varnum 46–55; Berthoff 72). Yet these efforts ignore the teachers' own repudiations of such codifications (Varnum 49–50) and have proved difficult to sustain. Varnum herself admits that Baird's relation to such figures is "difficult" to characterize, and confesses that in her attempts to trace Baird's influence on others, "there seems to be no one essential element of English 1–2 that 'Mafia' members carried away with them"; each of them has had "to work out his own relation" to the course (228, 229).

This refusal to acknowledge influence can be and has been understood as evidence of a masculinist ideology of self-reliance (see Varnum 3; Catano). However, from the perspective of current understandings of Composition history and its "professional development," it can also be seen as a repudiation by the teachers of attempts to view themselves as possessors of specialized professional expertise and their teaching as the transmission of commodified knowledge—as, say, sly instruction in the precepts of positivist operationalism. Baird's account of the course as "homemade" and of himself as "no philosopher" suggests such a repudiation, as do his and others' statements insisting on their own lack of expertise in the teaching of writing. Baird has linked himself with "a long tradition" at Amherst of "one man after another who was concerned about how you reach a class," but has also insisted, "Teaching is a mystery. Nobody knows how to teach. Nobody knows how to learn" (quoted in Varnum 55). While such statements can be taken as false modesty or as an attempt to preserve guild "mysteries" from the laity, other of Baird's statements suggest that they also articulate a rejection of any codification of teaching, since any knowledge about it exists, and has validity, only in specific circumstances. Asserting, "[T]here are no methods which will succeed in teaching everyone to spell correctly and to think straight," he insisted that any such methods "are means to an end, and come to life, if at all, only because of the energy which they generate in teacher and student" (quoted in Varnum 68). That it was the location of Baird and his staff within the dominant that made it possible for them to take such a stance toward professionalism and the commodification of knowledge is suggested in one of Baird's memoranda to his staff: "We take for granted," he reminded them, "that *at Amherst College* we can say boldly to everyone interested that no one knows how to teach writing" (quoted in Varnum 130, my emphasis). In other words, such resistance to commodification may well be a strategy affordable only to those in material social circumstances of significant privilege, and may itself reveal disdain for those requiring a more concrete, utilitarian approach to teaching and writing, as I'll argue in chapter 6.

This rejection of professional expert knowledge among the Amherst English 1–2 staff, and their position within the dominant, may explain in part the scarcity of their attempts to write about the course; if one rejects the abstraction of methods from the specific circumstances of their use by a teacher or student, then one has nothing to "sell" an audience, and if one is so positioned, one has no need to. Hence, while Baird was never bothered by attempts to describe the course, actively participating in Varnum's own efforts, for example, he had no "professional" investment in such projects, except to discourage efforts to turn accounts of the course into commodifications of it.

This same rejection of any commodification of teaching knowledge may also account for the communal treatment of the work associated with the course. We can see such treatment in a number of practices. First, all sections of the course in any given year used the same set of sequenced assignments. While an individual staff member produced the initial draft of the sequence, the staff as a whole was responsible for selecting and revising the assignments before they were given to students. At weekly staff meetings, teachers were to debate ways of addressing the students' papers and teaching the next assignments in the sequence. But the aim was to treat the course as a common project (Varnum 65, 69). As Baird put it, "the course would be as good as the instructors in it, working together. Ideally no one person would dominate. It would be a common action" (quoted in Varnum 66). Thus, at least ideally, neither the assignments and other course materials nor the ways of employing them in class were the property of anyone; rather, they belonged to all. The almost verbatim use of some of them, such as the course descriptions, in subsequent, published books by individuals attests to this view of them as "common" property (see Varnum 230–31).

Second, the practice of giving all first-year students in the college the same assignment the same week effectually rendered the students' own work part of the collective project. On the face of it, this structuring of coursework across sections might seem to be a prescription for alienated, alienating rotework. Neither students nor teachers had the choice of what they would be working on, either in individual assignments, class meetings, or the course as a whole. But this view assumes structure to function only as a barrier to action and agency rather than, as Giddens has it, "essentially involved in its production" (70). For in practice this "constraining" structure of assigned assignment sequences was also simultaneously potentially "enabling," highlighting as it did the dependence of the structure on agency—on what individual teachers and students made of the sequences, in individual class meetings, course sections, and papers. Varnum herself takes the Amherst pedagogy to have been intended to "spur student self-determination, to empower student resistance to normative pressures, and to promote a student's growth as a responsible personal agent" (3). In terms of my argument, the sequences can be seen as posing to both teachers and students the question of what use they might make, and how, of what otherwise would appear to be a call for the production of uniform themes, the ultimate in commodified writing (see Coles, "Freshman"). Further, while the giving of identical assignments to all students might appear to encourage competition among individual students, the sequencing of the assignments would undercut treatment of individual papers as more than segments of a larger, term-length process and project (see Varnum 137). And just as the course was not identified as belonging in its shape or meaning to any one instructor but as a "common" project, so responsibility for the "outcomes" of the course would belong to both teachers and students. As Baird warned in a description of the course given to students,

> The best we can do is treat writing—and the writer—with respect and imagination, and in our conversations about writing and the writer hope to say something. In the classroom we shall have good moments and moments not so good. . . .
>
> Every year, this teaching staff makes a new sequence of assignments, dealing with a new and different problem, so that for all concerned, teacher and student, this is a new course. . . .
>
> Whatever answers you reach in this course, they will be your own. You will do your own learning. (quoted in Varnum 250–51)

This location of the work of the course with its specific historical actors and circumstances may also be a way to account for the otherwise curious failure of its teachers to advertise their methods through publications, and by the resistance offered by those teachers who have published accounts of courses inspired by the Amherst course to taking those accounts as prescriptions. For the "methods" employed do not in fact "translate," their effects not commodifiable but tied to the circumstances in which and uses to which they have been put.

Resisting Tradition: Coles and Bartholomae

The writings of Bill Coles and David Bartholomae illustrate this resistance to commodification and show both the different forms which the Amherst "tradition" might take and the constitution of a tradition of resistance to "tradition" as ordinarily understood. The relationship of Coles and Bartholomae, in other words, demonstrates a literate practice enacting a different process of tradition articulating resistance to the commodification of pedagogy and composition theory. It is possible to see their writings as being "affiliated" with a particular tradition, commonly understood: the tradition associated with social-epistemic rhetoric. Both writers make statements that would appear to align them with that rhetoric, which James Berlin has argued holds that

> [K]nowledge is not simply a static entity available for retrieval. Truth is dynamic and dialectical. . . . It is a relation that is created, not pre-existent and waiting to be discovered. . . . Communication is always basic . . . because truth is always truth for someone standing in relation to others in a linguistically circumscribed situation. ("Contemporary Composition" 774)[5]

But what distinguishes Coles and Bartholomae from many other writers who profess such beliefs, and what aligns them with the Amherst tradition, as I am defining it, is the resistance they offer to having their statements understood as prescriptions or precepts. For when Coles and Bartholomae do offer statements, in what might appear to be efforts to transmit them, they regularly qualify the statements by offering critiques of them, disavowing them, framing them in forms that work against receiving the statements as "substantive," or employing paradoxical formulations that prevent any simple identification of the knowledge ostensibly to be transmitted.

For example, in one of his essays, Coles introduces what he calls a "Statement" that he first says contains knowledge that "one part of me believes all teachers of writing must know, subscribe to, and work out a set of classroom procedures in terms of." However, Coles immediately follows his "Statement" with a stinging critique of its logic, its oversimplifications of history, and its arrogance, and ends by confessing that in fact his "Statement" amounts to

> really no more than a massive rationalization of the practice of William E. Coles, Jr., himself and as is . . . [that] can in no sense be received as anything like substantive knowledge. Further, it would be no trouble at all for another kind of teacher with a quite different conceptual frame for seeing the activity of writing, to show first how my frame could be pedagogically ruinous, and then how *his* frame, on the basis of what he could prove it made possible, worked better. ("New Presbyters" 6–8)

More commonly, these writers regularly offer disavowals of and discouragement to any attempt to proselytize what they do present. For example, in one of Bartholomae's essays, he warns, "This paper is not meant to be in defense of any particular curriculum" (though he adds that he has one to defend if anyone's interested ["Wanderings" note 5]). Similarly, Bartholomae and Petrosky assert that "[t]he purpose of [the essays in *Facts, Artifacts, and Counterfacts*] is *not* to defend or explain a curriculum" (Preface; my emphasis). Coles likewise claims he does not intend *The Plural I* as a blueprint for others. Rather, he says,

> My intention . . . is to illuminate what is involved in the teaching (and learning) of writing *however* one approaches it, in hopes that this will enable other teachers to take a fresh hold on whatever they choose to do. . . . I have no desire to tell anyone else how he or she ought to go about handling the subject. (2)

Coles makes a similar disavowal in the preface to *Teaching Composing*, along with an explanation that his disavowal results directly from his philosophical position that writing *and* the teaching of writing are, or should be, self-creating activities. For neither students nor teachers, he claims,

> do I intend the approach and discussion to be seen as in any way prescriptive. . . . Thus, although I am concerned in this book with describing a way of introducing students to seeing *writing* as a creative process, . . . I am just as concerned with the *teaching of writing* as an activity to be seen in exactly the same terms.

And he claims in statements to students that echo those used at Amherst that his assignments

> are not an argument. They contain no doctrine, either individually or as a sequence. There is no philosophy in them . . . for a teacher to become aware of and give to students, for students to become aware of and give back to a teacher. . . . In fact, the assignments are arranged and phrased precisely to make impossible the discovery in them of anything like a master plan. They are put together in such a way as to mean only and no more than what the various responses they are constructed to evoke can be made to mean, a meaning that will be different for different teachers and students as well as differently come by. (*Composing* 3–4: rpt. *Teaching Composing* 11–12)[6]

To further discourage teachers from treating their works as commodities, Coles and Bartholomae, particularly Coles, have sometimes published in non-conventional forms. Coles has issued explicitly fictionalized, novelistic accounts of his courses, and an "essay" on the topic of "Literacy for the Eighties" that consists of a collage of fictional monologues of a writing teacher, a recovering alcoholic, and a racetrack "handicapper" (See *Plural I, Seeing Through Writing*, "Literacy for the Eighties").[7] In both *Facts Artifacts, and Counterfacts* and *Ways of Reading,* with its accompanying *Resources for Teaching Ways of Reading,* Bartholomae and Petrosky present odd comminglings of course materials and theoretical essays on teaching. And, again, they warn against reading those materials or essays as dogma, and even warn against any dogmatism that may have crept into their writing, by situating their comments in the context of their own history as teachers:

> We cannot begin to imagine all the possible ways that the essays [in *Ways of Reading*] might (or should) be taught. The best we can do is to speak from our own experience in such courses. If we seem at times to be dogmatic (to be single-minded in saying what should be done or how it should be done), it is because we are drawing on our own practices as teachers and they are grounded, finally, in our beliefs about what it means to read, write, and teach. We don't mean to imply that we have a corner on effective teaching or that there is no other way to help young adults take charge of what they do with texts. (*Resources* v)

Finally, both Coles and Bartholomae write in styles so densely textured as to provoke and require active readerly participation in response. Coles has described his own sentences as advancing "somewhat crabbedly from one notion in them to the next" ("Counterstatement" 208; quoted in Harris, "Plural" 159). Joseph Harris, one of the keenest readers of Coles' work, observes that Coles' sentences are

> [f]reighted with commas, qualifiers, rephrasings. . . . I find myself continually circling back in order to move forward, rethinking my place in the text, checking again to see how a certain word was used a line or sentence or paragraph before. His writing seems engineered to force a kind of rereading—or at least a very slow and close reading—from the start. His prose resists glossing; what it says seems peculiarly tied to the precise form of its saying. To use one of his own most characteristic phrasings, I like how Coles makes me aware of his writing *as writing*—as the tracing of the particular choices of a particular writer. ("Plural" 159–60)

And George Dillon, analyzing what he terms the "hard rhetoric" of *The Plural I*, observes that

> Coles has not courted the reader's approval any more than he has that of his students. . . . He is sometimes superior and

enigmatic. . . . Coles forces the reader, like his students, to draw her own conclusions about his style and methods. (*Rhetoric* 65)

Bartholomae describes himself similarly as trying in his writing

very hard to interfere with the conventional force of writing, with the pressure toward set conclusions, set connections, set turns of phrase. . . . What I learned first as a behavior . . . I've come to think of as a matter of belief or principle (working against the 'natural'—that is, the conventional—flow of words on the page). ("Against the Grain" 24)[8]

A remarkable passage in "Inventing the University" illustrates this strategy of interference. Bartholomae is describing the problems beginning college student writers have with establishing authority in their writing. In order to achieve that authority, he says, they must

speak not only in another's voice but through another's code; and they not only have to do this, they have to speak in the voice and through the codes of those of us with power and wisdom; and they not only have to do this, they have to do it before they know what they are doing, before they have a project to participate in, and before, at least in terms of our disciplines, they have anything to say. (156)

This is a curiously accretive passage. Each clause, while ostensibly adding an independent task for students to those mentioned in preceding clauses, functions instead semantically to qualify the meaning of the preceding clauses: students must speak in another's voice and through another's code, but in the voice and code of specific kinds of people, and under highly unpromising conditions. The addition of each subsequent clause interferes with the sense of closure suggested by the ending of the preceding clause (marked by each of the semicolons) by qualifying it. The cumulative effect of this passage is to render as increasingly difficult of resolution the dilemma these students face, an effect created through the insistent addition of a seemingly endless list of qualifiers. The sentences immediately following this passage give a further twist to this effect. A tentative resolution and conclusion to the dilemma is offered: "Our students may be able to enter into a conventional discourse and speak, not as themselves, but through the voice of the community." But the efficacy of this resolution is then immediately questioned: "the university, however, is the place where 'common' wisdom is only of negative value—it is something to work against" (156).

Bartholomae's refusal to offer closure goes hand in hand with a characteristic insistence on conflict and difficulty. He denies not only readers' desire for set conclusions but also their quite understandable desire for resolution of conflict and a quick, sure thing. He ends "Inventing the University" with a warning about such difficulties (and in an accretive structure that mirrors the first passage cited above):

> [The writer of the "White Shoes" paper] will have to be convinced that it is better to write sentences he might not so easily control, and he will have to be convinced that it is better to write muddier and more confusing prose (in order that it may sound like ours), and this will be harder than convincing the "Clay Model" writer to continue what he has already begun. (162)

Bartholomae's most characteristic strategy for interfering with set conclusions and insisting on difficulty, however, is to employ paradoxical formulations. "Inventing the University" itself represents an extended investigation of the paradox of "inventing" the already established.[9] But his other formulations of writing are also paradoxical, as when he describes writing as "an act of aggression disguised as an act of charity" ("Inventing" 140) or when, with co-author Petrosky, he describes his Basic Writing course as leading students to practice "imitative originality or . . . captive self-possession" (*Facts* 40). And Bartholomae and Petrosky do not reserve such formulations for teachers. In the introduction to *Ways of Reading*, they warn students:

> [O]ne of the difficult things about reading is that the pages before you will begin to speak only when the authors are silent and you begin to speak in their place, sometimes for them—

doing their work, continuing their projects—and sometimes for yourself, following your own agenda. . . .

There is a paradox here. On the one hand, the essays [anthologized in *Ways of Reading*] are rich, magnificent, too big for anyone to completely grasp all at once, and before them, as before inspiring spectacles, it seems appropriate to stand humbly, admiringly. And yet, on the other hand, a reader must speak with authority. . . .

From this pushing and shoving with and against texts, we come then to a difficult mix of authority and humility. (1, 10–11)

Such paradoxes place the work of resolution emphatically on readers—whether they are students or teachers. The task of making sense—of reading—becomes an active task for both as they encounter and wrestle with such paradoxes.

The resistance both these writers offer to ready commodification has, not surprisingly, made their work unusually liable to mixed, sometimes contradictory interpretations. Dillon offers two contradictory readings of Coles. On the one hand, he links him with writers who use "hard rhetoric" to evoke "the codes of 'manly' plain-spokenness and the courage of one's convictions" (*Rhetoric* 64), a reading difficult to square with either the opaque style Coles employs and encourages in students or Coles' explicit denunciations of advocates of the plain style ("New Presbyters" 6, "Freshman Composition"). On the other hand, Dillon also argues that Coles appeals in *The Plural I* to an "estheticizing school of prose criticism" that holds plain prose in contempt, seeking readers' "complex involvement in a sustained drama—a concrete universal, an esthetic object, the experience of which is self-validating" ("Fiction" 209, 205), a reading difficult to square with either Dillon's other argument or Coles' statement that he intends *The Plural I* not to give aesthetic pleasure but to "enable other teachers to take a fresh hold on whatever they choose to do [in teaching]" (*Plural I* 2). Coles' reluctance to offer explicit statements of his philosophical position leads Richard Young to identify Coles with those who hold that "the act of composing is a kind of mysterious growth" not susceptible to exposition (55). Berlin uses that same reluctance and Coles' emphasis on the "self" to link him with those Berlin calls the Expressionists, those who locate truth outside language, in personal experience that the writer must attempt to express authentically ("Contemporary Composition" 771–73; see also Courage note 2). Harris, on the other hand, argues that, for Coles,

> The task of writers is not to make language adhere to some mystic and wordless vision of their selves, but to use language in a way that begins to *constitute* a self. . . . [Berlin] sees [Coles] as starting with the self of the writer and then moving to the question of what language best expresses that self. The movement [for Coles] is actually the opposite. ("Plural" 162; see also Wiley 142)

Bartholomae, as Susan Wall and Nick Coles observe, has been interpreted as Coles' opposite, an advocate of an "unambiguously accommodationist Basic Writing pedagogy, a return to a new set of 'basics,' the conventions of academic discourse 'written out, "demystified" and taught in our classrooms' " (231).[10] And he is so identified in spite of evidence to the contrary from the course materials he and Petrosky provide in *Ways of Reading* and *Facts, Artifacts, and Counterfacts*. The paradoxical formulations he offers are frequently stripped of their sense of paradox and rendered unequivocal declarations.

It is of course possible to counter such readings. However, given the formulations of Coles' and Bartholomae's work, such counterings seem, if not unjustified, somehow out of place. The ways in which Coles and Bartholomae frame their statements position both badly, at best oddly, to complain, or to complain very loudly or directly, about misreadings of their work. Their dilemma is the dilemma of those Roland Barthes describes as attempting to resist the authority and law inherent in the teaching/speaking situation. As Barthes explains,

> Whoever prepares to speak (in a teaching situation) must realize the mise en scène imposed. . . . Either the speaker chooses in all good faith a role of Authority, in which case it suffices to 'speak well', in compliance with the Law present in every act of speech—without hesitation, at the right speed,

clearly (which is what is demanded of good pedagogic speech: clarity, authority). . . . Or the speaker is bothered by all this Law that the act of speaking is going to introduce into what he wants to say, in which case . . . he uses the irreversibility of speech in order to disturb its legality: correcting, adding, wavering, the speaker . . . superimposes on the simple message that everyone expects of him a new message that ruins the very idea of a message and . . . asks us to believe with him that language is not to be reduced to communication. . . . Yet at the end of all this effort to 'speak badly' another role is enforced, for the audience . . . receives these fumblings as so many signs of weakness and sends the speaker back the image of a master who is human, too human—*liberal*.

The choice is gloomy: conscientious functionary or free artist. . . . Nothing to be done: language is always a matter of force, to speak is to exercise a will for power; in the realm of speech there is no innocence, no safety. (*Image* 191–92)

What most interests me here is how to distinguish the tradition in which I'm placing Coles and Bartholomae from readings that commodify them and their work: Coles as the advocate of the search for a personal voice, Bartholomae as the drill sergeant of academic prose. Such commodifications depart from the resisting tradition by failing to enact that resistance in the formulations they offer. Instead, in their responses, such readings enact an alternative, far more dominant conception of tradition, the tradition that Barthes identifies with teaching and speech "in compliance with the Law" through its clear transmission of authoritative knowledge. By contrast, the tradition in which I am placing Coles and Bartholomae represents an alternative conception of tradition in writing opposed to the straightforward transmission of commodified knowledge. It represents an alternative conception of lore and of Practitioner inquiry generally and, as well, an important attempt to bridge, or rather erase, distinctions between teaching and scholarship through its writing practice. Finally, it demonstrates the need to recognize the imbrication of Composition traditions in material social practice.

I've argued above that the work of Coles and Bartholomae represents a "resistant" tradition identifiable not by its adoption of the precepts of an epistemic rhetoric but by the enactment of the implications of that rhetoric through resistance to direct transmission of particular beliefs, including beliefs about epistemic rhetoric. Like Barthes' unwilling speaker, they attempt to "speak badly," to convince that their language "is not to be reduced to communication" (Barthes, *Image* 192). Acutely aware of the power of language to enact "imperial domination" (Bartholomae, "Reply" 126), they work against the authority commonly granted the position of Barthes' teacher/speaker.

Taking this seemingly odd position offers an alternative to the picture North gives of "Practitioner inquiry" and a potential resolution to the difficulties which North sees Practitioners generally having in their relations to the other "methodological communities" in Composition. Virtually all of the work of Coles and Bartholomae, including material presented originally for students, addresses teachers, and virtually all of it is founded on teaching experience, as the frequent and lengthy quotations of student writing in the work of both demonstrates. It is thus possible to categorize their work as representations of what North calls "Practitioner inquiry." North himself identifies Coles as an exemplary Practitioner writer.

But the role their writing plays differs significantly from the role North imagines it can play in such inquiry. North sees writing as the medium "least amenable" to lore because it does not allow for the reciprocity crucial to Practitioner inquiry:

> The disclosure [in writing of results of Practitioner inquiry] will inevitably drift away from the sharing of accounts of inquiry—the confusions, the tentativeness, the recursiveness, the muddied uncertainty about successes—toward a neater, more linear, more certain prescription. (*Making* 53)

Yet at the same time, North claims that the virtue of the few successful Practitioner writers resides in the certainty they offer readers about the teaching experience and the pragmatic logic underlying their advice (52). Though North would seem to value "uncertainty" in the ordinary dissemination of lore, he praises successful Practitioner writing for its reduction of uncertainty. This contradiction stems in part from the assumption that in writing and reading, Practitioners accept, or must accept, Barthes' "Law" of the teaching mise en scène, what Carr describes as the false notion that "influence and tradition are produced in straight lines, that theories are uttered and then get 'implemented' somehow and the influence spreads down and out until it is diffused in the hinterlands" (97).

In other words, North conflates a restricted notion of writing and reading practice as the production and distribution of commodified knowledge with the full range of possible uses for writing and reading, and sees Practitioners' institutional structural position as fully determining their actions and desires. As a result, in spite of North's calls for respect for Practitioners, he derogates to them the role of unquestioning consumers. Interaction between other methodological communities and Practitioners, he observes, "tends to be top-down: the spoon-feeding of the lowly Practitioners with whatever they can handle of the findings of other communities" (372). Though North laments this style of interaction, it seems inevitable given his view of writing and of "lore" and its "pragmatic logic." But this has to be the case only if we confuse the "pragmatic logic" governing Practitioner inquiry with a search and desire for prescriptions. North describes Practitioners as hungry for those who will tell them "what to do," to the extent that they take descriptions for prescriptions (see 25–27). "Because lore is fundamentally pragmatic," he explains, "contributions to it have to be framed in practical terms, as knowledge about what to do" (25). To illustrate, North points to Shaughnessy's *Errors and Expectations*, whose popularity among Practitioners, he claims, arises from the fact that it tries "to tell practitioners what to do, and [Shaughnessy's] authority rests primarily . . . on our sense of her competence" (53).

North doesn't say what convinces him that this is Shaughnessy's appeal for Practitioners. He admits that, for himself, it is "[Shaughnessy's] attitude [that] is more valuable than any of her findings *per se*" (53). But it seems at least possible that this same "attitude" is what appeals to Practitioners as well. Bartholomae suggests that the appeal of Shaughnessy's book for Practitioners resides in the use to which it puts Practitioner knowledge and the model it provides for merging teaching and scholarship. Rather than praise the work for its "practicality," he admires it for the completeness of the picture Shaughnessy is able to give of writers at work, a completeness obviously made possible strictly by virtue of her teaching experience ("Released" 73–74). Comparing *Errors and Expectations* to statistical research on prose features, he notes that prior to the publication of *Errors and Expectations*,

> It was not uncommon . . . to hear statistical research being praised at the expense of the anecdotal accounts that had characterized another tradition of scholarship in composition. Much of that criticism . . . came from people who didn't teach writing and who lacked the day-by-day contact with writers and their problems that makes the impressions and speculations of writing teachers, at least the best of them, like Shaughnessy, so valuable. Shaughnessy, like Ann Berthoff, has demonstrated how teaching and research can together be part of a professional life. ("Released" 73)

Both Coles and Bartholomae imagine Practitioners receiving writing not as prescriptions to be swallowed, commodities to be consumed, but as enactments of a merged teaching and research, enactments that can then inspire or provoke enactments in response. It is that sort of writing and the sort of knowledge it produces that Coles values, writing that captures *in* writing what North describes as "the confusions, the tentativeness, the recursiveness, the muddied uncertainty about successes" of day-to-day teaching practice without transforming the account of that experience into prescription. As Coles observes in the introduction to *The Plural I*, while much has been written on how to teach writing, there is "surprisingly little" on "the actual doing, on . . . the continuing dialogue [between "non-mythic" teachers and students] at least as undramatic as it is dramatic in its workings, repetitive often, seemingly circular, inevitably messy, on the sheer dirty work of teaching and learning day by day, in this time, of that place" (3–4). What matters to Coles is not the sort of knowledge easily transmittable in clear, linear writing but the use made of that knowledge at individual locales of individual teachers with specific classes. As he argues in response to calls for defining what composition teachers yet need to know, "the only substantive knowledge connected with the teaching of writing that is worthy of the name is knowledge that has been made more than knowledge by the teacher himself" ("New Presbyters" 9). Hence Coles offers so little, really no, direct advice either to teachers or students on how to write, how to teach. Similarly, Bartholomae offers few prescriptions either to teachers or students on how to go about teaching or writing. Whereas other writers on teaching are commonly known for their advocacy of such techniques as free-writing and "believing games" aimed at smoothing the writing process, presumably anyone's writing process, neither Coles nor Bartholomae is associated with any comparable techniques. Both have described specific courses and assignment sequences, but as noted earlier, they bracket them with warnings about their use by others. William Irmscher's response to Coles' *The Plural I* illustrates an alternative image of how Practitioners might respond to books on teaching. Irmscher praises the book for telling him what not to do. As he explains,

> [What the instructor is like and how the students react] is so vivid that I know I don't want to be like Coles. I don't want to use his approach, and I don't want to treat students as he does. But I *know* all of this because he has dramatized the situation. (87)

In the resistant tradition I am tracing, such a response might indeed be a welcome one.[11]

I have argued that the work of Coles and Bartholomae represents a tradition resistant to common conceptions of tradition in Composition operant in recent studies of the field's history as the straightforward transmission of commodified knowledge, and I have suggested further that this "resistant" tradition poses an alternative "mode of inquiry" among Practitioners that merges teaching with scholarship while avoiding the pitfalls of Practitioner lore as North has described it. To identify this tradition, I've had to look at pedagogies, teaching materials, and statements of philosophy not as constative "statements" but as practices, as "performative," blurring imperceptibly into one another, and these practices as resisting rather than complying with the Barthesian "mise en scène" of teaching and speaking. In hooks' terms, I've had to look at not just the words but at how and why they are spoken, and to whom about whom.

This tradition's insistence that teachers re-invent the tradition both in their teaching of writing and in their writing about teaching means that this tradition resists the usual means of identification. In an overview of theories of composition, Richard Fulkerson describes no less than four elements or "components" constituting any theory of composition: axiology, or a belief about the goal or aim of writing; procedure, or a sense of the means by which writers achieve that aim; a pedagogical component, or how to teach writers to use those means; and an epistemology, a belief about what counts as knowledge (410–11). Fulkerson's analysis helps to resolve some of the confusion marring other analyses of the field, a confusion Fulkerson blames on the failure to recognize all of these elements and their independence (410, 420–21). But as my discussion of the Amherst tradition and of Coles and Bartholomae suggests, tradition represents an additional element distinguishing any theory from others.

In his essay, Fulkerson is interested only in categorizing composition "theory," abstractly understood, whereas a tradition—that is, the process by which a theory, and/or any component of that theory, is constituted and maintained—would seem to emphasize something non-theoretical, a *material practice*: the question, say, of whether one teaches a theory of composition by example or handouts or through refereed publications, of whether one's writing style is smooth or knotty, of the kind of publications in which one's theory is articulated. But as the Amherst tradition and the work of Coles and Bartholomae illustrate, the material practice of tradition—including writing and writing style—is not to be so easily divorced from theory or any of its "components." At least in the tradition I have traced, every component is imbricated with the others. This imbrication qualifies the now common advice from historians of Composition like Varnum and Gere to broaden our gaze to include material other than textbooks and journal publications. The question is not simply whether historians of Composition have done their homework. In attending to as broad a range of material documentation as possible, historians need to attend as well to the nature of such materials as a practice by which particular traditions are constituted and maintained. And, to the extent possible, we need to consider what the reception given those materials signifies. The very different public receptions given Coles and Bartholomae in spite of the close correlation of much of their work and in spite of Bartholomae's explicit acknowledgments of Coles' influence on him attest not only to the resistance their work offers to common conceptions of traditions in Composition as transmitted unproblematically in straight lines, as "theories [that] are uttered and then get 'implemented' somehow" (Carr 97). It attests as well to the power those common conceptions have exerted on historians of Composition, and to the engagement of historians in the selective process of constituting some traditions and denying others, and thus their own engagement in composing Composition.

In my engagement in that process, I have argued that the work of the Amherst tradition, extended in the writings of Coles and Bartholomae, constitutes a tradition that resists ordinary conceptions of tradition and provides an alternative model of the process by which Practitioners might share "lore" and by which teaching practice and scholarship might be reconciled. Attention to the variety of practices by which traditions are constituted and maintained can inform our understanding of those practices and of the daily work of composition teachers and scholars. Such attention is important not only as a technical matter of historiography but as a political matter. For such attention not only informs but also shapes theories of composition. As the tradition I've identified shows, theories inhere as much in such material practices as they do in statements.[12]

Further, these theories and practices inhere as much in the material conditions of *institutions* and *their* histories as they do in the work (teaching and writing) of individual "figures" in composition. If we take the *Facts* course, for example, to represent the work of powerful teachers like Bartholomae, Petrosky, and their colleagues at the University of Pittsburgh, and as the enactment of a particular "theory" of composition, we must also take it to represent a remarkable institutional commitment of resources to the course (see acknowledgments in the Preface to *Facts*). We will fail to see the full range of traditions in Composition, and we will exclude much of it from the "field" of Composition, if we think of "traditions of teaching" in traditional terms only. If we are to understand traditions of teaching, we need to look not just to statements of philosophy, nor to textbooks, nor to the paraphernalia of course materials, nor to the institutional and larger social historical conditions of the courses, nor even to the interaction of all these in relation to each other, but to the teaching all these enact on both students and teachers, immediately and in history. We need to see how these define, and define differently, what "tradition" means in the work of composition.

Tradition and Redefining Work in Composition

"Every instance of the use of language," Giddens observes, "is a potential modification of that language at the same time as it acts to reproduce it" (220). While Giddens makes this observation in accounting for the type of change obtaining, through tradition, in oral cultures, the observation applies to language users in all societies. Students and teachers have a practical knowledge of their role and capacity both to reproduce and change language, and so culture, which Composition can draw upon, a practical knowledge embodied in the practices of traditions of writing and the teaching of writing. Rather than displacing such knowledge with knowledge sanctioned by academic discipline, Composition can tap the knowledge of tradition, embodied in its practices. For "compositionists" to do so, however, means foregoing the usual distinctions between professionals and laity, renouncing intellectual property rights over writing instruction, and sharing responsibility for and control over our work with the public in ways for which academic professionalism has not prepared us, indeed which it has actively worked against (see Zeichner). It means, in short, redefining the work of Composition and ourselves as workers working with, rather than for, on, or in spite of, students and the public. Composition would have to recognize, and realign itself with, its teaching, not in opposition to research or theorizing, not as a new strategy to achieve distinction from the public as professionals, but as the primary site where such work took place, in concert with students.

In a critique of "careers" in composition, Bartholomae suggests the possibility of such a realignment when he observes that he regularly teaches the first-year writing course at his university not as a sacrifice or service, not as a gesture of solidarity with TAs, students, or teaching in opposition to research, but out of commitment to "a certain kind of intellectual project—one that requires me to think out critical problems of language, knowledge, and culture through the work of 'ordinary' or 'novice' or student writers. . . . a way of working on the 'popular' in relation to academic or high culture" ("What" 24). He proposes that we see Composition as undertaking just such projects, but he warns that while, so defined, Composition can be a "good field to work in," it means "you have to be willing to pay attention to common things" (28). This view offers an alternative to dominant definitions of intellectual work in Composition as the production of commodities: publications, academic credits, or abstract writing skills. It takes Composition's non-disciplinary status, its location on the margins between the academy and the "popular," not as a lack to be corrected or fate to be condemned, but as the basis for useful intellectual work involving both students and teachers as they confront the contact between academic and non-academic discourse and concerns.

I have posed an ideal of English 1–2 at Amherst as a tradition of teachers and first-year students aimed at also carrying out a project of such collective intellectual work that can stand as an alternative potentially disrupting the domination of professionalism in Composition. Other courses might carry out similar projects very differently. For example, Dennis Lynch, Diana George, and Marilyn Cooper have described first-year writing courses at Michigan Technological University (MTU) that teach argument as inquiry. Unlike the Amherst course, these courses involved students in using argument to explore an issue of current public concern and debate—the use of water resources, for example—in increasingly complicated ways. The courses required students to write far fewer papers than the Amherst course—four essays in one version, three of them essentially drafts for the final essay—and involved students in extensive research, again unlike the Amherst course (Lynch et al. 77). At the same time, the process engaged students in learning not only the formal modes of argumentation but in rethinking their knowledge about and positions on these issues, ultimately redefining them, and so treating knowledge as contingent (82). Further, it provided students with an opportunity to connect their academic work with their everyday lives, and their everyday lives with their academic work (Lynch et al. 82), in ways far more dramatic than the Amherst course encouraged.

But recognizing tradition not as a fixed body of knowledge but an action and ongoing project of reworking knowledge means rejecting advocacy of the dissemination of MTU- or Amherst-like courses, whatever we might admire about these courses or specific features of them. Instead, we can pursue the ways in which specific practices enact the relationship to knowledge characteristic of tradition, as at Amherst, MTU, and in other teaching traditions as yet unstudied. Any practice defines the work and the worker in relation to that work. For example, the Amherst practice of using a new assignment sequence each year was, according to Baird, a way of "always facing a new problem, and a problem that you didn't know how to solve. That way you never felt you were just a damned section man, or whatever, teaching a required course" (Varnum 112–13). Other traditions might well evidence different ways by which, operating in different specific conditions, teachers have defined their work, the work of their students, and so themselves and their students as workers in comparable terms, avoiding reification of work and the alienation attendant on such reification.

But again, if tradition as a practice is characterized by attention to the contingencies of immediate circumstance, then the various "practices" of various teaching traditions cannot be understood apart from the conditions of their employment. This is not to equate practices with those conditions. For example, while the teaching practices at Amherst cannot be understood outside the conditions of its relative isolation from pressures of research professionalism (Varnum 12, 29, 62), nor outside the conditions of class, race, and gender privilege obtaining at Amherst during midcentury for both its professors and its students, those conditions do not in themselves inevitably render the course ethically noxious: say, the playing of an elite game of collegewide "boot camp" hazing by those already in positions of social power to reinforce their positions of privilege (see Varnum 213–20). Such an analysis would derogate the actors involved by accepting that institutions "work 'behind the backs' of the social actors who produce and reproduce them" (Giddens 71). We can see the tradition embodied in certain practices of the English 1–2 course not simply as the result of allegiance to secretly held epistemological beliefs imposed by the teaching staff on students, nor simply as the result of the conditions of Amherst as an isolated elite, all-male, effectively all-white private college. Rather, it can also be seen as an attempt to mobilize existing residual values and conditions for alternative work. What distinguishes the course is the response of these teachers to conditions similar to those prevailing at many other colleges, just as the courses in argument described by Lynch and colleagues demonstrate a specific response to conditions presumably similar in some ways, different in others, to those prevailing at other schools, and just as the *Facts* course represents a response to unusual institutional circumstances of support, student populations, and faculty obtaining at the University of Pittsburgh. The Amherst course made possible not simply the reproduction of specific conditions—the enactment of ritual male hazing, say—but also a dialogical relationship between and among students and faculty the antithesis of the masculinist authoritarianism that boot camps are intended to foster, and an alternative to the increasingly dominant pressures to engage in research professionalism. Similarly, the MTU course makes possible not just students' enactment, or re-enactment, of *Crossfire*-like mud-slinging, nor simply a conservative's worst nightmare of students' conversion to PC positions on issues of current public debate, nor rote exercises in writing generic research papers, but also the use of conventions of writing argument turned to non-conventional ends, as suggested by the authors' terms for argument as "agonistic inquiry" and "confrontational cooperation." The overdetermined possibilities of these courses are demonstrated by the significant differences in the experiences reported to Varnum by the students who had taken the Amherst course and those who taught it—some decrying it as an exercise in humiliation, others avidly recalling its liberating effects.

Exploring the potential of such traditions of practice means addressing both the conditions making such work possible and the variety of ways of engaging in such work within and against such conditions. This will not be achieved as a byproduct of achieving academic professional disciplinary status, since the terms and conditions for achieving that status militate against such work. It will require, instead, insisting on a variety of different definitions of our work and the work of our students, definitions that may draw significantly and effectively on the authority of tradition as a continual process of collectively reworking, and rewriting, our knowledge. And it will require sturdy resistance to pressures to commodify that work, whether in such forms as publications, student test results, teaching evaluations, or "accountability." This is emphatically not to oppose publishing or evaluating, necessary to any reworking of knowledge, but to specific forms and uses of these that reify knowledge and work—most obviously for people "in" Composition, the use of these in reappointment and tenure review. Finally, it will require steady critique of the material conditions in which any teaching practices take place: admission standards, financial aid policies, and other factors producing student populations; class size; job security and salary; clerical support; computers, libraries, offices, paper, time.

Those pressures which appear to threaten the privileges and rights of Composition as an academic specialty might be harnessed to forge a different definition of our work and its worth. Composition courses are one of the few sites where those most marginal to the academy have a space—first-year students, especially those deemed "unprepared" for college, the "basic" writers thought to lack "the basics." It is also one of the few sites where these students and their writing are given serious, sustained attention, where the teacher is likely to know both students' names and their writing, and where the students, in turn, are likely to know their teacher in more than a superficial way. And it is, therefore, not surprisingly one of the courses that the public most remembers and with which it most identifies (see Bazerman 255). The public's claims on Composition can and have been mocked as merely "sentimental," evidence of their foolish commitment to a degrading initiation ritual or fond nostalgia for Mr. Chips figures (Crowley, "Personal" 156). But as I have suggested in chapter 4, those claims might be engaged seriously. Dominant public discourse identifies the course strictly as remedial, providing skills training for future workers. It is this "official" public demand on the course that has most fed calls to abolish the course, or the universal requirement to take it, usually out of either elitist disdain for such matters or rejection of the possibility of teaching general writing skills (see Russell, "Romantics"; *Reconceiving Writing*). But other strands of public discourse, less "official" and strident, recognize the course, and writing, as also an occasion for reflective thinking (Gere, Hollis). Indeed, it is difficult to imagine a public that would reject its own capacity or right to engage in such intellectual work, refuse an occasion to engage in such work, given the necessary material support, or discourage teachers from such engagement. The course could attend critically to the material practices of writing, providing training in and critique of those practices. But simultaneously, and in the process of doing so, it could engage students in the kind of "practical criticism" of and work on "popular" in relation to "academic" culture for which Bartholomae calls and at which courses like those at MTU aim. The public's claims on the course might also provide ammunition for improving the material conditions of its teaching. Rather than pleading for improved working conditions on the basis of Composition's putative status as a professional academic discipline involved in the disinterested pursuit of knowledge, I am arguing that we consider aligning ourselves with those most at risk because of those conditions: the students who have experienced the overcrowded classrooms, overworked teachers, limited computer access and supplies, and so on (cf. Final Report 28–29; Thompson A23).

In so doing, we can educate ourselves on the history of strategies employed for improvement of such conditions, especially unionization, by those teachers with whom we are simultaneously closest in our work (and in the public imaginary), yet put at most distance by our "professional" aspirations: primary and secondary school teachers. We might, in other words, mobilize the clash between sentimental public memories of traditional composition teaching and existing conditions to justify an improvement in these conditions, in the public's own interest as participants in, rather than objects of, the work of Composition. On the basis of his analysis of "social movement" unionism and the public workplace, Paul Johnston argues that, far more than workers in the private sector, public workers "are constrained to frame their claims as 'public needs' . . . and to align with and even assemble coalitions around these public needs, turning bargaining into a political debate over public policy" (12). For the fact is, such workers are always involved in public issues. They confront them, Johnston observes,

> face-to-face—at the point of production, so to speak, of society itself. . . . Thus, they are participants in the never-ending argument over "what is the public good" and join—and increasingly organize—coalitions on behalf of politically defined public goals associated with their work. (12–13)

While Johnston focuses primarily on such public workers as nurses, city streetsweepers, clerks and librarians, college faculty too, like primary and secondary school teachers, can be seen as confronting, at the point of production of society itself, the question of "what is the public good."[13] Rather than defining themselves as academic entrepreneurs pursuing private interests or engaging in purportedly "disinterested" scholarship, faculty could align with public constituencies in redefining and pursuing the public good, resisting reductively utilitarian definitions of those goods in terms of "growth" and the production of exchange value—that is, in terms of the accumulation of private capital—and fighting for education's use value for and by the public.[14]

Composition has always occupied a marginal position in the academy, justified by the lack of distinction between its knowledge and lay knowledge, by its focus on teaching, by its association with the public's interest in finding and keeping work. But margins, hooks reminds us, "have been both sites of repression and sites of resistance" ("marginality" 342). Rather than simply taking Composition's traditional marginality, a marginality intrinsic to its status as a tradition rather than profession, as a site and sign of deprivation only, of our oppression and means of oppressing others, I am arguing that we can take tradition in Composition as also a site of resistance, a means of recuperating the wholeness of our work with both the academic and the non-academic. We can take tradition as the site of radical possibility.

To recover that possibility, we need to rethink our notions not only of tradition but of writing, redefining notions of both these in which efforts at professionalizing Composition are invested. As I have argued throughout this chapter, Composition has understood writing only in terms of a limited range of writing practices, practices associated with writing that occurs only at specific sites, and has recognized only a narrow range of the work writing may accomplish. In the final chapter, I take up the task of how we might redefine not just Composition's traditions but writing, and, in so doing, recompose what we mean by Composition.

Chapter 6

WRITING

T here is an ambiguity in the term *writing*, like the term *work*, arising from its use to designate both an activity and the product of that activity.[1] Seen from the perspective of writing *as* work, this ambiguity calls into play questions about the commodification of that work: the "work" of writing may signify not the activity of production, distribution, and consumption but the commodity, removed ("alienated") from the social relations and means of its production.

Debate in Composition has sometimes seized on this ambiguity in references to the work of writing as the source of its troubles, and, to end them, has attempted to push one meaning or the other to the shadows, as in the slogan "process, not product." For example, recognizing the alienation of the labor—writing activity—and the laborer—the writer—from the product of her labor—the writing—obtaining in the commodification of writing, some attempt to counter that alienation by emphasizing process and de-emphasizing the object of commodification: the material form of the written product. Or, alternatively, and more sophisticatedly, others attempt to locate in the writing product the writing activity itself. Mina Shaughnessy's inferences about the "logic" governing the production of error-ridden student texts move from the written "product" to the imagined activity that produced them, thus revivifying those texts by locating within them the thinking of the "basic" writers who produced them. Both of these strategies represent alternatives to approaches focusing on characteristics of the writing (written) product alone. That focus is decried in terms of the bankruptcy of the formalist principles that seem to underlie it and its effect of privileging textual forms at the expense of denigrating the writer and her writing, that is, the labor of production. But those taking these more "formalist" approaches answer that to ignore the written product is to condescend to writers by treating their work as beneath serious attention, as well as ultimately doing a disservice to writers by denying the very real demands to be made on writing outside the composition course.

However, from the perspective that I have been advancing of writing as material social practice, all of these moves fall short. Most obviously, they mistake a highly circumscribed set of activities in the finite process of crafting a single text or set of texts for the full material social process of writing: a process that includes the technology of writing, the material conditions enabling and constraining its practice, the historical location of any act of writing in the history of writing practices and cultural meanings for them, and the modes of the distribution and consumption of writing. Those focusing attention on the writing process at the expense of attention to the written product ignore the full material social process of the production of writing, which extends beyond an individual's or group's composition of a single text to include the history of the formation of the text's genre, and the text's distribution and reception. Those focusing attention on the written "product" ignore both their own participation in the production of the form through their reception of it and, typically, much of the materiality of the "product" examined, attending in fact to a highly restricted set of abstracted formal "product features." In this focus, written "error," for example, is typically defined in ways that ignore such matters as faint print, smudges, missed deadlines, or illegible handwriting, not to mention errors in "content."

I have touched on these limitations in chapter 2 in my critiques of both "practical" "nuts and bolts" pedagogies and the various alternatives to them represented by versions of expressivist, process, collaborative, and contact-zone pedagogies. For the purposes of the present argument, the circumscription of the full mode of production of writing in all such pedagogies leads to a false sense of the commodification of writing and so to misguided strategies of resistance to that commodification. More damagingly, in adopting such a restricted view of the production of writing, these approaches tend in fact to contribute to its commodification.

Two limiting assumptions in particular underlie this effect. First, a linear, sequential model of writing production is assumed: production is imagined to be followed by commodification, distribution, and consumption (cf. Marx, *Critique* 193–205; Trimbur, "Whatever"). It is only within this view of writing production that its commodification, and so the alienation of the writer from the writing, are seen as occurring *after* the concrete labor of writing, hence something which can be avoided through delay. This strategy neglects the ways in which the modes of distribution and consumption enter into the very processes and conditions of writing's production, from the "start." And it is misguided as well in treating the (imagined as subsequent) commodification of the writing as inevitable and total, to be delayed but not overcome. For, secondly, both those advocating strategies of delay and those insisting on attention to the formal features of the written "product" forget that both use and exchange value reside within the commodity: that "nothing can be a value without being an object of utility. If the thing is useless, so is the labour contained in it; the labour does not count as labour, and therefore creates no value" (Marx, *Capital* I, 131; cf. Kusterer 192). If one cannot forever delay the commodification of the work of writing, nor can one deny the continuing potential use value of that work even in its commodified form. In chapter 2 I have critiqued the "delaying" strategies associated with expressivist and process pedagogies. In the present chapter, I explore the implications of denying, and of recognizing, this complex interdependence of concrete and abstract labor, use and exchange value, for our understanding of the materiality of writing and our engagement with it in both our teaching and our writing. Specifically, I examine the implications of this interdependence for how we define the subject of the composition course, composition scholarship, and debate over the forms of writing that scholarship.

Teaching Writing and Writing

"The subject of a writing course is writing" (David et al. 525). This seemingly obvious, tautological statement, offered by Denise David, Barbara Gordon, and Rita Pollard in an attempt to find "common ground" among composition teachers, in fact conceals as much as it reveals, and what it both conceals and reveals is disturbing. For it turns out that by "writing" David and colleagues seem to mean a highly restricted set of concerns aimed at the development of abstract writing "skills." This is indicated by the first "guiding assumption" they identify for writing courses: "The development of writing ability and metacognitive awareness is the primary objective of a writing course" (525; for similar statements, see Hairston, "Diversity"; Fulkerson 414–16). Sharon Crowley has pointed to the pervasiveness within Composition, and within American culture generally, of this restricted sense of writing as a set of abilities to be developed, which she identifies as "writing" in contrast to "Writing":

> there's writing, which is the simple ordering and recording of thoughts or information and which can be done as easily by a secretary or a committee or a machine or a technical writer, since its author-ity [sic] is not relevant to its status as text; and there's Writing [sic], what Authors (and authors) do. ("writing" 97)

"writing" here is mechanical, identified with easily acquired skills and the production of a commodity. The teaching of "writing," as opposed to "Writing," is thus the teaching of commodification: both the production of written commodities (texts) and the commodification of the writer into a bundle of skills for subsequent exchange on the job market. This is contrasted with Writing, produced by Authors (usually invisible and dead), or at least authors (aspiring Writers), as "Great Works" (Crowley, "writing" 95–96).

This distinction between "writing" and "Writing," students and Authors, is part of a chain of binaries separating the non-literary from the literary, craft from art, labor from work, skill from genius. In response to Composition's relegation by the dominant to a focus on only the first of the terms of these binaries, Composition has either accepted that relegation as a "practical" measure or attempted to overthrow that relegation by appropriating the latter terms for Composition. We can see the same binaries invoked in William E. Coles, Jr.'s insistence, back in the late '60s and early '70s, that "the teaching of writing as writing is the teaching of writing as art," for "when writing is not taught as art, . . . it is not writing that is being taught, but something else" (*Plural I* 11). "writing," for Coles, is Crowley's "Writing," an "art" that, as art, is "unteachable" ("Freshman" 136), just as, Crowley notes, to effectively prevent student "writers" from "Writing," current-traditional rhetoric holds in reserve instruction in invention, seen as something "that cannot be taught but must nonetheless be learned" ("writing" 97). Its unteachability is seen as a guarantee of its resistance to commodification. The alternative to teaching the unteachable art of "Writing," conversely, is an exercise in mutual degradation of teacher and student, the doing of what anyone can do. For Coles, it is "turning the activity of writing . . . into a kind of computerized skill," "a trick that can be played, a device that can be put into operation, . . . a technique that can be taught and learned—just as one can be taught or learn to run an adding machine, or pour concrete" ("Freshman" 136, 137). Michael Holzman argues similarly against teaching writing as pure "technique," teaching "a specific skill, suitable for those who will be filling out forms, producing technical writing, and drafting urban planning proposals" (132). Holzman's worry is that doing so will fail to prepare students to be active participants in the Jeffersonian ideal of "a citizenry not merely skilled, but one which can think critically and responsibly" (133).

The assumption governing these arguments is that to teach writing as technique, as mechanical skill, is to be complicit in the degradation of the writer and the writing—to substitute, in Coles' terms, "a process for an activity, perhaps a product for a process" ("Freshman" 136). There is a slippage in such arguments: the historical fact of the degradation of those involved in certain forms of work—such as running adding machines, being mechanics, pouring concrete, or even filling out forms—is taken as evidence that such work is inherently alienating and degrading. The historical fact of the dominant commodification of skills used in such work is assumed to exhaust the full potential of that work. And the effect, historically, of the social relations of production in such work is then identified with the actual labor performed (cf. Marx, *Capital* 1038–49). Features in the work of writing taken as analogous to these other types of work—technical skills, attention to physical properties (forms, the "mechanics" of a task)—are then derided as in themselves degrading. To avoid such degradation, emphasis is placed on an abstraction of the activity—writing as an "action" (for Coles)—which displaces concern for use: for, in short, the materiality of writing.

As Susan Miller has observed, writing in such pedagogies becomes "intransitive," having "no particular products as results" (*Textual* 97). For in the production of writing as art such concerns presumably have no place. The full material social process of writing is in these pedagogies reduced to the process of producing an individual text and its reading, and efforts are directed at shifting the emphasis of concerns within that scope: to encouraging what Bourdieu describes as the "aesthetic" disposition, in which works are considered "in and for themselves." There is a clear class basis for this disposition: it is "the paradoxical product of conditioning by negative economic necessities—a life of ease—that tends to induce an active distance from necessity" (Bourdieu, *Distinction* 3, 5; see also 54–55).

Significantly, however, the same focus on "process" invoked in this aesthetic disposition is also invoked by those arguing for the teaching not of "Writing" but "writing." Eleanor Agnew, for example, concludes from her recent study of the workplace writing experiences of former basic writing students that

> the conditions and writing practices of the workplace which are both possible and appropriate for the classroom are inherent in many of the innovative pedagogies spawned by the process movement over the past two decades. . . . collaborative writing, peer editing, sequenced assignments, multiple drafting, varied writing formats, fewer grades and more conferencing, and informal, student-centered classes. (35–36)

Agnew recommends these pedagogies not as a means of teaching "Writing" but "writing," that is, of ensuring a closer fit between the writing environment of basic writing courses and the writing environment students will encounter in their subsequent employment.

Similarly, Maxine Hairston advocates "process" pedagogy not as a strategy of subversion but as part of a "practical enterprise" of better preparing students for the work they may expect to do in their subsequent academic and postacademic careers: that is, to teach craft, not art, writing skills, not literature ("Breaking" 276, 280; "Diversity" 180, 186, 189, 192).

That roughly the same pedagogy can be invoked in the name of achieving distinctly opposed ends shows the dominance of both the restricted sense of the "process" of writing production and the confusion about the relationship between use value and exchange value. Most obviously, the distinction between Writing and writing, art and craft, the literary and the non-literary obscures the full sociality of Authorship, (i.e., of "Writing"). As Raymond Williams notes, while there is general recognition of the simplest sense of Authors' need to respond in their Writing to pressures from the "political economy of writing," in the form of pressures on its distribution and even on the language and discursive conventions employed in Authorial composition, this recognition retains the ordinary sense of the author as autonomous, operating within and responding to the social but not, himself, in his consciousness socially produced (*Marxism* 192–93). Those advocates of "process" pedagogy attempt either to preclude the effects of this political economy, simplistically understood, on the student writer, thereby rendering them Authors, or assume that the students enact their autonomy in acceding to what are thought to be the demands of that economy. Both thus deny the operation of the social in producing the consciousness of writers and Writers, and so its presence already in the classroom and in the very minds of the students.

A variety of barriers stand in the way of theorists accepting the social production of writers' individual consciousness. First and foremost is the monolithic understanding of the social (and hegemony) and so of what the social production of individual consciousness might involve. Williams has in mind a dynamic dialectical relationship between the social and the individual, not Marxist variants of structuralism "in which the living and reciprocal relationships of the individual and the social have been suppressed in the interest of an abstract model of determinate social structures and their [individual] 'carriers' " (*Marxism* 194). The more common, deterministic understanding of the social production of consciousness testifies most obviously to the dominant's seizure of the definition of the social as uniform, all-encompassing and static rather than as a dynamic ongoing process of struggle among heterogeneous and conflicting forces. It is this seizure which suppresses the "living and reciprocal relationships of the individual and the social" in favor of imagining consciousness to be determined by external, fixed social conditions. Faced with this understanding of the impact of hegemony, Williams remarks, "it is not surprising that many people run back headlong into bourgeois-individualist concepts, forms, and institutions" (*Marxism* 194).

Secondly, scholars resist recognizing the social production of consciousness, Williams explains, because of the extraordinary difficulty of grasping the "emergent" arising out of "practical consciousness" that is part of the process of the social production of consciousness. Williams argues that while "[s]ocial forms are evidently more recognizable when they are articulate and explicit," "[t]here are the experiences to which the fixed forms do not speak at all, which indeed they do not recognize" (*Marxism* 130). That difference represents the gap between official and practical consciousness:

> practical consciousness is what is actually being lived, and not only what it is thought is being lived. . . . It is a kind of feeling and thinking which is indeed social and material, but each in an embryonic phase before it can become fully articulate and defined exchange. Its relations with the already articulate and defined are then exceptionally complex. (*Marxism* 130–31)

The very complexity of grasping this practical consciousness stands in the way of recognizing its sociality, given the dominant's consignment of such consciousness to the realm of the "individual," "personal," "private," "emotional," "feminine," "irrational," "traditional," "experience," and especially when the embryonic thoughts and feelings of what is actually being lived remain unarticulated and undefined while competing with the already articulate and defined. Official consciousness both interferes with and substitutes for the articulation of practical consciousness. Those accepting this substitution define as "individual" what is in fact socially produced—through material social practices—if officially unrecognized as such.

Finally, recognizing the social production of consciousness meets with resistance because it undermines the concept of the Author as a quintessentially autonomous individual on which English literary study specifically but also academic institutions and capitalist ideology generally depend. Co-extensive with this concept of the Author is the removal of "Writing" from the material social world, redefining it from being a socially located activity to an aestheticized, idealized art object—from writing as an activity engaged in to meet human needs as part of a larger social process to writing as an object produced for the sake of "art." As Williams explains, in the process of this removal of "Writing" from the material social world, "The properties of 'the medium' [of art] were abstracted as if they defined the practice, rather than being its means," thus suppressing the full sense of practice, and "art was idealized to distinguish it from 'mechanical' work" (*Marxism* 160). We can see the evocation of just such a process of idealization in the statements from Coles cited above.

Historically, one motive for this redefinition has been "a simple class emphasis, to separate 'higher' things—the objects of interest to free men, the 'liberal arts'—from the 'ordinary' business ('mechanical' as manual work, and then as work with machines) of the 'everyday world'" (*Marxism* 160). This redefinition is marked by the isolation of and concentration on language forms and the "evacuation of immediate situation" (*Marxism* 156). The materiality of writing and the conditions of writing as a social practice are thus evaded. For to recognize writing fully as a material social practice would be to undermine the autonomy of both the author and the "work" of writing, and so the ideological mechanism separating work from labor, thought from experience, the academic, intellectual, and spiritual from the political, economic, commercial, and physical.

Williams notes that nineteenth-century craftsmen participated in this idealization of the work of art, in the form of its removal from the material social process, as a protest against the commodification of work within capitalist production that displaced them and their work:

> The protest in the name of "art" was . . . at one level the
> protest of craftsmen—most of them literally hand-crafts-
> men—against a mode of production which steadily excluded

them or profoundly altered their status. But at another level it was a claim for a significant meaning of work—that of using human energy on material for an autonomous purpose—which was being radically displaced and denied, in most kinds of production, but which could be more readily and more confidently asserted, in the case of art, by association with the "life of the spirit" or "our general humanity". (*Marxism* 161)

The point of such protests was not against work per se. Rather, in such arguments, art was "exempted from, made exceptional to, what 'work' *had been made to mean*" (*Marxism* 161, my emphasis). Thus, if, for Coles, the work of pouring concrete, say, seems inherently degrading because of its undeniable materiality (physicality and use), these nineteenth-century craftsmen, recognizing the degradation of their work through its commodification, attempted to counter that degradation by claiming for their work an idealized status as art. There is in such moves a struggle over meaning but also, unfortunately, an acceptance of the equation of the physical materiality and use of work with its degradation. This equation leads to the assumption that the value of work is in inverse relation to its human usefulness, and to the move to increase the value of one's work by aestheticizing it.[2] That is, the terms of valuation remain unchallenged; only the attribution of them is in dispute.

In such arguments, the usefulness of writing to others is evidence of its complicity in unjust social relations. Writing is ideally to be of no use, in that sense, but for the writer herself. Thus Peter Elbow poses the issue of the first-year writing course as one of choosing between offering students the chance of writing for themselves rather than meeting the demands of readers ("Being" 72–73, 76–77). Hairston offers a somewhat different version of this when she insists on teaching "writing for its own sake," a practice she sees as threatened by a model that "doesn't take freshman English seriously in its own right but conceives of it as a tool, something to be used. . . . for social reform" ("Diversity" 179, 180). The former, she insists, answers "the educational needs of the students," their "values, preferences, or interests," whereas the latter model addresses the needs of the teacher, unfairly imposed on the students and the course ("Diversity" 180, 181). What Hairston does, in effect, is see in the exchange value of the teaching of writing skills only the use value of these for the students, and in the use value of teaching the ideological implications of writing only its exchange value for teachers. She does so by equating the demands of businesses with students' ostensible desires and needs (see her earlier "Not All Errors"), and denying the possible overlap between the political interests of teachers and the needs or desires of the students. Conversely, arguments like Holzman's and Coles' identify in the use value of writing techniques only their exchange value, while ignoring the exchange value in the use value of teaching writing as art.

The difference between the two positions, to the extent that there is one, resides in the kinds of capital recognized. Hairston et al. recognize (to decry) the *cultural* capital teachers (if not students) might gain, at least within certain economies, from a politicized or aestheticized composition curriculum; Coles et al., blind or at least inattentive to this form of capitalization, emphasize (and decry as base and degrading) the *economic* capitalization of a curriculum devoted to teaching writing skills. That is, both positions recognize only the use value of one curriculum and only the exchange value of another. The effect of this is that the commodification of the work of writing—whether conceived as art or as technique—goes on undeterred in the curriculum advanced by either. For the value of the work is identified not with the social relations of its production (including its consumption) but with the form of the product.

That is commodification. As Marx explains, it is only when "the labor expended in the production of a useful article [is presented] as an 'objective' property of that article, i.e. as its value. . . . that the product of labour becomes transformed into a commodity" (*Capital* I, 153–54). The "aesthetic gaze" is complicit in such commodification by its rejection of the functionality, for someone in some circumstance, of the article produced, and of the social relations of its production. Production, instead, is assumed to be autonomous (Bourdieu, *Distinction* 3). Composition's history of fetishizing specific textual forms, illustrated by its fascination both with "error" and with experimental textual forms, gives ample evidence of its neglect of the relations of production, as does its almost complete neglect until recently of the technological and human physiological demands of writing (see Haas 5, 36). In that history, textual forms are imagined in themselves to produce specific effects, good or bad, rather than being seen as notations which depend for their production and effect on specific practices with them. This is what Marx terms commodity fetishism, in which "the commodity reflects the social characteristics of men's own labour as objective characteristics of the products of labour themselves, as the socio-natural properties of these things. . . . the products of the human brain appear as autonomous figures endowed with a life of their own, which enter into relations both with each other and with the human race" (*Capital* I, 164–65). Calls for and attempts at more experimental writing forms (most prominently, but not exclusively, in ethnographic writing) make a fetish of specific "experimental" textual forms as commodities having the power in themselves to accomplish valuable work. The diffident treatment of "error" by both those advocating writing as art and those advocating writing as technique also illustrates this fetish. Error is seen in itself as evidence of the writing's exchange or use value, forgetting that use values, including the use value of written forms designated as in error, "are only realized in use or in consumption" (Marx, *Capital* I, 126). A comma splice is only a comma splice when produced as such through a particular reading, enacted to achieve a particular aim, as Joseph Williams demonstrated some time ago ("Phenomenology").

Two strategies for teaching authority in writing exemplify the limitations in these perspectives. The aim of these is to address the disparity between Authors and student writers and the resulting disparagement of students, one by teaching students to produce texts that enact conventions for establishing rhetorical authority, the second by having students produce texts that break from conventions of writing. What links both, however, is their identification of Authorship with (objectified) texts that students are then expected to produce. As Ann M. Penrose and Cheryl Geisler, for example, have observed, some of the pedagogies aimed at "teaching towards authority" engage students in the rhetorical analysis of texts to learn strategies they can then use in their own writing (517). However, as they and others acknowledge, authority in writing in fact seems to have much more to do with "a number of complex variables": age, gender, and perhaps most powerfully, schools' teaching about authority (Penrose and Geisler 507). As Stuart Greene has also observed, while most studies of authorship focus on the formal structures of texts or individuals' writing processes, "authorship is a *relational* term that calls attention to the fact that writers are always situated within a broad sociocultural landscape" (213, my emphasis). Pedagogies aiming to teach students to achieve "authority" through adopting strategies found in already authorized texts sidestep the social relations inherent in the authorizing of those texts while attempting to assimilate students to conventional textual representations of authority. They thus perpetuate the commodification of the work of writing by identifying its significance as an objective property of the text.

Pedagogies encouraging students to break from such conventions, while avoiding this assimilationist move, nonetheless risk a similar commodification of the work of writing, locating it in novel text-objects which students are then encouraged to produce. I take calls for such textual experimentation to be aimed at exploring the tension felt in practical consciousness "between the received interpretation and practical experience," the "experiences to which the fixed forms do not speak at all, which indeed they do not recognize" (Williams, *Marxism* 130). Lillian Bridwell-Bowles suggests this aim when she observes that "students may need new options for writing if they, too, are struggling with expressing concepts, attitudes, and beliefs that do not fit into traditional academic forms" ("Discourse" 350). She describes courses in which she engages students in considering and producing various writings about, and illustrating, difference in language. Nonetheless, she remains skeptical, and reports skepticism among her students, concerning the value of "simply changing the surface of our academic language" ("Discourse" 350; Bridwell-Bowles's course does not require, only encourages, students to engage in experimental writing). She reads her students' skepticism to speak to their fear that their experiments with writing will lack currency outside her course, that they need to master conventional writing for academic survival, if not "success" ("Discourse" 351, 361). That is to say, her students worry about the lack of economic capital accorded experimental writing. But I would suggest that another cause for skepticism is that courses in "experimental," different writing are equally complicit in identifying the significance of the work of writing with written forms in and of themselves rather than with material social practices and conditions. In other words, students' experiments with discourse conventions need to be placed in the context of the larger social power relations within which any such experiments might take place. It is perhaps telling that Bridwell-Bowles' experimental writing courses appear to be restricted to the graduate and advanced undergraduate level ("Freedom" 56). It may well be that her students' breaks with conventions of writing are effectively "contained" by being so situated, just as her own breaks with convention in her writing may speak primarily to her present professional status, representing more a luxury she can now afford, as she herself suggests ("Discourse" 366). In such cases, the "novelty" of the writing reinforces, rather than working against, social relations in which writing represents a commodity, carrying cultural capital, both drawing on and adding to the status of the product and its "producer."

I don't mean here to dismiss attempts to teach students either to learn the rhetorical gestures that can help establish a writer's authority or to experiment with discourse conventions, but to argue that such attempts need to be part of a larger strategy in which "authorship" and the work of writing are investigated as socially, historically mediated. As Williams warns, we should look "not for the components of a product but for the conditions of a practice" (*Problems* 48). This is somewhat different from Penrose and Geisler's recommendation to "create a context in which students see themselves as authors, reading and writing alongside other authors in the development of community knowledge and norms. . . . helping students see themselves as insiders" (518). The aims of such recommendations are impressive—both to demystify a sense of authors as unquestionable sources of truth and to allow students to learn to make good use of their own experiences to contribute meaningfully to "textual conversations." But efforts to achieve such aims risk lapsing into bracketing the work of the classroom from the social and re-inscribing the status quo of the "author." These efforts do so by naming *as* the social a uniform official view of the classroom, unless they are accompanied by students' critique of the conditions of the various practices by which that—and other—types of "authorship" are socially produced and the work of writing commodified, as well as by critiques of the conditions and practices responsible for the production of its opposite, the "student writer" and the commodification of "writing skills."

Scholarship on Writing as Writing

The commodification of writing that obtains through pedagogical strategies that restrict their focus to following or breaking from formal written conventions has its parallel in debate over the production of Composition scholarship. In chapter 1, I have critiqued the identification of academic work outside the realm of ongoing, everyday material life in disembodied texts: journal essays, research reports, books, or, more specifically, in the arguments distributed by these material artifacts. It is this same understanding of work as commodity that limits debate over theory and research in Composition scholarship.

This is, perhaps, most evident in the refusal to recognize the material conditions making possible the work of conventional theory and research. As A. Suresh Canagarajah has observed, while scholars have long recognized the "sociality" of scholarly "knowledge-production," they have typically ignored the material constraints on such production—what he terms its "nondiscursive" requirements. So, for example, in a recent study of "Novelty in Academic Writing," David Kaufer and Cheryl Geisler, drawing on a rich literature in the sociology of scientific discourse, emphasize that "novelty" in academic writing is "less a property of ideas than a relationship between ideas and communities": "cutting edge" thus "depends as much on [a discipline's] social organization as on where any particular individual would like to position it" (288). To produce novelty, they argue, authors must have "mastered a set of tacit practices and conventions that enable them to 'use' the past in order to transcend it"; there must be a market for their innovations; and they must use social networks and read literature to develop an acceptable synthesis of "what everyone knows" (288, 289, 290). Drawing on his own experience and that of other non-Western scholars, Canagarajah, by contrast, while not disputing such arguments, notes that they ignore the "nondiscursive" requirements and conventions of knowledge-making. These include, but are not limited to, requirements of access to scholarly books and journals and a community of scholars familiar with these; access to "conventional" word-processing technology, including photocopying machines, quality paper, computer hardware and software, and fresh typewriter ribbon; reliable communication facilities, including

access to electric power, telephone, fax, and electronic and (affordable) surface mail service; (political and material) freedom to travel;
and quiet, stable, peaceful living and working conditions supportive
of scholarship. Lack of the ability to meet these "nondiscursive" requirements makes it difficult for scholars to materially produce,
send, and have their writing read by journals and publishers (451).
Moreover, Canagarajah notes, these "nondiscursive" requirements
also affect "discursive" requirements of academic publishing, in
terms of the conventionally understood "manifest content" of their
writing. For example, because scholars on the geopolitical "periphery" often lack access to both past and more recent scholarly literature, their writing may well sound like "old news," and their ability
to produce an acceptable "review of the literature" standard in
many scholarly publications may well be hampered (448). Thus
they are less able to produce the "new," defined as what is recognizable as new within and by the scholarly community (Kaufer and
Geisler 289, 293).

   While Cangarajah's argument is directed primarily to the difficulties posed for "Third World" or "periphery" scholars, he notes
that his arguments "are applicable as well to the periphery within
the center: the marginalized communities and poorly facilitated institutions in the technologically advanced nations that might also
face [similar] disadvantages" (447). Interestingly, however, the pervasive idealization of academic scholarship prevents even those
within such communities from recognizing, and so from addressing,
the material obstacles to their participation in scholarly practices
and communities. For example, in their introduction to *Writing
Ourselves into the Story: Unheard Voices from Composition Studies*,
a collection designed explicitly to include voices commonly "unheard" in Composition, Sheryl Fontaine and Susan Hunter define
the barriers to including such voices almost exclusively in terms of
the control exercised by dominant voices over the themes and discursive conventions of writing. They critique a contradiction between prominent claims of the field's commitment to multivocality
and the limitations set on the field's discourse through such practices as defining a specific theme for the annual Conference on
College Composition and Communication, the valuing of particular
kinds of research and pedagogies over others, editorial policies
defining the content and form of journal essays, and the pursuit of

the "new" at the expense of established knowledge (6–9). As evidence of the exclusionary effects of these practices, they note the small percentage of the field's membership represented by the authorship of published essays and the lopsided (over two to one) ratio of male to female authors in scholarly journals (7–8).

But while these practices indisputably limit scholarly discourse in Composition, it would also seem to be the case that *non*-discursive requirements, of the sort Canagarajah details, pose far more serious restrictions to entering that discourse.[3] It is just this neglect of the power of such requirements, attributable to a denial of the materiality of scholarly writing, that accounts for how Fontaine and Hunter can express wonder "why more two-year college faculty did not respond, why ethnic voices are so conspicuously absent" from the numbers of those who did answer their call for submissions to their collection, a collection explicitly aimed at giving voice to those typically "unheard" (11–12). Imagining the discourse community of Composition in abstract terms ignores the ways in which, as Canagarajah observes, material conditions shape the knowledge construction activities of disciplinary communities (445). Valorizing the place of language and discourse in knowledge production, in poststructuralist/postmodernist fashion, either elides such conditions entirely or "collapse[s] [them] into language/discourse," with the consequence that their power operates all the more powerfully because unobserved (Canagarajah 445, 439).[4]

This commodified view of scholarship provides a different perspective from which to understand the theory/practice debate. The work of theory, or, better, "theorizing," is not typically imagined as material practice but as commodity whose properties reside in the "theory" itself, understood as existing outside the material realm. As a consequence of adopting this idealized conception of theory, theorists can account for readers' difficulties with theory only in terms of the readers' willful resistance or pathology: theory "phobia" or a knee-jerk, anti-intellectual, antitheory posture (see Lu and Horner, "Problematic" 267–68). This perspective neglects the specific material conditions necessary for carrying out the work of understanding as well as producing theoretical texts, such as time, quiet, access to texts, training (cf. Canagarajah). Instead, the work of theory is seen not as theorizing—that is, as involving specific material social relations of production, distribution, and consumption of writing—but as commodity: a theory, opposed or accepted, current (and thus possessing "currency") or past (and therefore lacking value). Postmodern critiques of theory, while insisting on the necessity for self-reflexivity on the theorist's discursive position, have not extended that call to include reflexivity on the theorist's material social position (cf. Faigley 111–12).

In an attempt to resolve the theory/practice debate, it is sometimes argued that theory is, after all, endemic, residing even in "practice" (cf. Dobrin 9–10). And indeed, I have argued throughout previous chapters that in work "practice" workers regularly theorize: they develop and possess a "working knowledge" about their work that both guides and enables their practice. Recognizing such theorizing, however, does not in itself resolve the theory/practice debate, so long as it overlooks the material differences in what is produced and processes of capitalizing on those products: a book articulating a theory, say, versus no document, and no recognized theory (workers' "working knowledge" typically going unrecognized by both the workers and those studying them). Those who do grant such material differences to the product use them to denigrate the latter as not true knowledge or theory. In either case, however, the full material social process of the work of theorizing is elided; in the first strategy, by equating the two very different material practices of writing theory and developing working knowledge; in the latter, by ignoring the differences in the material conditions that would account for differences in the theories produced and the different forms of their distribution and consumption. "Theory," in other words, remains a commodity whose value is divorced from the conditions of its production and reception.

This commodified view of theory dominates arguments concerning the use of theory in Composition. In Sidney Dobrin's review of that debate, he notes the common criticism leveled by the "antitheory" position that theory, or at least the theories being critiqued, have no use for Composition practitioners (17–24). That is to say, it has no use value in, say, helping practitioners understand their students' writing or how to address that writing. Instead, these critics charge, the theories have only exchange value as cultural capital for the theorists. Thus Hairston complains about articles "that are larded with the fashionable names and terms but which, in my opinion, seek more to serve the ambitions of the authors than the needs of the readers" ("Comment" 696; quoted in Dobrin 18). These critics attribute to a desire for accruing cultural capital the opacity of much of the language used in theory, criticizing it as exclusionary, meaningless, and arrogant in its implications. Or, put more mildly, the pursuit of theory in Composition is viewed as reflecting the reigning zeitgeist, as when Lester Faigley suggests, "The quick-changing fashions of thought within composition studies and the continuous searching for new discourses about writing and ways of representing writing might be considered as part of a postmodern sensibility that delights in ephemerality and the commodification of culture" (16).

In response, defenders of theory argue that often theory does have implications for use in the classroom, that the insistence that all theory must be of direct use to teaching practitioners ties Composition unduly to its service role, or that theory for theory's sake is in itself valuable, if not directly for teaching, then to the "discipline" (Dobrin 28, 63–64). More specifically, the seeming opacity of much theoretical discourse, the defenders argue, does not inhere in the discourse but in the relation of the reader to that discourse. For example, the term "prewriting," Dobrin observes, is of great use to those in Composition despite its status as jargon for laypersons (23). That is to say, the use value of "jargon" terms does not inhere in the terms themselves but in their use, and thus cannot be assessed through scrutiny of the terms themselves, as commodities. The same argument, however, must be made of theory generally. The use value of "theory," or, better, a theory, resides not in "theory" itself or even a theory itself but in the material social practices with it. Further, and following this, the exchange value of a theory does not exhaust its potential, any more than its use value in a given situation exhausts its full use value nor prevents its susceptibility to commodification.

This same understanding of value must be applied to practitioner work. The dismissal of Composition's service function in defenses of theory betrays theorists' own blindness to the use value of practitioner work for both theorists of writing and for the practitioners and students themselves. That is, if the anti-theorists tend to see only the exchange value of theory, and not its potential use value, theorists tend to see only the exchange value of "service" work and not its use value: they recognize only its reification into commodified writing skills realized as economic capital (in the "service" economy). However real such exchange value may be, service work may also possess use value for students and teachers in helping them think through and address, by means of their writing, immediate issues confronting them. Further, this blindness among theorists is particularly galling given the needs of many practitioners, and their students, for the capitalization of their work to ensure their material survival, needs that are met "silently" for many theorists through their institutional positions (in which cultural capital is exchanged for economic capital). Ignoring the use value of practitioner work for the teachers and students, and recognizing only its exchange value, theorists denigrate pursuit of that exchange value, in a classically classist manner made possible by their own class position. In the process, they return the anti-theorists' treatment of theory as commodity by treating practitioner work as itself a commodity.

In chapter 3 I argued that power in pedagogy, rather than being understood as reified monolith, has to be understood as contingent and relational. In the same way, here I would argue that we need to understand the work and value of our scholarly writing as equally contingent and relational. Such an understanding does not absolve writers (or readers) of responsibility for work but changes the specific kind of responsibility they can and should take. Locating the work of scholarly writing in the full material social process may better enable writers and readers to address questions of the specific kinds of work specific kinds of writing can do, under what conditions, for whom, and how.

These questions have been addressed most explicitly in debate over the form and use of critical ethnographic work. Critical ethnography has attracted compositionists because of its attention to issues of textual representation of experience, its concern to honor the interests of research "informants," and its commitment to intervention in the lived experience of those represented in the process of ethnographic work. Such concerns and commitments link it to many compositionists' own commitments to exploring the relation of writing to experience, to enacting participatory democratic relations with students, and to using pedagogy as a site for social emancipation (Lu and Horner 257–58, 264–65). Taken together, however, these commitments pose a dilemma. As Roger Simon and Donald

Dippo warn, there is a contradiction between critical ethnography's aims of social emancipation, democratic participation and challenges to conventional representations of experience, on the one hand, and the exclusionary effects of some of its discursive forms:

> the [ethnographic] work must find ways of communicating that do not simply reaffirm old "ways of seeing"; it must challenge the very foundations of our experience of ourselves yet be understandable and sensible. . . . Yet to challenge familiar assumptions and values through a discourse which, to be understood, is compelled to reproduce in its very content and organization the assumptions and values of the discourse itself, presents enormous difficulty. . . . To challenge common sense is at times to challenge the syntax and semantics of common sense, remembering when we do we always run the risk of speaking to ourselves. (200)

This dilemma has led to both calls for and the production of new textual forms. For example, Ruth Solsken, observing that "poststructuralist perspectives call for a new kind of multivocal dialogue in which differences are not resolved but problematized, and in which ambivalence and open-endedness are more valued than closure and coherence," calls for the creation of "spaces for deliberate experimentation and reflection, among them spaces where we can tell stories and reflect on our stories" (320–21). Michael Kleine, arguing for a radical critique of ethnographic discourse, says we must "allow ourselves to write even more in the first-person singular, to write personal diaries—even confessions—about our experiences as ethnographers," and that these might even "supplant formal academic articles for awhile" (124). Linda Brodkey calls for the writing of "critical ethnographic narratives" in which narrators' "self-consciousness about ideology makes it necessary for them to point out that all stories, including their own, are told from a vantage point, and to call attention to the voice in which the story is being told" ("Writing Critical" 71). And Gesa Kirsch and Joy Ritchie encourage researchers to "allow multiple voices to emerge in their research studies, an act that will require innovation in writing research reports" (19). In response, a host of experiments with new forms of writing and reporting research have appeared (see Kirsch 191–93).

However, innovative, experimental texts, at least for ethnographers of education, confront a stumbling block. In an essay on the place of ethnography in research on writing, Ralph Cintron, like Solsken, Kleine, Brodkey, and others, acknowledges that "the new ethnography, in keeping with postmodernist fragmentation and scepticism, can no longer convincingly present a whole or 'totalizing' portrait of a given culture. Rather, it should attempt a multiplicity of interpretations" (378). But, similarly to Simon and Dippo, he concludes that the "pragmatic needs of education . . . inhibit ethnographic experimentation" (401). As he explains,

> Teachers, principals, school boards, government agencies, the public, and even the media want to know what the language situation is and how to deal with it. . . . how well their programs are working or how well their money is being spent. To a significant degree, then, the audience for writing research imposes on researchers a normative discourse that lacks elasticity. The result is that textual experimentation is confined to those ethnographies that have the luxury to experiment. Such writers need not answer to institutions that are significantly controlled by "bottom-line" economics. (401; see also Kirsch 197)

What is striking here is that those difficulties to which Cintron and others point arise precisely when the work of ethnography is located wholly or primarily in the (published) research text aimed at fellow researchers and, particularly for Cintron, policy makers. Without discounting such difficulties and the importance of overcoming them, I would urge that these may better be addressed by rethinking the location the work of ethnography. Teacher-researchers have observed that whereas traditional research identifies its "results" with the published text, at least some of the results of their work can more readily be identified with the process of conducting the research (Bissex 14). The use value of the research, in other words, is realized as it is consumed in the conduct of the research; the research report, at least to the teachers, is often of secondary importance. This is not to deny the potential use value, for others, of the published research text but to recognize the contingency of its use value: the whole range and complexity of its use value, contingent on specific material social circumstances. And it is to put a different kind of pressure on the work of writing such texts. Of new textual practices in writing and reporting research, Kirsch has recently warned,

> They can disguise writers' continuing authorial control, they can fail to provide the theoretical framework and cultural context necessary for understanding the multiple voices emerging in a single text, they make new and difficult demands on readers, they require tolerance for ambiguity and contradictory claims, and they easily become elitist and exclusionary. (193–94)

I am arguing, indeed, that these effects result not simply from these specific textual forms but from the commodified view of the work of ethnography impelling the use of such forms. In effect, the pressures placed on the writing result from asking too much of it, which comes from imagining characteristics of ethnographic work to reside as objective properties of the (commodified) ethnographic text. The identification of the character of ethnographic work in terms of its textual features distances that work from the specificities of ethnography as material social practice. It can thus lead to attempts to substitute complexities of textual notation for the complexities of the experience of face-to-face encounters. This puts undue pressure on the work of writing while putting at risk the writing's critical social effectivity by reinforcing hierarchical social relations that critical ethnography is explicitly committed to altering. This then invites criticisms of elitism similar to those lodged against "theory." The production of an "open" text, for example, assumes a disposition of detachment from material necessity that permits the valuing of form over use, including the "elementary" use of writing for "representing, signifying, saying something" (Bourdieu, *Distinction* 3).

Alternatively, the experiences of those engaged in teacher-research suggest that, indeed, some, perhaps much, of the work of such research may not take form in published texts but rather will be located at the research site of the classroom, in the consciousness and pedagogical and reading and writing practices of those living at the "site." If we locate that work in such practices, then innovations in published textualizations of that work could be directed not only at problematizing representation but at producing not multivocal but multiple texts: different texts doing different work, used differently, by different types of readers, reading under different circumstances. Innovative work would be located not simply in texts but in practices, both textual and non-textual. This might lead to less confusion of innovative textual forms with innovative practice. The "community literacy" projects described by Wayne Peck, Linda Flower, and Lorraine Higgins, discussed in chapter 2, are suggestive in this regard. In pursuing specific projects, such as addressing high-school suspension policies or landlord/tenant disputes, project participants produced a variety of texts focused not simply on representation but on action. Some of the texts produced, drawing on an array of other texts and different discourses, led to the construction of hybrid, "intercultural" discourses (Peck et al. 209–13). But the "difference" between these texts and those following the conventions of academic discourse or the "home" discourses of the participants was valued not in and of itself, for its "hybridity," but in terms of the "difference" it made in the life and lives of the community: that is, for its specific use to them (220–21).

Teaching Writing, and the Teaching of Writing, as Material Social Practice

If, as seems inarguable, the subject of a writing course is writing, then writing must be understood as material social practice; further, I am arguing, so must the writing course and writing in and for Composition. It is by treating the writing course as material social practice that writing can itself be taught as such. Part of treating writing and the teaching of writing in this way will, of course, involve confronting dominant tropes for writing and its teaching, including the views of writing critiqued above. First and foremost among these is the view of writing as commodity divorced from the conditions of its production and use, for that view is concomitant with the trope of literacy as mark of civilization, culture, intelligence, even full humanity (see Brodkey, "Tropics"). It renders writing (and the writer) autonomous, literacy an attribute residing objectively in the writing (or writer) rather than in material social relations. The teaching of writing, insofar as it calls attention, explicitly or implicitly, to the material production of writers and writing, and so to the material contingencies of "civilization," challenges dominant identifications of class, race, ethnic, and gender differences as natural (cf. Bourdieu, *Distinction* 67–69). And hence, for example, to stifle that challenge, the longstanding dominant trope of writing as marker of racial difference, illiteracy used as evidence of black inferiority, literacy instruction forbidden to slaves, literacy used by blacks in an attempt to acquire social capital (see Gates 1–15).

Teaching writing, and the teaching of writing, as material social practice would involve teaching the contingent nature of the specific exchange and use values of those activities. I am not suggesting a course in which the teacher lectures students on the sociology of literacy, enlightening them about the commodification of writing and contingencies in the capitalization of literacy, demystifying the ideology of Authorship, and so on. While, as should be obvious, I see value in studying the sociology of literacy and these topics in particular, I do not recommend such a pedagogy for a writing course. This is not because I think students in such courses are unprepared to understand such subjects but because such subjects are better addressed through enabling students to articulate the practical consciousness of such matters they have that they can explore in and through their writing in a writing course.

As a way of suggesting what this can involve, I want to look at some student writing. My aim is not to offer testimony to the efficaciousness of my teaching or, worse, a teaching method understood transhistorically, but to locate the argument I have been presenting in the experience of the work in which my students and I have been engaging in first-year writing courses. Below, for example, is a collation of the original and revised version of a student text. The text was written in response to an assignment asking students to make sense of the relationship between Paulo Freire's arguments regarding "banking" versus "problem-posing" education and Freire's writing style.[5] I had hoped the assignment would draw students' attention to the effect of style. By shifting their focus away from the manifest "content" of writing—the "thesis" of an argument, its "main points," or the facts it conveyed—I wanted them to consider the politics of stylistic stance. That is, I see in hindsight, I was encouraging students to adopt an "aesthetic disposition" to writing focused on the significance of reified form. Since Freire's analysis focuses not on the "content" of teaching but on pedagogical style, it seemed especially appropriate, in a writing course, to have students adopt a similar focus on the "pedagogical" style of Freire's writing. Indeed, such a focus is one I have commonly aimed at encouraging in students in my writing courses as one appropriate to the "subject" of writing. It is useful in moving students away from questions about the veracity or sincerity of what's said in their writing to questions about how it is constructed and the meaning of its stylistic construction. Further, by directing students to analyze the style of Freire's writing, I wanted not only to encourage such a focus on style, but also to demystify Authorship and demonstrate the relevance of such a focus for all writers and writing.

In response, I received the following paper and revision (plain text appeared in both versions, italicized text only in the original, underlined text only in the revision, and bracketed text moved from one place in the original to another in the revision):

In Paulo Freire's essay "The 'Banking' Concept of Education," he discusses the "evils" of educating the oppressive "banking" way. By stating his opinions, Freire examines the two methods of education: the "banking" way and the "problem-posing" method. Freire attempts to teach the reader about his principles of education in a format that at moments seems to contradict his ideas about education. While trying to teach about his concepts of education, his writing style itself can appear to be going against his own beliefs. Yet, on a more in-depth examination of the writing, Freire's format could actually help to prove his point.

When first reading through Freire's essay, I could only see his writing style as narrative and static. *Yet his writing style can only be seen as narrative and static in my opinion.* Freire simply writes his opinion and never once questions his beliefs. Instead of having a "conversation" with the reader, Freire sits the reader down and tells them how it is, how it should be, and what the reader needs to do to correct it. For example, with statements like "Education must begin with the solution of the teacher-student contradiction" (208), Freire tells the reader the definition of the teacher-student contradiction and then proceeds to tell the solution. Like the educational style he opposes, his writing seems to be "an act of depositing" (208).

At the same time, however, Paulo Freire's writings and ideas do indeed challenge us. His opinions make the reader reconsider their own beliefs held about education. In this way, I believe the writing could be stretched to be considered "liberatory" writing. Since his ideas about education are so revolutionary and going against the typical grain of thought, his writing does pose the reader a problem. [See * below]

Paulo Freire writes that banking education attempts "to conceal certain facts" (216). Yet this is exactly what he appears to do in his essay. He does not tell the entire story: he leaves out the pros and tells only the cons of banking education. We are told that only the "oppressors" use the banking concept and that the "liberators" use the problem-posing technique. *He writes about how writing must be liberatory, and that "one does not liberate men by alienating them.* Authentic liberation—the process of humanization—is not another deposit to be made in men" (213). Ironically, this is exactly what Freire seems to be doing in his writing—depositing his ideas in the reader.

Instead of allowing for a partnership between writer and reader, Freire often appears to force *forces* his opinions on what he seems to consider *considers* the "ignorent" readers. Freire tells the reader what he or she "must" do and "cannot" do. *The solution may not be "found in the banking concept" (209), like Freire says, but the solution is definitely not found in his writings. The solution can only be found in a problem-posing environment that allows the reader to learn and doesn't impose another person's viewpoints on them.*

However, in an essay such as Freire's, I have found it is difficult to write in a format other than banking. A writer can only state what he knows or believes and let the reader decide for themself whether or not to believe it. Freire's only problem is that he doesn't question his ideas, but constently asserts them as facts. By using direct statements like he does, Freire seems to consider every thought he's ever had as an obvious fact. Instead of offering his opinions as an interpretation of what he sees, he offers them solely as truths. He forcefully insists to the reader that his interpretation is correct and never once mentions that his ideas are nothing but opinions. Everything Freire writes appears to be opinion, for he never mentions any personal experience with banking or problem-posing education. Never does Freire say that he has found what he thinks to be true because of past experiences. Never does he have any personal examples that would back up what he writes. For example, his opening paragraph is not about his horrible confrontations with banking education as a kid, but a series of statements telling the reader what to believe. Freire's introductory sentence starts out, "A care analysis of the teacher-student relationship . . ." (207); this is what Freire's entire essay seems to be based on, his critical, opinionated "analysis."

One could argue that Freire's banking format is necessary to state his "revolutionary" problem-posing ideas. Yet, according to Freire himself, "Those truly committed to liberation must reject the banking concept in its entirety" (213). The "educational goal of deposit-making" must be, says Freire, abandoned entirely for one to intelligently educate. Therefore, even if his ideas are liberatory, using the banking format to present them would be contradictory.

[*At the same time, however, Paulo Freire's ideas should indeed challenge most readers. His opinions make the reader reconsider their own beliefs about education. Since Freire's ideas are so revolutionary, they pose the reader a problem.] Yet Freire's ideas are only revolutionary if the reader does not already see the educational system as Freire does. Freire's ideas can only be considered problem-posing if they are different enough to make the reader reconsider his own beliefs about education. In the context of now, I believe his ideas are revolutionary enough to be considered problem-posing. However, every reader is different—if Freire's ideas do not strike the reader as challenging then he has failed in his quest to educate the reader in a liberatory style.

Freire states that as students in a problem-posing environment are posed with problems, they will feel "increasingly challenged and obliged to respond to that challenge. . . . Their response to the challenge evokes new challenges, followed by

new understandings" (215). This is what I believe Freire was
going for in his essay. When reading it, I felt challenged and
did respond; as a result, I found I had a better understanding
about education. Like the problem-posing method he talks
about, Freire's essay seems to strive for the "emergence of consciousness" (215) in the reader. In this way, his writing can be
considered "liberatory." By stating that "Liberating education
consists in acts of cognition, not transferrals of information"
(214), I believe Freire is telling the reader to think about his
ideas: Freire doesn't want the reader to simply accept his
viewpoints on education, he wants to be challenged back. He
wants us to participate in stimulating thought and definately
succeeds; he "liberates" us in our learning. Although Freire's
writing style appears to be narrative and static, I believe that
his ideas clearly challenge most readers and invite the readers
to challenge them back. Freire states that "the role of the
problem-posing educator is to create, together with the students, the conditions under which knowledge at the level of
the doxa is superseded by true knowledge, at the level of the
logos" (215). And this is exactly what Freire does. Through his
writings, he creates a healthy, stimulating environment in
which knowledge can be learned.

When I received the revised version of this paper, I was impressed
not just by the amount of work the student had invested in the revision, illustrated most concretely by the additions of the underlined passages, but by the student's reformulation of the issue of
the relation of writing style to its effect posed by the assignment. In
an argument that informs the one I have been advancing here, the
student distinguishes effect from style, redefining effect in terms of
historical contingencies. This is not what I had expected.

In the original, the student did indeed overcome any compunc-
tion about criticizing Freire he may have had, despite Freire's certifiable Authorship. (I have found many students in fact relish the
opportunity to engage in such criticism.) While the student accepts
the limitations of the "banking" style of education, he also rejects
Freire's writing for its enactment of the same style: the "solution,"
he concludes, "is definitely not found in [Freire's] writings." There
is a kind of glee being taken here at the irony, or what students

have sometimes described as the "hypocrisy," of Author Freire being caught at what he criticizes others for doing: banking, depositing his ideas into readers. And it is that irony I had hoped students would discover through their analysis.

In the student's revision, however, he foregoes these pleasures for a different one: the pleasure of offering and enacting a different theory about how writing works. Specifically, rather than settling for deciding whether Freire's writing style is banking or liberatory, he concludes that the effect depends on the context of readers' beliefs about education when reading Freire. In the context of "now," he says, Freire's ideas "are revolutionary enough to be considered problem-posing." That same view of the significance of context leads not only to the student's criticisms of Freire's failures to locate his own theorizing in the context of his experiences but also to adding references to passages in Freire that, to the student, have led him to his interpretations of Freire (as in the additions to the second and fourth paragraphs, and in the student's references to his own writing experiences at the opening to the long underlined section that concludes the paper, and to his experience of finding Freire challenging, in the final added paragraph). In other words, Freire's theory on banking versus liberatory pedagogy, as constructed by the student, has had use value for the student realized through the perspective it provides for his understanding both of Freire's writing and his own writing practice, informing and changing what and how he writes. As the student explained in a paper reviewing his work for the course, "Freire's writing had an impact on me: by reading and writing about Freire, I constructed a new writing style" (see appendix B). He was thus engaged in what Judith Goleman terms the necessary *"double activities* of 'learning about' and 'making something of' " knowledge to achieve and maintain critical consciousness (72, 73).

We can understand the student's qualification of taking his position in the context of "now" as a useful perspective with which to view not only the work of Freire's writing but the student's work, the work of the paper for the class, and for understanding my work on it subsequently. The student's analysis suggests that the value of Freire's text does not reside in properties located objectively in the text, understood outside the realm of material social practice: that is, as a "deposit," in Freire's terms, though Freire's text is certainly susceptible to commodification. (This is a perspective with which Freire, I think, would agree.) If we apply this perspective to the student's text(s), this means, however, that, similarly, the value of the student's text resides not in itself, as an "impressive" (or flawed) work, but in the use made of it for the writer (in the context of "now"), fellow students reading it, me as teacher of that course, and now for my writing of the present text. This perspective does not preclude the commodification of the student's writing. At the very least, it contributed to his acquisition of academic credits and his grade point average, presumably to be exchanged subsequently for employment opportunities, a wage or salary, and so on. And within the (largely underground) status economy of the classroom, my "publishing" his text, in the format presented above, for discussion presumably led to his acquisition of some kind of social capital. But if work carries both potential use and exchange value, its commodification does not preclude its use value. Any likely capitalization of the student's work did not eliminate its uses for the student, described above, or for others.[6]

How does this apply to the use made of these texts in the course? To some readers the most salient feature of the revision may be that it fails to conform to a dominant view of revision as "cleaning up" matters of "form" at the sentence and larger levels. The word "ignorent" remains misspelled in both versions, for example. More importantly, in moving from the original to the revision, the writer retains much of the perspective on Freire's style as ironically "banking" that obtained in the original, rather than replacing the presentation of that perspective with the alternative perspective for which he argues in the long, underlined section added to the end, especially the final two paragraphs. This feature troubled the student's peers in our discussion of the revision. They objected that the paper was confusing, and argued that the writer ought to have made up his mind whether Freire's style was liberating or banking, rather than being "wishy-washy." In a debate closely paralleling the student discussion of a paper described in chapter 2, student demands for the paper conflicted with my own desire to hold up the revision as a model for what the other students could do, showing the daring of a writer for breaking with conventional expectations for revisions and risking the loss of a clear and coherent argument for the sake of better understanding the issues raised by the assignment. And student demands conflicted with my excitement about the argument I saw the writer making, an excitement I wanted to share with the students. In other words, some of the very features of the paper to which students objected were those that had impressed me.

From the perspective of the argument I have been making in this chapter, however, both the students and teacher were, to borrow a phrase from the student paper presented in chapter 2, "both right in their opinions, but at same time also wrong." Students were, and always are, acutely aware of the potential exchange value of any student writing and its conversion to capital. But my sense of the pervasiveness of their concern with that value blinded me to the use value that they also sought from the paper, one that, for them, given their reading practices and histories, would have been increased by the writer's clarification of his argument. Students were also acutely aware of the labor demands required in producing the kind of revision represented by the paper, demands to which I, as reader and not writer, was relatively indifferent. I could afford, in other words, to adopt an "aesthetic" disposition toward the writing that they could not. And that disposition led me to neglect the conditions and means of its production. I was, in short, treating the revision as an exciting commodity.

Conversely, students might well see in the attributes of the paper I praised only their exchange value within the economy of the course, while neglecting its potential use value. There is plenty to support such a view. The course description, handed out to the students at the beginning of the term, explained what writing would be valued within the economy of the course. It told them to "think of the papers you write for this course as attempts not to present the 'final word' on the subject but as stages in an ongoing process of learning what can be said about the subject," on the assumption that "your writing is central to [the academic processes of interpretation and intellectual inquiry]." And it promised, or warned,

[T]he grade you earn for the course is intended to represent the degree of sophistication about writing and reading you achieve as a whole, not to represent a sum of quantified achievements. . . .

[Therefore] [i]n evaluating your own performance, it will be more useful for you to think of becoming a better writer and reader as a gradual process of becoming familiar with complexity rather than as a simple matter of a set of problems to be solved.

In an in-class written evaluation of his revision, the writer of the paper presented above describes his revision in just such terms (see appendix A). Citing phrases from the course description, he says that, in keeping with the stated design of the course, the challenges posed by Freire and his responses to them led him through a " 'process of interpretation and intellectual inquiry' " to re-evaluate his position on the " 'relationship between writing and learning, writing and knowledge,' " and to write a revision that is "much more sophisticated." Thus, in a familiar narrative of before/after transformation, he aligned his work in producing the revision with the official goals of the course, and, therefore, in terms that helped define its exchange value in the economy of grades.[7] Without discounting the exchange value of the paper within this economy, students' (and others') recognition of that value may have overshadowed the use value of the revision for the writer in understanding his writing, or, for that matter, its potential use value for others. That is, the revision's susceptibility to commodification does not exhaust its use value. In the writer's final paper for the course, he attests to the use value of both the "new" style of writing evinced in his revision and a more traditional style (see appendix B). While the "new," "open-minded" writing style, he says, "allowed for much more interaction between reader and writer," "[i]f I needed [to] make my opinions clear to the reader and my ideas were considered challenging or problem-posing enough to strike the reader as revolutionary in the context of when I was writing it, I would opt for a more direct style of writing, similar to that of Freire or Adrienne Rich [in "When We Dead Awaken"]." While he describes these in terms of "success," success here means not simply what will "sell" within either the economy of the course or the more general political economy of writing, but also what will be more useful for given purposes, within given contexts.

The student's final evaluation points implicitly to a potential conflict between the use value and exchange value of writing both within the economy of the writing course and the larger economy of

writing. What seems necessary in teaching writing as material social practice is to confront this conflict in value directly. Thomas
Fox, in his account of a course in which students directly addressed
the relation of writing practice to class, race, and gender, argues
that to tap the potential of the classroom and school for social liberation, we need to practice a "double curriculum" addressing "both
the inequalities that exist outside the classroom and the effect
those inequalities have on literacy, *and* a concurrent focus on classroom activities and procedures" (*Social Uses* 116). While a focus on
the former may seem to threaten to transform the composition
course into a course on the sociology of literacy, and the latter to
transform it into a course on the politics of pedagogy, I would argue
that we may avoid those threats by focusing on students' writing as
the site where both sets of pressures get negotiated. Fox notes that
students and teachers "already [continually interpret and critique
the classroom as it evolves] all the time. . . . [b]ut especially in the
classroom, these activities are kept guardedly secret" (116). They
are kept secret because they conflict with the ideal images of
Studenthood and Teacherhood, in which, most obviously, both
teachers and students deny the pressure of grading and the pursuit
of grades in favor of a more flattering image of classroom work as
the disinterested pursuit of knowledge (Fox, *Social Uses* 46). The
assumptions driving this denial appear to be that the pursuit of one
inevitably cancels out the other, and that a "pure" pursuit of knowledge is possible, though only outside of material social contingencies (hence their presence is denied). That is, the institutional
structure, such as the course, is seen as militating against students'
and teachers' autonomous agency. The argument I have been advancing, however, is that we need to understand such pursuits as
enacted only through structures, whose effects are indeterminate.
If the dominant recognizes only the exchange value of classroom
work, we should not perpetuate that tendency by denying the potential use value of that work as well. And in fact, so long as the
only alternative to valuing that work for its economic capitalization
(as skills instruction, say) is seen as its aestheticization, we have
simply traded in one commodification of composition for another:
economic for cultural capital, skills for art.

Students (as well as teachers) appear to have a practical consciousness of the tension between the use and exchange value of

their work. As Fox points out, students and teachers already, albeit "secretly," address such matters. In class discussions of student papers, the tension produced by that conflict is always palpable, as arguments arise about what the teacher wants or what is, indeed, "good" writing. To teach composition and the composition course as material social practice means tapping that consciousness to investigate how to negotiate these in the work of writing and learning about writing. In terms of my argument, in *Social Uses of Writing*, Fox importantly emphasizes the need for students and teachers to explore how contingencies of social capital associated with gender, race, and class affect the exchange value of literacy. The emphasis I am urging, in what I believe to be complementary to his, is the need for students and teachers to explore the contingencies of economic and social capital associated with student, teacher, and, more broadly, academic identities for both the exchange and use value of specific writings, for students, teachers, schools, and larger social formations.

To put it another way, rather than using the composition course as an occasion for teaching culture, as some have argued, I am arguing that we use the course as an occasion to teach the culture of composition. If Fox has students investigate the impact of gender, race, and class on their reading and writing, I am advocating that we also have students investigate the impact that being students, in composition courses, has on their writing, including the impact of what Fox calls the ideology of Studenthood (9–10). For if examining one's experience of the social categories of race, gender, and class provides an opportunity for students to turn what is often viewed as a liability or disadvantage into a source of strength (Fox, *Social Uses* 21), so, too, examining the experience of the social categories of student, teacher, the composition course, and school can occasion resistance to dominant, limiting definitions of the potential use value to be produced within these institutional categories. That is, rather than attempting to extend the reach, or scope, of Composition and the composition course by naming as texts, or "compositions," the full range of cultural artifacts, and thus turning students' gaze outward from their position as students in a composition course, we may better use composition and the teaching of composition to focus on the cultural work of and in composition. In so doing, the subject of the writing course remains writing, which,

after all, through study and experience, writing teachers and scholars know best and in which they are invested, as writing teachers,
in continually re-investigating. Composition—the institution, the
course, the text, the practice—remains the site for the investigation
and revision of culture, as practiced in and through composition.

In chapter 2, I've described what it might mean to approach the work
of student writing as material social practice in which structure and
agency meet. That approach, we've seen, focuses not so much, or not
only, on the object produced in class—a student text and the readings
of it—but on the practices by which they are produced and the conditions of those practices, so that we may understand their conditionality. Here let me extend that argument by describing my
experience with teaching a first-year writing course aimed at enabling students and teachers to develop the potential hidden by dominant definitions of students, authors, teachers, and composition.[8]

In my attempts, I've focused the course explicitly on student/au-
thor relations and the role of conventions in reading and writing.
Many of the activities in which we've engaged have remained traditional—students read texts and wrote, revised and discussed papers about them in response to a sequence of assignments I
designed; I commented on their writing, gave them a grade at the
middle and the end of the term, and led class discussions. However,
I attempted to complicate their and my evaluation of these activities with a sense of their conditionality, foregrounded by continual
reflection on these evaluations and the roles to be played by individuals positioned within the institution of school and, more specifically, composition courses as students, teachers, and authors.

I've had students confront and attempt to counter the reading
practices producing both authorship and student writing by comparing their responses to unconventional published writing to their
responses to breaks with convention in the writing of their peers.
For example, asked to identify problems they've experienced with
Virginia Woolf's *A Room of One's Own*, my students have reported
difficulties making sense of her statements, apparent contradictions
in what she says, lack of transitions, and the relevance of various
details on which she focuses. They have frequently reported similar
difficulties when reading their fellow students' essays. Initially, how-

ever, they have accounted for those difficulties very differently. They explained the difficulties they have with Woolf in one of two ways: more commonly, they alluded to their own defects as readers—they were just freshmen, didn't know much about her references, have never encountered writing like Woolf's before, and haven't had a chance to give her writing the attention it so obviously deserves. Or alternatively, they have invoked unified but complex intentions ascribed to Woolf to account for the features of her writing that troubled them. Woolf's writing lacks transitions, for example, because, some students have explained, "It seems she is taking us through her day and gives thoughts on the different things she sees. The different things in the places [where] she was, brought about extra thoughts. They were not forced but brought about by surroundings."

On the other hand, students initially explained difficulties they had with their fellow students' writing primarily in terms of the student writers' lacks: lack of effort, thought, ability, understanding. Unlike Authors' breaks with convention, students' breaks with convention were typically seen as mistakes, evidence of one or more such lacks. In short, students' initial responses to Authorized and student writing—at least those student responses given official articulation in my classroom—have mirrored those that have been critiqued in Composition, representing the operation of the "author-function" in maintaining hierarchized relations between Authors and students, with the twist that students have come to see that they themselves participate in maintaining such relations, to their own apparent detriment (see Stygall).

The aim of having students compare their different ways of responding to the difficulties they experience with published and student writings is not to shame students for failing to grant authorial status to their peers or for being fulsome in their responses to published writings. I would not, for example, encourage students to use their difficulties reading Woolf as a reason to denounce her as an hysterical "illiterate" woman, nor would I encourage them to interpret every comma splice or lack of transition in their own writing as an act of political daring or artistic innovation. Rather, this confrontation is meant to lead to investigating the complex of immediate and ongoing material conditions of practices that produce the differences in responses and possible alternative conditions of practices—the various conditions of practices that produce the "student writer," "student writing," the "author" and "authored" writing, and alternatives to these. In the case of Woolf, this would involve having students both recognize the differences between how they have responded to their difficulties with Woolf and how they have responded to their difficulties with the writings of their peers, and the various conditions in which they find themselves—and Woolf— they as students in a first-year required composition class, Woolf as a writer featured in a required textbook (about whom even a play seems to have been written, some have reported), their writing reproduced anonymously on ditto sheets. And it would involve having them also investigate the practices to which those conditions have led them—for example, the kind of writing they've learned to produce—and the uses and limitations, under specific conditions, of continuing or resisting such practices.

What such investigations can do first and foremost is locate writing materially—for student writing, in the specifics of the students' lives, the classroom, the course, the institution, and ongoing immediate history, in the forces that seem to have led or required them to be enrolled in a college composition course in the first place. This has required no Marxist-inflected lecturing to students on the history of literacy and schools as the site for the reproduction of hegemonic discourse. Students have a practical consciousness of these matters; it is simply a consciousness all too rarely tapped. Such investigations can be the occasion for considering as well the "practical" matter of writing "process," here, however, considered not simply as either "successful" or "poor," the processes of "experts" versus the "inexperienced," but as integrally related to specific material conditions. Those same investigations can address the various practices by which such matters are obscured to produce a sense of "authorship" for writings by folks like Woolf: the status they acquire as required readings, the presentation of their writings in "finished" form in "readers," with admiring introductions, the questions students are encouraged to ask of these writings versus those they are encouraged to ask about their own writings; the canonizing effects generally of schools and the interests served by such effects. Their confrontation with Woolf's *A Room of One's Own* has a particularly ironic appositeness here, given the way in which those practices efface the material conditions enabling and constraining her writing of a text aimed at emphasizing just such conditions. While drawing attention to these practices risks simply impressing upon students the limitations of their positioning as student writers, it can also impress upon them the historicity, and therefore the malleability or conditionality, of that positioning and the positioning of Authors such as Woolf—and thus the possibility of working against the limitations and exploiting the strengths of both such positions, and so, in the process, transforming what it means to write and read as either a student or an author.

Secondly, investigating such conditions and practices can help combat the strong pressure among both students and teachers to reify the work of student writing even while acknowledging that pressure. It can do this by locating that work not as an objectified entity, in the text produced, but in the process of mediation. Williams notes that in considering the production of society itself, "the most important thing a worker ever produces is himself, himself in the fact of that kind of labour" (*Problems* 35). Writing is one site for such self (re)production: the place for the mediation of one's position, responding to and re-creating the context of its production. As Fox argues,

> Contexts . . . do not precede language, but are in part created by it. . . . Although . . . students' interpretation of the classroom context is not freely chosen, but influenced by the student's history, it does not follow that students, even with their shared histories, will necessarily interpret the context in the same way. Students construct and revise the classroom context through the continual interaction of teacher and student. (*Social Uses* 16)

An approach to writing as both a response to and creation of context by both writers and readers would not deny the powerful effects of social, historical and institutional positionings on the relations writers and readers produce but would reject the absoluteness with which those positionings determine meaning. In Fredric Jameson's words, "The literary . . . act . . . always entertains some active relationship with the Real. . . . [It] brings into being that very situation to which it is also, at one and the same time, a reaction. It articulates its own situation and textualizes it" (81, 82). Focusing attention on the work of student writing as the mediation of one's situation is one way of identifying that work as and with the conditions and practices of such mediation: the modes by which a writer articulates the situation to which the writing is simultaneously a reaction. I have attempted to make that an explicit focus of the course by sequencing assignments so that subsequent assignments have students revisit and revise the positions they have taken in earlier papers, explicitly experiment with different positions and discourse conventions, and reflect on the significance of these experiments. Further, I have had students address the articulations of situation represented in the course description, the texts of the assignments, and in my written and oral comments on their writing. In their revisitations and experiments, students have reacted to and revised their positioning as student writers vis-à-vis myself as teacher, other student readers, and the writing of published authors.

In the shifting mediation of a second student's relations as a student to writings of published authors and to his readers in the following excerpts, we can see the changing situation of the student himself and his "textualization" of that situation through the course of his experiences as a student:

Essay 7
In looking at the way Pratt and Fish conceive groups of people, I see somewhat different characteristics. It seems that Fish groups people in such a way that all members think and act in a similar fashion, whereas Pratt recognizes the presence of a contact zone in which the members clash and opinions do not generally coincide.

Essay 9
My writing as a student can be compared to the previous point. Just as Woolf was subordinate to men and had to change her style accordingly, I too, as a student, must change or at least be cautious in my writing. And this is hard to describe. Maybe I subconsciously feel that I can't come off as arrogant to professors or to more experienced writers. So I am cautious.

Essay 10 (revising Essay 7)
After reading the essays of Stanley Fish and Mary Louise Pratt and writing several essays of my own in response to

theirs, I have come to a conclusion about their ideas: Pratt makes sense and Fish does not. It's as simple as that. Now one might say, "[————], you're just a lowly English I student. You're in no position to determine such things." And to this, I would have to respond, "I beg to differ, my friend. I have discussed, analyzed, and written about these essayists to the extent of which I have appointed myself a certifiable expert on the matter." A bold statement?

For Essay 7, in which students were asked to use their experience as students to make better sense of the approaches Mary Louise Pratt (in "Arts of the Contact Zone") and Stanley Fish (in "How to Recognize a Poem When You See It") take to the significance of groupings of people, the student positions himself as a commenter outside the arena of debate simply describing, in fairly neutral fashion, what he sees as some characteristics distinguishing Fish's views from Pratt's. For Essay 9, in which students were asked to draw conclusions about what they might learn about writing in the contact zone from analyzing Woolf's writing in such terms, the student draws a correlation between the subordinate position of Woolf as a woman writer and his own as a student. This leads him to recognize that he feels, if only (until now) subconsciously, that he must be "cautious" in his style. It's unclear to him exactly how that caution manifests itself—it's "hard to describe." Interestingly, in writing about that caution he is, in a sense, less cautious. He is thus maintaining an "active relationship to the Real," both responding to and re-articulating—revising—that situation of being a student in a composition course reading the works of authors like Fish, Pratt, and Woolf. In Essay 10, in which students were asked to experiment with various conventions of writing associated with different social groups or genres of writing in revising an earlier paper, the student actively works against such cautiousness. He attempts, in spite of his admitted status as "just a lowly English I student," to speak more boldly about how he views the arguments of Fish and Pratt, and justifies his boldness on the basis of his changed situation of now having "discussed, analyzed, and written about these essayists" extensively. He thus redefines the context in which he writes, and so his position as a student writer.

Because the arrangement of these excerpts and the order in which they were written might suggest otherwise, I want to be clear that I am not arguing here for a narrative of a writer gradually learning, with just the right help from his inspiring teacher, to throw off the shackles of unjust "lowly English I" status and boldly take his rightful place as a keen judge of folks like Fish and Pratt, thus emerging as a true Author producing Essay 10, a product remarkable for its insights. Even putting aside the idealization of the student as autonomous "author" of the papers in such a narrative, it is not clear that the stance he adopts in the excerpt from Essay 10 is somehow inherently preferable to that he adopts in the excerpt from Essay 7 (or that the readings of these presented above are the only possible ones). The student himself poses the "boldness" of his statements as a question, not a fact. But such questions are immaterial from the perspective that the student's work is not, strictly speaking, located in these papers but in his mediation of social relations as they occur in the practices of his writing and reading of others and in my (and his fellow students') mediation of those papers in reading them in particular ways. Hence some readers may prefer the latter to the earlier paper, and some the reverse, for various reasons. But in each case the student is producing different versions of himself as a student in response to the changing conditions of his life in the course. I present excerpts from these papers because they explicitly address this production and these conditions. The work of his writing, however, takes place in that mediation of relations rather than being located in the papers he gives to me. And therefore it is variable, dependent on how the meanings of his papers are made both by him and by readers, in his writing and in the various readings by him (of his own papers) and by his teachers and fellow students (and now by you), and the varying conditions of such readings. That Essay 10 was produced intentionally as an "experiment" with writing conventions (as directed by the assignment) for commentary is meant to encourage reflection on such mediation.

These excerpts do suggest that there are moments in student writing that we can use to relocate the work of writing in material conditions and practices. However, I find that in attempting to relocate that work in material conditions and practices, I must be careful both to avoid the reification of writing that can occur in glorifications of experimental writing and to recognize the work that occurs in the practice of conformity of some student writing to particular conventions. Indeed, I and my students have found that locating writing in material conditions radically problematizes the application of the terms "conventional" and "unconventional" to specific notations. As some of my students have observed, a request by a teacher to experiment with writing conventions makes any ostensible "break" from such conventions an exercise in conformity to the social convention of students fulfilling teachers' requests— hence the student's explicit ambivalence regarding the "boldness" of his Essay 10. In other words, the value of these breaks from convention becomes a question for discussion: what is the relationship between its exchange value within the economy of the course (as a fulfillment of course requirements generally and assignment requirements specifically), its exchange value within larger economies, and its potential use value for the student writer in learning about writing and his subject, or its potential use value for his fellow students, or for his teacher? What would be an appropriate comment for his peers and his teacher to make in defining/producing the specific value of the work accomplished? In the case of the student writings I have been discussing, these questions would have to address conditions of relative freedom granted to both composition students and their instructors in the kinds of writing assigned and produced and in selecting and implementing criteria for evaluating that writing and grading students.

I am suggesting, in other words, that we (students and teachers) should question the use of and breaks from discourse conventions in terms of what all is at stake for what writers and readers, under what conditions (cf. S. Miller, *Textual* 112). As Goleman warns regarding students' critiques of the essay form, "Critical understanding of the . . . form's ideological effects cannot be achieved all at once or once and for all. Subject to ongoing determinations, the ideological effects of a genre on a writer will always be eminently specific, and the meaning that these effects have for students will often be ambiguous" (68). Rather than assuming that the significance of any particular notation or other textual form resides in the form itself, the significance of specific forms needs to be understood as mediated by writers and readers in particular situations.

It is noteworthy, in this regard, and a subject for further inquiry for me and my students, that even within the confines of an assignment explicitly soliciting such experimentation with conventions, those of my students most seemingly "daring" in their breaks

with formal conventions of writing have been those students located socially in positions of privilege—whites, males, middle or up-
per-middle class. In contrast, women, non-traditional students,
students of color, and those apparently of working-class backgrounds have engaged far less in that sort of daring. This does not,
however, mean that such students were simply not yet "ready" to be
"daring" in some abstract sense. Rather, their own writing practices, however seemingly "conventional" in aim and form, could be
for them and for readers as much "daring" if not more so than the
other students' production of more formally unconventional writing,
as artful a writing as any more apparently transgressive writing.
Transgressive writing, in short, as the first student paper suggests,
must be identified materially, not with specific written forms but in
the specifics of time and place and subject, and the social locations
of specific writers and readers.

This points to a limitation in both the course Fox describes and
the one I've been describing above.[9] Whereas Fox's course asked
students explicitly to investigate their language use in relation to
the social categories of race, class, and gender, it did not ask them
to investigate it in relation to the social categories of student,
teacher, school, or composition. While Fox in his book gives ample
attention to the impact of these latter categories on students' language use (and his own as teacher), that was not a focus of the
course. Conversely, the course I've described, while asking students
explicitly to investigate their language use in relation to the social
categories of student, teacher, school, and composition, addressed
the impact of such larger categories as class, race, and gender on
writing only tangentially, as these issues arose in responses to the
readings (e.g., Woolf's *A Room of One's Own* and Adrienne Rich's essay "When We Dead Awaken").

These converse approaches parallel the approaches characteristic
of compositional research. As Glynda Hull, Mike Rose, Kay Losey
Fraser, and Marisa Castellano have observed, much literacy research
adopts either a micro- or a macro-perspective: either "fine-grained
analyses of texts or of the cognitive processes involved in text com-
prehension and production *or* . . . studies of wider focus of the social
and political contexts of reading, writing, and schooling" (321).
However, what is needed, they argue, are studies that move "between
micro-level, close examination of oral or written discourse and macro-

level investigations of society and culture. . . . Without the microperspective, one runs the risk of losing sight of the particulars of behavior; without the macroperspective, one runs the risk of missing the social and cultural logic of that behavior" (321–22; see also Rodby 111). Much recent ethnographic research has taken up such calls, examining the inscription of material cultural conflict in students' writing and classroom discourse.[10] To this research and to these calls I would add that such work is appropriate not only for composition researchers but also teachers and their students, as the subject of writing. For their institutional positions as students and teachers of composition both enable and impel such movement between the micro-analyses of particular writing practices and the location and participation of such practices in macro-level, ongoing material history.[11] Composition courses taking up such a call would not, indeed no course could, eliminate hegemonic notions of "authors," any more than any pedagogy can effectually "authorize" students, free composition teachers from the official duties of their institutional roles as teachers, or purge students, teachers, or the culture at large of racism, sexism, or classism. But courses could have students and teachers investigate the operation of such forces in their responses to student and non-student texts, and the operation of these and other institutions in constructing writing, rather than allowing these to be accepted as mystified "givens." The result would presumably be neither the derogation or elevation of some writing and writers at the expense of others but the placement of the work of writing in specific material history as participating in that history, with the writing imagined not as reified text-objects but as work—that is, as practices within and on the social that function not only materially but on one's consciousness, or sense of self. In this way, students and teachers could connect their "personal" experiences with writing and reading practices to the social and institutional forces shaping those practices and to which those practices respond.

In his famous essay "From Work to Text," Roland Barthes describes a move in how language and literary work are conceived (*Image* 155–64; cf. "De l'oeuvre au text"). Whereas the work (*"l'oeuvre"*), traditionally conceived, is a "fragment of substance," found in books, the Text is a "methodological field" (*Image* 156–57). While the work can be "held in the hand, the text is held in language" (157), the Text "cannot stop . . . its constitutive movement is that of cutting across (in particular, it can cut across the work, several works)" (157). It *"is experienced only in an activity of production"* (157). Whereas the work "closes on a signified," the Text "practises the infinite deferment of the signified, is dilatory" (158). The Text is "an *irreducible* . . . plural" (159).

In proposing a "theory of the Text," Barthes argues for a different "practice of writing" (164). Such a practice would undermine hierarchical relations between Authors and writers, canonical and non-canonical writings, and undermine restrictive disciplinary boundaries separating the study of literature from the study of communication, art, music, architecture, history, and so on. It would seem, in short, to liberate traditional reifications of these and the unequal social relations embodied in hierarchical relations between types of textual practices, distinctions now erased under the rubric of Text, or "discourse." However, the terms by which Barthes distinguishes Text from work deflect such a practice. Work is identified with consumption and the commodification of the product of writing. Text, by contrast, while associated with the "activity of production," is im-material. One cannot hold Textual production in one's hand, only "in language." Text tries to eliminate or diminish the distance between reading and writing by defining both as "signifying practice" (162). In postulating Text as distinct from work, Barthes is arguing against a traditional notion of the literary work as authored commodity (160–61). In so doing, however, he encourages a dematerialized view of writing and its practice. Recognizing the commodification of material manifestations of writing (e.g., in the form of books), he argues for an idealization of writing removed from material exigence, and so in effect encourages a commodification of Text as the sublime experience of "play," an experience requiring the distancing from material exigency epitomized in the "aesthetic" disposition. But in resisting the commodification of writing through postulating Text, he abandons the materiality of the work of writing to just such commodification.

In this chapter, and in this book, I argue for a conception of the work of writing different from both Text and the literary work (*oeuvre*) as traditionally conceived. In so doing, I join the very different efforts of other composition scholars to locate writing in the realm of the material. The potential of both *work* and *writing* to designate either an activity or the product of that activity, rather than as both, has, in practice, led to the domination of one of these meanings over the other: "work" as concrete labor *or* the "product" of that labor, "writing" as aestheticized practice *or* as a "paper." *Composition*, while liable to the same ambiguity in its use, also encompasses in its signification both work and writing while adding to these the dominant institutional location at which the work of writing, however understood, is found: not just *composition* but *Composition*. Thus Composition—as a term designating an historically situated institution, activity and object of that activity, has within it the potential to allow recognition of the continual negotiation of the value and meaning of the work of writing, understood not simply as activity nor as product but as material social practice. The subject of Composition—its work—is, or can be, the exploration and negotiation of that meaning: to continually redefine, in and through its practices, its work.

Appendix A

This paper, written by the student author of the essay revision presented and discussed on pages 233–42, is the student's account of that revision.

In my revision, I made several significant changes. My original paper focuses mainly on Freire's banking format and how I saw it as contradicting his ideas on education. In my revision, I tried to figure out how one can avoid writing in a banking format or, if they must write that way, how Freire could use the format to his advantage and help prove his point. I discovered that, by looking at specific quotes in his essay, Freire's banking format still seems to be contradictory even if his ideas themselves are liberatory. However, unlike in my original, I did this by pointing to direct quotes from the text and applying those quotes to my ideas.

Another major revision I made was that I added to my paper the fact that Freire uses no personal examples in his essay to help prove his points. This fact was made clear to me by our out of class discussion about my revision and by closer, more in-depth examinations of the text.

I tried to avoid writing in a banking format by discussing Freire's essay on a more personal level—how *I* read it and saw it, and by pointing to more quotes to explain my thoughts. Although my attempt to avoid writing in a banking format may have not worked, I believe it is a somewhat dramatic change from my original.

In revising my paper, I found that I became, as Freire puts it, "increasingly challenged and obliged to respond to that challenge" (215). Throughout these challenges and problems, and my responses to these problems, I found I had a better understanding about reading and writing. The process through which I went when revising my papers led me to rethink and reevaluate my position on the nature of not only reading & writing, but on the "relationship between writing and learning, writing and knowledge" ([course description] 1).

My paper written for Assignment # 7 is, in my opinion, much more sophisticated than my previous papers. By experimenting and refining my theories & writing styles, I have come to a better realization of what an essay should consist of. Instead of seeing writing as a narrative effort, I have learned to see it as a "conversation" with the reader. No longer does writing simply consist of throwing my thoughts down on paper, but instead I discuss my thoughts, how I came to believe them, and other possibilities that I might consider. This "process of interpretation and intellectual inquiry" (1) that I have gone through so far in this class has given me a better understanding of the relationship between writing and learning and I believe it shows in my writing practice.

Appendix B

This was the final paper written by the student author of the essay revision presented and discussed on pages 233–42, and it presents the student's review of his work for the course.

In this final paper written for the course, I will discuss the history of my own writing practice in relationship to particular traditions of writing as seen in both my past writings and the readings we have completed. I will look at some patterns I see in my past writings and compare them to patterns seen in the various readings for the course. All of this will be done in an effort to explore my own writing practice and the transition it has gone through, if any, in the course of this class.

When reading through papers I have completed early in the semester, it becomes clear to me that I have indeed gone through a dramatic transition in my writing style. My first paper on Bartholomae and Petrosky's inroduction to *Ways of Reading* was primarily done in a writing style that I have been writing in since high school. The paper consisted mainly of paraphrases of Bartholomae and Petroskys' writing—instead of an interaction occuring between myself and the writers, I simply summarized what I saw to be the writers' main points. The few opinions I had about Bartholomae and Petroskys' ideas were stated as facts; I took for granted that they held one viewpoint and that was it. Later in the course I learned that the authors' viewpoints themselves can indeed change with each re-reading. By revising and re-reading, I in turn learn to re-interpret what the writers' main ideas might be. In this way, I discovered the "social interaction" that takes place between the reader and writer and how the reader can continually learn more and more as he examines and evaluates the writers' texts.

According to Bartholomae and Petrosky, a "reader must speak with authority" (11). While reading through my early papers, I do get a sense of authority in my writing, but it is a close-minded authority that does not consider more than one viewpoint. My papers were written direct and to the point; my opinions on the subject matter were obvious and stated with authority. However, I never questioned my thoughts or ideas. Not only did this make my writing one-sided, but it was also boring to the reader. My writing was similar to that of an instruction manual: factual and technically correct, but written without the intrest of the reader in mind.

In reading Paulo Freire, I found a writer who wrote in a writing style quite similar to my own. Freire, although actually arguing against it in his paper, writes in what I would consider a "banking" style of writing. He "deposits" his ideas in the reader, ideas that seem to be opinions, yet he continually asserts them as facts. This is exactly what I used to do in my papers until I wrote against Freire for doing the same thing. I came to the opinion that Freire's banking format is necessary to argue his "revolutionary" problem-posing ideas. In my paper on Freire, I avoided his "banking" style of writing by considering more than one perspective. Instead of sticking to my traditional style of writing by forming one opinion on the subject and arguing that one opinion directly throughout my paper, I developed a somewhat new style by considering as many viewpoints as possible. This created a much more "liberatory" effect in my writing. No longer was I forcing my one-sided opinions on the reader like Freire, but I was offering to the reader a broad variety of ideas, allowing the reader themself to form their own conclusions. Freire's writing had an impact on me: by reading and writing about Freire, I constructed a new writing style that allowed for much more interaction between reader and writer.

This new non-biased, open-minded style of writing has its advantages and disadvantages, which I began to discuss in my last paper. This particular style does not allow me to "conceal certain facts" (216) and can in no way be considered "an act of depositing" (208)—all features of the banking style of writing, which Freire denounces. This style is definately not "oppresive" in any way. Yet, much is lost in this liberatory style. As noted in my previous paper, it is "extremely difficult to become passionate or angry about a subject when you have to turn around and argue the other side of the issue." It is almost impossible to hold a strong opinion about something when you force yourself to consider every perspective. If I were to be writing about a hotly debated or "revolutionary" subject, this non-banking style of writing would probably not be as successful. If I needed my make my opinions clear to the reader and my ideas were considered challenging or problem-posing enough to strike the reader as revolutionary in the context of when I was writing it, I would opt for a more direct style of writing, similar to that of Freire or Adrienne Rich. But while my subject matter remains less radical or argumentive than that of Rich's or Freire's, I believe that the more open-minded style of writing displayed in my recent papers is more successful than my previous "traditional" style of writing.

Notes

Introduction

1. On the distinction between Composition and composition, see chapter 1, note 1.

2. See, for example, James Berlin's series of historical studies on composition, including his *Rhetoric and Reality: Writing Instruction in American Colleges, 1900–1985*; *Writing Instruction in Nineteenth-Century Colleges*; and *Rhetorics, Poetics, and Cultures: Refiguring College English Studies*; Lester Faigley's *Fragments of Rationality: Postmodernity and the Subject of Composition*, Susan Miller's *Textual Carnivals: The Politics of Composition*, and Stephen North's *The Making of Knowledge in Composition: Portrait of an Emerging Field*.

3. See, for example, Sidney Dobrin's *Constructing Knowledges: The Politics of Theory-Building and Pedagogy in Composition*, Joseph Harris' *A Teaching Subject: Composition since 1966*, Marguerite Helmers' *Writing Students: Composition Testimonials and Representations of Students*, *Keywords in Composition Studies*, and Min-Zhan Lu and Bruce Horner's *Representing the 'Other': Basic Writers and the Teaching of Basic Writing*.

4. See, for example, such works as Deborah Brandt's *Literacy as Involvement: The Acts of Writers, Readers, and Texts*, Evan Watkins' *Work Time: English Departments and the Circulation of Cultural Value*, Thomas Fox's *The Social Uses of Writing*, J. Elspeth Stuckey's *The Violence of Literacy*, and *The Politics of Writing Instruction: Postsecondary*.

5. See, for example, the essays in *Feminism and Composition Studies: In Other Words* and in *Feminisms and Critical Pedagogy*; Sue

Ellen Holbrook's "Women's Work: The Feminizing of Composition"; Susan Miller's "The Feminization of Composition"; and Eileen Schell's recent *Gypsy Academics and Mother-Teachers: Gender, Contingent Labor, and Writing Instruction*.

Chapter 1. Work

1. Bowing to this first usage, I employ the upper-case designation *Composition* to identify the field of activities associated with teachers and researchers—those sometimes labeled "compositionists"—officially recognized by the public, the academy, and professional composition organizations, as distinct from the full range of activities that might fall under the rubric *composition*: all the activities and conditions connected in some way to the engagement of students, teachers, and others in writing. The argument of this book, however, is that Composition must recognize its work as composition.

2. On actual faculty commitments to teaching and research, see Oakley 274–77.

3. In a study of 212 collective bargaining agreements for faculty in the 1990s, Gary Rhoades finds, in fact, that instructional technologies are being introduced as a "means by which managers can bypass full-time faculty's influence and claims on the curriculum," in effect becoming a means of "electronic subcontracting" (265).

4. Recent debates over the institutional ownership of intellectual property in which faculty have had a hand illustrate the contradictions to which such denials can lead. On these debates, see Lunsford and West. For an insightful analysis of the role material social circumstance plays in scholarly production, see Canagarajah.

5. Conversely, Rhoades finds that those faculty whose work has greater commercial value are also more closely regulated (254).

6. There is, of course, debate within literary study over treatment of TAs, but that debate typically is not contained *within* literary study but intersects with debate between literary study and Composition, the latter of which TAs are expected to teach while pursuing the former.

7. Cary Nelson's *Manifesto* and Evan Watkins' *Work Time* represent recent exceptions.

8. For a sense of just how overdetermined work in Composition and the academy generally is, see Alexander Astin's attempts to correlate a host

of variables to explain the effects of college experiences on undergraduates to answer the question posed by his title *What Matters in College*.

9. For a brief, updated account of faculty unions, especially in relation to adjunct and part-time faculty, see Schell 109–13.

10. For a concise account of this debate, see Schell 91–99.

11. Cf. Samuel Totten's discussion of such matters in the situation of primary and secondary school teachers (16–17).

12. For a more recent example of such strategies, see Sullivan et al., which I discuss in chapter 4.

Chapter 2. Students

1. See, for example, accounts of teachers and students in Tate et al.'s "Class Talk."

2. See, for example, Bruffee's "Writing and Reading as Collaborative or Social Acts."

3. For a critique of the alignment of such pedagogies with the goals and values of the "new capitalism," see Gee, Hull, and Lankshear, chapters 1 and 2.

4. See, in this regard, M. L. Pratt, "Daring to Dream" 8–12.

5. On the limitations of this approach, see Walters 828.

6. On composition as "women's" work, see S. Miller, "Feminization," and Schell.

7. In this tradition I would place the work of such figures as David Bartholomae and Bill Coles discussed in chapter 5. For specific articulations of this tradition, see my essay "Rethinking" 188–96, and Lu's "Writing as Repositioning" and "Professing Multiculturalism."

8. Shared not only among teachers but among students, many of whom, in my experience, view any praise of their writing with deep suspicion rather than pleasure, often to the extent of taking statements of praise (from me or their peers) as "sarcastic" statements of condemnation.

9. This paper was in response to "Making Connections" Assignment no. 1, in *Ways of Reading* 154. The writer of this paper granted permission to reproduce it on condition of anonymity. The paper's page references are to essays reprinted in *Ways of Reading*.

10. On the relation between writing technologies, cognition, and rhetoric, see Haas.

Chapter 3. Politics

1. Luke herself argues that this second view restricts feminists to the "good girl" posture of maternal, nurturing, self denial ("Feminist Pedagogy" 284, 298–302).

2. Ironically, it is just such a discourse which Brodkey and her colleagues intended to counter in their course through teaching argument "as inquiry rather than advocacy" (Brodkey, "Making" 239–41), an intention so at odds with conventional understandings of political discourse as to be unimaginable to opponents.

3. For a full-length account of a composition pedagogy focusing explicitly on the ubiquity of the political in writing, see Thomas Fox's *The Social Uses of Writing*.

4. On debate responding specifically to Ellsworth's account, see, for example, in addition to works discussed in this chapter, Giroux, "Border"; McLaren; Burbules and Rice, "Dialogue across Differences" and "Can We Be Heard"; Lather; and Leach.

5. Ellsworth restricted her research on critical pedagogy to thirty articles in "major educational journals" published between 1984 and 1988 (298 n. 2), a restriction for which she has been criticized by Henry Giroux, "Border" (178), and Peter McLaren (72).

6. For a different account of black ambivalence toward schooling, see hooks, *Talking* 98–100.

7. My argument here is aligned with some of the criticisms leveled at weak versions of "reproductive" theories of education, which seem to leave no room for resistance or agency. For a useful analysis of such theories, see Morrow and Torres.

8. For an account of faculty success in battling injustice, see L. R. Pratt (43–45).

9. The very different history of a course at the University of Massachusetts, Amherst similar to the proposed UT Austin course illustrates the operation of such contingencies (see Dietz-Kilen; Beverly Watkins).

10. For a different argument on the relation of adopting a "practical" pedagogy to the marginality of teachers' institutional position within the academy, see my "Discoursing Basic Writing" (207–19).

11. This is emphatically not to argue that attention to error in writing (understood here as the use of unconventional spelling, syntax, and punctuation) is either inappropriate or evidence of complicity with dominant oppressive social forces. As I have argued in "Rethinking the 'Sociality' of Error," error in writing (and ways to correct it) can and must be addressed in composition pedagogy; to do so, however, its "sociality" must be explicitly confronted.

Chapter 4. Academic

1. Elbow also sees the convention of "explicitness and straightforward organization in academic discourse" teaching a "version of reality" holding "that we can figure out what we really mean and get enough control over language to actually say it—directly and clearly" (146). Tellingly, however, he does not object to this effect.

2. Originally published as "The Idea of Community in the Study of Writing," *College Composition and Communication* 40 (1989): 11–22. Page references are to the version reprinted in Harris' book *A Teaching Subject*.

3. For a more general critique of such efforts, associated with the critical linguistics movement, see chapter 3 of Lester Faigley's *Fragments of Rationality*.

4. Hill and Resnick don't deny the legitimacy of other purposes for college composition but see these as additional to, if no less central than, the purpose of preparing students for workplace writing (145 n. 1).

5. Stephen Orgel's "What Is a Text?" is one example of scholarship drawing on such an array of work.

6. The history of cultural studies instruction in Britain's Open University is instructive here. As Richard Miller notes, the "openness" to inspection of cultural studies courses led instructors to design their course materials in ways that would meet with the approval of scholars, whatever difficulties this posed for the students for whom the materials were ostensibly intended (" 'A Moment' " 422–23). In short, its pursuit of exchange value led it to undermine the use value of its pedagogical work.

7. In light of the discussion of revisions to Drake's English curriculum that follows, it bears noting that I had at least an equal hand in all deliberations and decisions about the revisions and their implementation. For a different account of the revisions to Drake's English curriculum, see Mahala and Swilky.

8. I detect a further parallel in the contemptuous attitude disciplines take toward schools of education, which, at a further remove than Composition in attending to primary and secondary education, and so more closely associated with "mothering," also have a hand in the material reproduction of academic subjects—students and fields of knowledge. Composition's obvious association with education has always served to devalue it, hence its own habitual distancing of itself from education.

9. In his posthumously published *Rhetorics*, Berlin's descriptions of ways to enact such a rhetoric are restricted to individual courses rather than department curricula. Cf. Sidler and Morris.

10. In her earlier "(Dis)Missing Compulsory First-Year Composition," Brannon presents SUNY's original justification for abolishing its first-year composition course.

11. For work that appears to have no apparent use value, workers may hypothesize a use to give it meaning (Kusterer 154–55).

12. A recent advertising campaign for my own institution, for example, presented D-R-A-K-E as "letters of recommendation."

Chapter 5. Traditional

1. In *Domination and the Arts of Resistance: Hidden Transcripts*, James A. Scott points to a parallel phenomenon in the failure to acknowledge discrepancies between "public" and "hidden" transcripts among and between members of dominant and subordinate groups (3–4, passim).

2. A. Suresh Canagarajah makes a similar argument for the strategic value, as well as the limitations, of the independence and detachment afforded those scholars working in communities peripheral to the Western academic world (464–65).

3. Sullivan et al. note that professionalism and disciplinarity are not synonymous: the former is typically defined in terms of an ethic of using one's expertise to serve clients, the latter in terms of the production of academic knowledge (385–86). However, within the academy, professionalism

is typically conflated with disciplinarity: the primary "client" is identified *as* the discipline, which one "serves" through producing academic knowledge. Throughout this book I am, of course, arguing against this conflation and for a different view of the work of composition.

4. For an account of engagement with such demands, see Sullivan et al., and my discussion of their work in chapter 4.

5. The text cited identifies this as "New Rhetoric," but Berlin has earlier in the same essay identified New Rhetoric as "what might be called Epistemic Rhetoric" (773). He reproduces the description cited in only slightly altered form as a description of epistemic rhetoric in his later *Rhetoric and Reality* (166). See also his yet later description of what he terms "social-epistemic" rhetoric in "Rhetoric and Ideology" (488). For Coles' statements aligned to this view of knowledge, see *Composing* 1, "Sense" 28, *Plural I* 12, 13. For statements by Bartholomae aligned to this view, see "Writing" 69, 78, and Bartholomae and Petrosky's *Facts* 8, 41.

6. In *Composing II*, perhaps as part of a continuing attempt to "be as straight as possible" with students about what he is doing (*Composing II* 9), Coles qualifies this assertion by admitting that the assignments do rest on the assumption that "language using (in its broadest sense) is the means by which all of us run orders through chaos thereby giving ourselves the identities we have," and that they offer "writing as an activity of language using intended to provide you with a way of seeing how getting better at writing can have something in it for you" (18). See also the later variant in his *Seeing Through Writing* (9–10).

7. See Joseph Harris' remarks on the "blurring of boundaries" in Coles' writing ("Plural" 160), and George Dillon's exploration of the rhetorical significance of Coles' use of fiction in *The Plural I* ("Fiction in Persuasion" 203–9).

8. See also Bartholomae's admiration of such stylistic gestures in student writing ("Inventing the University" 159).

9. Elsewhere Bartholomae observes, "I intended the title of ["Inventing the University"] to be read ironically, since I was arguing that academic discourse could never be invented, only appropriated" ("Reply" 130).

10. Wall and Coles are playing off Bartholomae's statement in "Inventing the University" that "[o]ne response to the problems of basic writers . . . would be to determine just what the community's conventions are, so that those conventions could be written out, 'demystified' and taught in our classrooms" (147). As Wall and Coles note, Bartholomae does

not advocate this response; rather, he goes on immediately afterwards in the essay to pursue a different one. See also Slevin's discussion of the reception given "Inventing" ("Genre" 23–24).

11. In "Looking Back on *The Plural I*," Coles quibbles only with Irmscher's identification of the persona of *The Plural I* with Coles himself (273).

12. Cf. Harris, "The Rhetoric of Theory"; Raymond (94); and Phelps's discussion of the relationship between reflection and experience (69–76).

13. In light of government funding for research and tuition at all types of postsecondary institutions and in light of the public good to which all such institutions are thought to contribute (which is the justification for that government support), I take the common distinction between "public" and "private" postsecondary schools to be one without a difference for the argument advanced here, however significant in other regards.

14. On the political difficulties of defining these goods, see Johnston 30–31.

Chapter 6. Writing

1. The same ambiguity obtains with the term *composition*, which suffers from the ambiguity of referring not only to an activity and the product of that activity but also to the teaching of that activity and to the academic field devoted to studying that activity, the product of that activity, and the teaching of it.

2. For recent illustrations of such moves in that struggle, see Todd Jailer's poems "Bill Hastings" and "The Aesthetics of Line Work," *Working Classics* 114, 117.

3. Clare Frost, whose essay is included in the Fontaine/Hunter collection *Writing Ourselves into the Story*, does address the role of both discursive and non-discursive constraints on her abilities to participate in Composition scholarly discourse.

4. For an argument on the material constraints on Composition scholarship parallel to and informing the one I have been making, see John Trimbur's "Writing Instruction" (139–42).

5. The original paper was written in response to an assignment adapted from "Questions for a Second Reading" no. 3, *Ways of Reading* 220. Page references are to that edition. Both versions of the paper are

reprinted here by permission of the author on condition of anonymity. In collating the two versions, I have added the underlining, square brackets, and italicizing but have not otherwise changed the texts of the originals.

6. Cf. Goleman's warnings about the tension between the use value and foundational value of dialectical knowledge, and of mistaking the "process of ideological becoming with a cultural artifact" through valorizing students' performance of dazzling cultural criticism (100, 88–89).

7. On the before/after trope in freshman writing, see Faigley 129; Goleman 70–71.

8. Judith Goleman argues similarly for the composition course as the site for students and teachers to "analyze the social functions of their current reading and writing practices and the subject positions they define; and to reconstruct these practices for different social functions and subject positions, as they can and as they choose. . . . using writing to discern the lineaments of their 'situations' . . . [to work] the writing that has been working them—studying, in various contexts, what this writing does, how it does it, and what the available or yet-to-be imagined alternatives might be" (106–7).

9. Fox is explicitly and refreshingly clear that, while he is arguing for following certain principles for writing pedagogy, he is not prescribing his course as a model for others to follow (see *Social Uses* 123).

10. See, for example, such studies as Brodkey, "On the Subjects"; Ewald and Wallace; Faigley; Goleman; Haas; Hull and Rose, " 'This Wooden Shack Place' " and "Rethinking Remediation"; and Stygall.

11. For an analysis of such pedagogical efforts, see Lu and Horner, "Problematic" 269–75.

Works Cited

Adler-Kassner, Linda, Robert Crooks, and Ann Watters. "Service-Learning and Composition at the Crossroads." *Writing the Community* 1–18.

Agnew, Eleanor. "Basic Writers in the Workplace: Writing Adequately for Careers after College." *Journal of Basic Writing* 11.2 (Fall 1992): 28–46.

Anokye, Akua Duku. "Housewives and Compositionists." *College Composition and Communication* 47 (1996): 101–3.

Astin, Alexander W. *What Matters in College? Four Critical Years Revisited.* San Francisco: Jossey-Bass, 1993.

Atkins. Response to John T. Day. *ADE Bulletin* no. 111 (Fall 1995): 39–41.

Bacon, Nora. "Community Service Writing: Problems, Challenges, Questions." *Writing the Community* 39–56.

Baker, Houston A. *Blues, Ideology, and Afro-American Literature: A Vernacular Theory.* U of Chicago P, 1984.

Barthes, Roland. "De l'oeuvre au text." *Revue d'esthetique*, 1971. Repr. *Le Bruissement de la langue: essais critiques IV.* Paris: Editions du Seuil, 1984. 69–77.

———. *Image—Music—Text.* Trans. Stephen Heath. New York: Noonday, 1977.

Bartholomae, David. "A Reply to Stephen North." *PRE/TEXT* 11 (1990): 121–30.

———. "Against the Grain." *Writers on Writing.* Ed. Tom Waldrep. New York: Random, 1985. 19–29.

————. "Inventing the University." *When a Writer Can't Write: Studies in Writer's Block and Other Composing Problems*. Ed. Mike Rose. New York: Guildford, 1985. 134–65.

————. "Released into Language: Errors, Expectations, and the Legacy of Mina Shaughnessy." *The Territory of Language: Linguistics, Stylistics, and the Teaching of Composition*. Ed. Donald A. McQuade. Carbondale: Southern Illinois UP, 1986. 65–88.

————. "The Tidy House: Basic Writing in the American Curriculum." *Journal of Basic Writing* 12.1 (Spring 1993): 4–21.

————. "Wanderings: Misreadings, Miswritings, Misunderstandings." *Only Connect: Uniting Reading and Writing*. Ed. Thomas Newkirk. Upper Montclair, NJ: Boynton/Cook, 1986. 89–118.

————. "What Is Composition and (if you know what that is) Why Do We Teach It?" *Composition in the Twenty-First Century* 11–28.

————. "Writing with Teachers: A Conversation with Peter Elbow." *College Composition and Communication* 46 (1995): 62–71.

Bartholomae, David, and Anthony R. Petrosky. *Facts, Artifacts, and Counterfacts: Theory and Method for a Reading and Writing Course*. Upper Montclair, NJ: Boynton/Cook, 1986.

————. *Resources for Teaching Ways of Reading: An Anthology for Writers*. 2nd ed. Boston: St. Martin's, 1990.

Bazerman, Charles. "Response: Curricular Responsibilities and Professional Definition." *Reconceiving Writing* 249–59.

Bell, John. "Re-presenting Remediation." *College Composition and Communication* 47 (1996): 412–14.

Benjamin, Ernst. "A Faculty Response to the Fiscal Crisis: From Defense to Offense." *Higher Education under Fire* 52–72.

Berlin, James A. "Composition Studies and Cultural Studies: Collapsing the Boundaries." *Into the Field: Sites of Composition Studies*. Ed. Anne Ruggles Gere. New York: Modern Language Association, 1993.

————. "Contemporary Composition: The Major Pedagogical Theories." *College English* 44 (1982): 765–77.

————. "Rhetoric and Ideology in the Writing Class." *College English* 50 (1988): 477–94.

————. *Rhetoric and Reality: Writing Instruction in American Colleges, 1900–1985*. Carbondale: Southern Illinois UP, 1987.

————. *Rhetorics, Poetics, and Cultures: Refiguring College English Studies*. Urbana, IL: National Council of Teachers of English, 1996.

————. *Writing Instruction in Nineteenth-Century Colleges*. Carbondale: Southern Illinois UP, 1984.

Berthoff, Ann E. "I. A. Richards." *Traditions of Inquiry* 50–80.

Bissex, Glenda L. "Why Case Studies." *Seeing for Ourselves: Case Study Research by Teachers of Writing*. Ed. Glenda Bissex and Richard H. Bullock. Portsmouth, NH: Heinemann, 1987. 7–19.

Bizzell, Patricia. "Marxist Ideas in Composition Studies." *Contending with Words* 52–68.

————. "Power, Authority, and Critical Pedagogy." *Journal of Basic Writing* 10.2 (1991): 54–70.

Bledstein, Burton. *The Culture of Professionalism: The Middle Class and the Development of Higher Education in America*. New York: Norton, 1978.

Bleich, David. "Feminist Philosophy and Some Humanists' Attitudes Towards the Teaching of Writing." *Journal of Advanced Composition* 13 (1993): 137–52.

Bloom, Lynn Z. "Freshman Composition as a Middle-Class Enterprise." *College English* 58 (1996): 654–75.

Blumenstyk, Goldie. "Colleges Wonder if Microsoft Is Their Next Competitor." *Chronicle of Higher Education* 24 April 1998: A33.

Bourdieu, Pierre. *Distinction: A Social Critique of the Judgement of Taste*. Trans. Richard Nice. Cambridge, MA: Harvard UP, 1984.

————. *Homo Academicus*. Trans. Peter Collier. Stanford UP, 1988.

————. *In Other Words: Essays Towards a Reflexive Sociology*. Trans. M. Adamson. Stanford UP, 1990.

————. "The Corporatism of the Universal: The Role of Intellectuals in the Modern World." Trans. Carolyn Betensky. *Telos* 81 (Fall 1989): 99–110.

Brandt, Deborah. *Literacy as Involvement: The Acts of Writers, Readers, and Texts*. Carbondale: Southern Illinois UP, 1990.

Brannon, Lil. "Confronting the Logic of Instrumentalism: Using Rhetoric for Social Change." Conference on College Composition and Communication. Phoenix, AZ, 13 March 1997.

———. "(Dis)Missing Compulsory First-Year Composition." *Reconceiving Writing* 239–48.

Brereton, John C., ed. *The Origins of Composition Studies in the American College, 1875–1925: A Documentary History*. U of Pittsburgh P, 1995.

Bridwell-Bowles, Lillian. "Discourse and Diversity: Experimental Writing within the Academy." *College Composition and Communication* 43 (1992): 349–68.

———. "Freedom, Form, Function: Varieties of Academic Discourse." *College Composition and Communication* 46 (1995): 46–61.

———. "Service-Learning: Help for Higher Education in a New Millennium?" *Writing the Community* 19–28.

Broderick, James H. "A Study of the Freshman Composition Course at Amherst: Action, Order, and Language." *Harvard Educational Review* 28 (1958): 44–57.

Brodkey, Linda. "Making a Federal Case out of Difference: The Politics of Pedagogy, Publicity, and Postponement." *Writing Theory and Critical Theory* 236–61.

———. "On the Subjects of Class and Gender in 'The Literacy Letters.' " *Becoming Political: Readings and Writings in the Politics of Literacy Education*. Ed. Patrick Shannon. Portsmouth, NH: Heinemann, 1992. 97–112.

———. "Tropics of Literacy." *Rewriting Literacy* 161–68.

———. "Writing Critical Ethnographic Narratives." *Anthropology & Education Quarterly* 18 (1987): 67–76.

Bruffee, Kenneth A. "Collaborative Learning and the 'Conversation of Mankind.' " *College English* 46 (1984): 635–52.

———. "Writing and Reading as Collaborative or Social Acts." *The Writer's Mind: Writing as a Mode of Thinking*. Ed. Janice N. Hayes et al. Urbana, IL: National Council of Teachers of English, 1983. 159–70.

Bullock, Richard, John Trimbur, and Charles I. Schuster. Preface. *Politics of Writing Instruction* xvii–xx.

Burbules, Nicholas C. "A Theory of Power in Education." *Educational Theory* 36 (1986): 95–114.

Burbules, Nicholas C., and Suzanne Rice. "Can We Be Heard? A Reply to Leach." *Harvard Educational Review* 62 (1992): 264–71.

———. "Dialogue across Differences: Continuing the Conversation." *Harvard Educational Review* 61 (1991): 393–416.

Campbell, Dianna S., and Terry Ryan Meier. "A Design for a Developmental Writing Course for Academically Underprepared Black Students." *Journal of Basic Writing* 2 (Fall/Winter 1976): 20–30.

Canagarajah, A. Suresh. " 'Nondiscursive' Requirements in Academic Publishing, Material Resources of Periphery Scholars, and the Politics of Knowledge Production." *Written Communication* 13 (1996): 435–72.

Carlson, Dennis. *Teachers and Crisis: Urban School Reform and Teachers' Work Culture*. London and New York: Routledge, 1992.

Carr, Jean Ferguson. "Rereading the Academy as Worldly Text." *College Composition and Communication* 45 (1994): 93–97.

Catano, James V. "The Rhetoric of Masculinity: Origins, Institutions, and the Myth of the Self-Made Man." *College English* 52 (1990): 421–36.

Changing Work, Changing Workers: Critical Perspectives on Language, Literacy, and Skills. Ed. Glynda Hull. Albany: State U of New York P, 1997.

Cintron, Ralph. "Wearing a Pith Helmet at a Sly Angle: Or, Can Writing Researchers Do Ethnography in a Postmodern Era?" *Written Communication* 10 (1993): 371–412.

Clanchy, M. T. "Hearing and Seeing *and* Trusting Writing." *Perspectives on Literacy* 137–58.

Coles, William E., Jr. "An Unpetty Pace." *College Composition and Communication* 23 (1972): 378–82.

———. *Composing: Writing as a Self-Creating Process*. Rochelle Park, NJ: Hayden, 1974.

———. *Composing II: Writing as a Self-Creating Process*. Rochelle Park, NJ: Hayden, 1981.

———. "Counterstatement." *College Composition and Communication* 29 (1978): 206–09.

———. "Freshman Composition: The Circle of Unbelief." *College English* 31 (1969): 134–42.

———. "Literacy for the Eighties: An Alternative to Losing." *Literacy for Life: The Demand for Reading and Writing* 248–62. Rpt. as "Writing as Literacy: An Alternative to Losing." *The Plural I—and After* 278–98.

———. "Looking Back on *The Plural I*." *The Plural I—and After* 271–77.

———. "New Presbyters as Old Priests: A Forewarning." *CEA Critic* 41.1 (1978): 3–9.

———. *Seeing Through Writing*. New York: Harper, 1988.

———. *Teaching Composing: A Guide to Teaching Writing as a Self-Creating Process*. Rochelle Park, NJ: Hayden, 1974.

———. "Teaching Writing, Teaching Literature: The Plague on Both Houses." *Freshman English News* 9.3 (1981): 3–4, 13–16.

———. *The Plural I: The Teaching of Writing*. New York: Holt, 1978.

———. *The Plural I—and After*. Portsmouth, NH: Boynton/Cook, 1988.

———. "The Sense of Nonsense as a Design for Sequential Writing Assignments." *College Composition and Communication* 21 (1970): 27–34.

Collins, Terence G. "A Response to Ira Shor's 'Our Apartheid: Writing Instruction and Inequality.'" *Journal of Basic Writing* 16.2 (Fall 1997): 95–100.

Composition in the Twenty-First Century: Crisis and Change. Ed. Lynn Z. Bloom, Donald A. Daiker, and Edward M. White. Carbondale: Southern Illinois UP, 1996.

Connors, Robert J. "Mechanical Correctness as a Focus in Composition Instruction." *College Composition and Communication* 36 (1985): 61–72.

———. "Textbooks and the Evolution of the Discipline." *College Composition and Communication* 37 (1986): 178–94.

Contending with Words: Composition and Rhetoric in a Postmodern Age. Ed. Patricia Harkin and John Schilb. New York: Modern Language Association, 1991.

Courage, Richard. "Basic Writing: End of a Frontier?" *Journal of Teaching Writing* 9 (1990): 247–60.

Crowley, Sharon. "A Personal Essay on Freshman English." *PRE / TEXT* 12 (1991): 156–76.

———. "Around 1971: Current-Traditional Rhetoric and Process Models of Composing." *Composition in the Twenty-First Century* 64–74.

———. "Composition's Ethic of Service, the Universal Requirement, and the Discourse of Student Need." *Journal of Advanced Composition* 15 (1995): 227–39.

———. "The Perilous Life and Times of Freshman English." *Freshman English News* 14 (1986): 11–16.

———. "writing and Writing." *Writing and Reading Differently: Deconstruction and the Teaching of Composition and Literature*. Ed. Douglas Atkins and Michael L. Johnson. Lawrence: UP of Kansas, 1985. 93–100.

Darrah, Charles. "Complicating the Concept of Skill Requirements: Scenes from a Workplace." *Changing Work, Changing Workers* 249–72.

David, Denise, Barbara Gordon, and Rita Pollard. "Seeking Common Ground: Guiding Assumptions for Writing Courses." *College Composition and Communication* 46 (1995): 522–32.

Day, John T. "Rethinking Graduate Education in English: The Liberal Arts College Perspective." *ADE Bulletin* no. 111 (Fall 1995): 33–37.

Deans, Tom. "Writing Across the Curriculum and Community Service Learning: Correspondences, Cautions, and Futures." *Writing the Community* 29–37.

Desy, Jeanne. "Reasoned Writing for Basic Students: A Course Design." *Journal of Basic Writing* 2 (Fall/Winter 1976): 4–19.

Dietz-Kilen, Jim. "PC or not PC: Is That the Question?" *Iowa English Bulletin* 40 (1992): 32–38.

Dillon, George L. "Fiction in Persuasion: Personal Experience as Evidence and as Art." *Literary Nonfiction: Theory, Criticism, Pedagogy*. Ed. Chris Anderson. Carbondale: Southern Illinois UP, 1989. 197–210.

———. *Rhetoric as Social Imagination: Explorations in the Interpersonal Function of Language*. Bloomington: Indiana UP, 1986.

Dobrin, Sidney I. *Constructing Knowledges: The Politics of Theory-Building and Pedagogy in Composition*. Albany: State U of New York P, 1997.

Donahue, Patricia, and Ellen Quandahl. "Reading the Classroom." *Reclaiming Pedagogy: The Rhetoric of the Classroom.* Ed. Patricia Donahue and Ellen Quandahl. Carbondale: Southern Illinois UP, 1989. 1–16.

Dorman, Wade, and Susann Fox Dorman. "Service-Learning: Bridging the Gap between the Real World and the Composition Classroom." *Writing the Community* 119–32.

Drake University General Catalog, 1996–98. Des Moines, IA: Drake University, 1996.

Duffey, Suellynn. "Mapping the Terrain of Tracks and Streams." *College Composition and Communication* 47 (1996): 103–7.

Dunn, Patricia. Comment. *College English* 54 (1992): 731–33.

Ebert, Teresa L. "Quango-ing the University: The End(s) of Critique-al Humanities." *The Alternative Orange* 5.2 (Summer/Fall 1997): 5–47.

Eddie, Gary, and Jane Carducci. "Service with a Smile: Class and Community in Advanced Composition." *The Writing Instructor* 16.2 (Winter 1997): 78–90.

Ede, Lisa, and Andrea Lunsford. *Singular Texts/Plural Authors: Perspectives on Collaborative Writing.* Carbondale: Southern Illinois UP, 1990.

Elbow, Peter. "Being a Writer vs. Being an Academic: A Conflict in Goals." *College Composition and Communication* 46 (1995): 72–83.

———. "Reflections on Academic Discourse: How It Relates to Freshmen and Colleagues." *College English* 53 (1991): 135–55.

———. "Response." *College Composition and Communication* 46 (1995): 87–92.

Ellsworth, Elizabeth. "Why Doesn't This Feel Empowering? Working through the Repressive Myths of Critical Pedagogy." *Harvard Educational Review* 59 (1989): 297–324.

Ewald, Helen Rothschild, and David L. Wallace. "Exploring Agency in Classroom Discourse or, Should David Have Told His Story?" *College Composition and Communication* 45 (1994): 342–68.

Faigley, Lester. *Fragments of Rationality: Postmodernity and the Subject of Composition.* U of Pittsburgh P, 1992.

Feminism and Composition Studies: In Other Words. Ed. Susan Jarratt and Lynn Worsham. New York: Modern Language Association, 1998.

Feminisms and Critical Pedagogy. Ed. Carmen Luke and Jennifer Gore. New York: Routledge, 1992.

Final Report. Modern Language Association Committee on Professional Employment. New York: Modern Language Association, December 1997.

Fish, Stanley. "The Unbearable Ugliness of Volvos." *English Inside and Out: The Places of Literary Criticism.* Ed. Susan Gubar and Kamholtz. New York: Routledge, 1993. 102–8.

Fontaine, Sheryl, and Susan Hunter. "Introduction: Taking the Risk to Be Heard." *Writing Ourselves* 1–17.

Fox, Tom. *Defending Access: A Critique of Standards in Higher Education.* Portsmouth, NH: Boynton/Cook Heinemann, 1999.

———. "Proceeding with Caution: Composition in the 90s." *College Composition and Communication* 46 (1995): 566–78.

———. *The Social Uses of Writing: Politics and Pedagogy.* Norwood, NJ: Ablex, 1990.

Freedman, Aviva. "The What, Where, When, Why, and How of Classroom Genres." *Reconceiving Writing* 121–44.

Freedman, Carl. "Marxist Theory, Radical Pedagogy, and the Reification of Thought." *College English* 49 (1987): 70–82.

Friend, Christy. "The Excluded Conflict: The Marginalization of Composition and Rhetoric Studies in Graff's *Professing Literature.*" *College English* 54 (1992): 276–86.

Frost, Clare A. "Looking for a Gate in the Fence." *Writing Ourselves* 59–69.

Fulkerson, Richard. "Composition Theory in the Eighties: Axiological Consensus and Paradigmatic Diversity." *College Composition and Communication* 41 (1990): 409–29.

Gadzinski, Eric. "The Year of Living Dangerously; or, Not Just an Adventure, but a Job." *ADE Bulletin* no. 117 (Fall 1997): 35–37.

Gardner, Janet E. "Trained in Theory, Hired in Literature." *ADE Bulletin* no. 117 (Fall 1997): 31–34.

Gates, Henry Louis, Jr. "Introduction: Writing 'Race' and the Difference It Makes." *"Race," Writing, and Difference.* Ed. Henry Louis Gates Jr. U of Chicago P, 1985. 1–20.

Gee, James Paul. "Discourse Systems and Aspirin Bottles: On Literacy." *Rewriting Literacy* 123–35.

Gee, James Paul, Glynda Hull, and Colin Lankshear. *The New Work Order: Behind the Language of the New Capitalism.* Boulder, CO: Westview, 1998.

Geisler, Cheryl. "Writing and Learning at Cross Purposes in the Academy." *Reconceiving Writing* 101–20.

Gere, Anne Ruggles. "Kitchen Tables and Rented Rooms: The Extra-curriculum of Composition." *College Composition and Communication* 45 (1994): 75–92.

Gibson, Walker. "Theodore Baird." *Traditions of Inquiry* 136–52.

Giddens, Anthony. *Central Problems in Social Theory: Action, Structure and Contradiction in Social Analysis.* Berkeley: U of California P, 1979.

Giroux, Henry. "Beyond the Ivory Tower: Public Intellectuals and the Crisis of Higher Education." *Higher Education under Fire* 238–58.

———. "Border Pedagogy in the Age of Postmodernism." *Journal of Education* 170.3 (1988): 162–81.

Goggin, Maureen Daly. "The Disciplinary Instability of Composition." *Reconceiving Writing* 27–48.

Goleman, Judith. *Working Theory: Critical Composition Studies for Students and Teachers.* Westport, CT: Bergin, 1995.

Goody Jack, and Ian Watt. "The Consequences of Literacy." *Literacy in Traditional Societies.* Ed. Jack Goody. Cambridge UP, 1968. Rpt. *Perspectives on Literacy* 3–27.

Gore, Jennifer. "What We Can Do for You! What *Can* 'We' Do for 'You'?: Struggling over Empowerment in Critical and Feminist Pedagogy." *Feminisms and Critical Pedagogy* 54–73.

Graff, Gerald. *Professing Literature: An Institutional History.* U of Chicago P, 1987.

———. "The Politics of Composition: A Reply to John Rouse." *College English* 41 (1980): 851–56.

Graff, Harvey J. *The Labyrinths of Literacy: Reflections on Literacy Past and Present*. Rev. ed. U of Pittsburgh P, 1995.

Gramsci, Antonio. *An Antonio Gramsci Reader*. Ed. David Forgacs. New York: Schocken, 1988.

Greenberg, Karen L. "A Response to Ira Shor's 'Our Apartheid: Writing Instruction and Inequality.' " *Journal of Basic Writing* 16.2 (Fall 1997): 90–94.

———. "The End of Open Admissions at CUNY." Conference on Basic Writing listserv posting, 27 May 1998.

Greene, Stuart. "Making Sense of My Own Ideas: The Problems of Authorship in a Beginning Writing Classroom." *Written Communication* 12 (1995): 186–218.

Grego, Rhonda, and Nancy Thompson. "Repositioning Remediation: Renegotiating Composition's Work in the Academy." *College Composition and Communication* 47 (1996): 62–84.

Guernsey, Lisa, and Jeffrey R. Young. "Who Owns On-Line Courses?" *Chronicle of Higher Education* 5 June 1998: A21–23.

Guillory, John. "Literary Critics as Intellectuals: Class Analysis and the Crisis of the Humanities." *Rethinking Class: Literary Studies and Social Formations*. Ed. Wai Chee Dimock and Michael T. Gilmore. New York: Columbia UP, 1994. 107–49.

Gunner, Jeanne. "The Fate of the Wyoming Resolution: A History of Professional Seduction." *Writing Ourselves* 107–22.

Guskin, Alan. "Learning More, Spending Less." *About Campus* July-August 1997: 4–9.

Haas, Christina. *Writing Technology: Studies in the Materiality of Literacy*. Mahwah, NJ: Erlbaum, 1996.

Hairston, Maxine. "Breaking Our Bonds and Reaffirming Our Connections." *College Composition and Communication* 36 (1985): 272–82.

———. Comment and Response. *College English* 52 (1990): 694–96.

———. "Diversity, Ideology, and Teaching Writing." *College Composition and Communication* 43 (1992): 179–93.

———. "Not All Errors Are Created Equal: Nonacademic Readers in the Professions Respond to Lapses in Usage." *College English* 43 (1981): 794–806.

Hansen, Kristine. "Serving Up Writing in a New Form." Interchanges: Reforming Writing Programs. *College Composition and Communication* 49 (1998): 260–63.

Harkin, Patricia. "The Postdisciplinary Politics of Lore." *Contending with Words* 124–38.

Harris, Joseph. *A Teaching Subject: Composition Since 1966.* Upper Saddle River, NJ: Prentice Hall, 1997.

———. "The Plural Text/The Plural Self: Roland Barthes and William Coles." *College English* 49 (1987): 158–70.

———. "The Rhetoric of Theory." *Writing Theory and Critical Theory* 141–47.

Heath, Shirley Brice. *Ways with Words: Language, Life, and Work in Communities and Classrooms.* Cambridge UP, 1984.

Heilker, Paul. "Rhetoric Made Real: Civic Discourse and Writing Beyond the Curriculum." *Writing the Community* 71–77.

———. "Students." *Keywords in Composition Studies* 225–27.

Helmers, Marguerite H. *Writing Students: Composition Testimonials and Representations of Students.* Albany: State U of New York P, 1994.

Herndl, Carl G. "Teaching Discourse and Reproducing Culture: A Critique of Research and Pedagogy in Professional and Non-Academic Writing." *College Composition and Communication* 44 (1993): 349–63.

Herzberg, Bruce. "Composition and the Politics of the Curriculum." *Politics of Writing Instruction* 97–117.

———. "Michel Foucault's Rhetorical Theory." *Contending with Words* 69–81.

Higher Education under Fire: Politics, Economics, and the Crisis of the Humanities. Ed. Michael Bérubé and Cary Nelson. New York: Routledge, 1995.

Hill, Charles A., and Lauren Resnick. "Creating Opportunities for Apprenticeship in Writing." *Reconceiving Writing* 145–58.

Hofstadter, Richard. *Anti-Intellectualism in American Life.* New York: Knopf, 1962.

Holbrook, Sue Ellen. "Women's Work: The Feminizing of Composition." *Rhetoric Review* 9 (1991): 201–29.

Hollis, Karyn. "Liberating Voices: Autobiographical Writing at the Bryn Mawr Summer School for Women Workers, 1921–1938." *College Composition and Communication* 45 (1994): 31–60.

Holzman, Michael. "Writing as Technique." *College English* 44 (1982): 129–34.

hooks, bell. "marginality as site of resistance." *Out There: Marginalization and Contemporary Cultures*. Ed. Russell Ferguson, Martha Gever, Trinh T. Minh-ha, and Cornel West. New York: New Museum of Contemporary Art; Cambridge, MA: MIT P, 1990. 341–43.

———. *Talking Back: Thinking Feminist, Thinking Black*. Boston: South End, 1989.

———. *Yearning: Race, Gender, and Cultural Politics*. Boston: South End, 1990.

Horner, Bruce. "Discoursing Basic Writing." *College Composition and Communication* 47 (1996): 199–222.

———. "Mapping Errors and Expectations for Basic Writing: From the 'Frontier Field' to 'Border Country.' " *English Education* 26 (1994): 29–51.

———. "Rethinking the 'Sociality' of Error: Teaching Editing as Negotiation." *Rhetoric Review* 11 (1992): 172–99.

Hull, Glynda. "Hearing Other Voices: A Critical Assessment of Popular Views on Literacy and Work." *Changing Work, Changing Workers* 3–39.

Hull, Glynda, and Mike Rose. "Rethinking Remediation: Toward a Social-Cognitive Understanding of Problematic Reading and Writing." *Written Communication* 6 (1989): 139–54.

———." 'This Wooden Shack Place': The Logic of an Unconventional Reading." *College Composition and Communication* 41 (1990): 287–98.

Hull, Glynda, Mike Rose, Kay Losey Fraser, and Marisa Castellano. "Remediation as Social Construct: Perspectives from an Analysis of Classroom Discourse." *College Composition and Communication* 42 (1991): 299–329.

Irmscher, William F. "Finding a Comfortable Identity." *College Composition and Communication* 38 (1987): 81–87.

Jameson, Fredric. *The Political Unconscious: Narrative as a Socially Symbolic Act.* Ithaca, NY: Cornell UP, 1981.

Janangelo, Joseph. "Pedagogy of the Rich and Famous: Stories of a Class(room) Struggle near Beverly Hills." *Iowa English Bulletin* 40 (1992): 87–96.

Jay, Gregory, and Gerald Graff. "A Critique of Critical Pedagogy." *Higher Education under Fire* 201–13.

Johnston, Paul. *Success While Others Fail: Social Movement Unionism and the Public Workplace.* Ithaca, NY: Cornell UP, 1994.

Jones, Danell. "Crossing the Great Divide: From Manhattan to Montana." *ADE Bulletin* no. 117 (Fall 1997): 42–44.

Kaufer, David, and Cheryl Geisler. "Novelty in Academic Writing." *Written Communication* 6 (1989): 286–311.

Keywords in Composition Studies. Ed. Paul Heilker and Peter Vandenberg. Portsmouth, NH: Boynton/Cook, 1996.

Kirsch, Gesa E. "Opinion: Multi-Vocal Texts and Interpretive Responsibility." *College English* 59 (1997): 191–202.

Kirsch, Gesa E., and Joy S. Ritchie. "Beyond the Personal: Theorizing a Politics of Location in Composition Research." *College Composition and Communication* 46 (1995): 7–29.

Kleine, Michael. "Beyond Triangulation: Ethnography, Writing, and Rhetoric." *Journal of Advanced Composition* 10 (1991): 117–25.

Knapp, James E. Response to John T. Day. *ADE Bulletin* no. 111 (Fall 1995): 47–48.

Kramnick, Jonathan Brody. "Origins of the Present Crisis." *Profession* 1997: 84–92.

Kusterer, Ken C. *Know-how on the Job: The Important Working Knowledge of "Unskilled" Workers.* Boulder, CO: Westview, 1978.

Lalicker, William B. "The Material Culture of the Department of English and the Epistemological Situation of Composition." Penn State Conference on Rhetoric and Composition. State College, PA, 8 July 1997.

Lather, Patti. "Post-Critical Pedagogies: A Feminist Reading." *Feminisms and Critical Pedagogy* 120–37.

Lauter, Paul. " 'Political Correctness' and the Attack on American Colleges." *Higher Education under Fire* 73–90.

Lave, Jean. *Cognition in Practice: Mind, Mathematics and Culture in Everyday Life*. Cambridge UP, 1988.

Leach, Mary S. "Can We Talk? A Response to Burbules and Rice." *Harvard Educational Review* 62 (1992): 257–63.

Literacy for Life: The Demand for Reading and Writing. Ed. Richard W. Bailey and Robin Melanie Fosheim. New York: Modern Language Association, 1983.

Lu, Min-Zhan. "Conflict and Struggle: The Enemies or Preconditions of Basic Writing?" *College English* 54 (1992): 887–913.

———. "Professing Multiculturalism: The Politics of Style in the Contact Zone." *College Composition and Communication* 45 (1994): 442–58.

———. "Redefining the Legacy of Mina Shaughnessy: A Critique of the Politics of Linguistic Innocence." *Journal of Basic Writing* 10.1 (Spring 1991): 26–40.

———. "Representing and Negotiating Differences in the Contact Zone." *Reflections on Multiculturalism*. Ed. Robert Eddy. Yarmouth, ME: Intercultural P, 1996. 117–32.

———. "Writing as Repositioning." *Journal of Education* 172.1 (1990): 18–21.

Lu, Min-Zhan, and Bruce Horner. *Representing the "Other": Basic Writers and the Teaching of Basic Writing*. Urbana, IL: National Council of Teachers of English, 1999.

———. "The Problematic of Experience: Redefining Critical Work in Ethnography and Pedagogy." *College English* 60 (1998): 257–77.

Luke, Allan. "Genres of Power? Literacy Education and the Production of Capital." *Literacy in Society*. Ed. Ruqaiya Hasan and Geoff Williams. New York: Longman, 1998. 308–38.

———. "Getting Over Method: Literacy Teaching as Work in 'New Times.' " *Language Arts* April 1998: 305–13.

Luke, Carmen. "Feminist Pedagogy Theory: Reflections on Power and Authority." *Educational Theory* 46 (1996): 283–302.

———. "Feminist Politics in Radical Pedagogy." *Feminisms and Critical Pedagogy* 25–53.

Lunsford, Andrea A., and Lisa Ede. "Representing Audience: 'Successful' Discourse and Disciplinary Critique." *College Composition and Communication* 47 (1996): 167–79.

Lunsford, Andrea A., and Susan West. "Intellectual Property and Composition Studies." *College Composition and Communication* 47 (1996): 383–411.

Lynch, Dennis A., Diana George, and Marilyn M. Cooper. "Moments of Argument: Agonistic Inquiry and Confrontational Cooperation." *College Composition and Communication* 48 (1997): 61–85.

MacDonald, Heather. "Why Johnny Can't Write." *Public Interest* Summer 1995: 3–13.

Mahala, Daniel. "Writing Utopias: Writing Across the Curriculum and the Promise of Reform." *College English* 53 (1991): 773–90.

Mahala, Daniel, and Jody Swilky. "Remapping the Geography of Service in English." *College English* 59 (1997): 625–46.

"Making Faculty Work Visible: Reinterpreting Professional Service, Teaching, and Research in the Fields of Language and Literature." Report of the MLA Commission on Professional Service. New York: Modern Language Association, 1996.

Marx, Karl. *Capital, I: A Critique of Political Economy*. Trans. Ben Fowkes. New York: Vintage, 1976.

———. *A Contribution to the Critique of Political Economy* (1859). Trans. S. W. Ryazanskaya. Ed. Maurice Dobb. New York: International, 1970.

Marx, Karl, and Friedrich Engels. *The German Ideology, Parts I & III*. Ed. R. Pascal. New York: International, 1947.

Mauzerall, Jorgette. "Taking the Plunge off the Ivory Tower." *ADE Bulletin* no. 117 (Fall 1997): 38–41.

McConnel, Frances Ruhlen. "Freeway Flyers: The Migrant Workers of the Academy." *Writing Ourselves* 40–58.

McLaren, Peter. "Schooling the Postmodern Body: Critical Pedagogy and the Politics of Enfleshment." *Journal of Education* 170.3 (1988): 53–83.

McLaughlin, Thomas. *Street Smarts and Critical Theory: Listening to the Vernacular*. Madison: U of Wisconsin P, 1996.

Miller, Richard E. " 'A Moment of Profound Danger': British Cultural Studies away from the Centre." *Cultural Studies* 8 (1994): 417–37.

———. "Composing English Studies: Towards a Social History of the Discipline." *College Composition and Communication* 45 (1994): 164–79.

——. "Fault Lines in the Contact Zone." *College English* 56 (1994): 389–48.

Miller, Susan. " 'Is There a Text in This Class?' " *Freshman English News* 11 (1982): 20–24.

——. *Textual Carnivals: The Politics of Composition.* Carbondale: Southern Illinois UP, 1991.

——. "The Feminization of Composition." *The Politics of Writing Instruction* 39–53.

Mines, Luke. "Globalization in the Classroom." *The Nation* 1 June 1998: 22, 24.

Morrow, Raymond Allan, and Carlos Alberto Torres. *Social Theory and Education: A Critique of Theories of Social and Cultural Reproduction.* Albany: State U of New York P, 1995.

Mortensen, Peter. "Going Public." *College Composition and Communication* 50 (1998): 182–205.

Nelson, Cary. *Manifesto of a Tenured Radical.* New York UP, 1997.

Nelson, Cary, and Michael Bérubé. "Introduction: A Report from the Front." *Higher Education under Fire* 1–32.

Noble, David F. "Digital Diploma Mills: The Automation of Higher Education." *Monthly Review* February 1998: 38–52.

North, Stephen M. *The Making of Knowledge in Composition: Portrait of an Emerging Field.* Upper Montclair, NJ: Boynton/Cook, 1987.

Nystrand, Martin, Stuart Greene, and Jeffrey Wiemelt. "Where Did Composition Studies Come From? An Intellectual History." *Written Communication* 10 (1993): 267–333.

Oakley, Francis. "Against Nostalgia: Reflections on Our Present Discontents in American Higher Education." *The Politics of Liberal Education.* Ed. Darryl J. Gless and Barbara Herrnstein Smith. Durham, NC: Duke UP, 1992. 267–89.

Ogbu, John U. "Literacy and Schooling in Subordinate Cultures: The Case of Black Americans." *Literacy in Historical Perspective.* Ed. Daniel Resnick. Washington, DC: Library of Congress, 1983. Rpt. *Perspectives on Literacy* 227–42.

Ohmann, Richard. *English in America: A Radical View of the Profession.* New York: Oxford UP, 1976.

———. Foreword. *Politics of Writing Instruction* ix–xvi.

Ong, Walter J., S.J. *Orality and Literacy: Technologizing the Word*. London: Methuen, 1982.

Orgel, Stephen. "What Is a Text?" *Research Opportunities in Renaissance Drama* 24 (1981): 3–6.

Peck, Wayne Campbell, Linda Flower, and Lorraine Higgins. "Community Literacy." *College Composition and Communication* 46 (1995): 199–222.

Penrose, Ann M., and Cheryl Geisler. "Reading and Writing without Authority." *College Composition and Communication* 45 (1994): 505–20.

Perspectives on Literacy. Ed. Eugene R. Kintgen, Barry M. Kroll, and Mike Rose. Carbondale: Southern Illinois UP, 1988.

Petraglia, Joseph. "Writing as an Unnatural Act." *Reconceiving Writing* 79–100.

Petrosky, Anthony. "Rural Poverty and Literacy in the Mississippi Delta: Dilemmas, Paradoxes, and Conundrums." *The Right to Literacy* 61–73.

Phelps, Louise Wetherbee. *Composition as a Human Science: Contributions to the Self-Understanding of a Discipline*. New York: Oxford UP, 1988.

Plater, William M. "Future Work." *Change* May/June 1995: 22–33.

Poirier, Richard. "Hum 6, or Reading before Theory." *Raritan* 9.4 (Spring 1990): 14–31.

The Politics of Writing Instruction: Postsecondary. Ed. John Trimbur and Richard Bullock. Portsmouth, NH: Boynton/Cook, 1991.

Pollitt, Katha. "Why Do We Read?" *The Nation* 23 September 1991. Rpt. *Debating P.C.: The Controversy over Political Correctness on College Campuses*. Ed. Paul Berman. New York: Bantam, 1992. 201–11.

Pratt, Linda Ray. "Going Public: Political Discourse and the Faculty Voice." *Higher Education under Fire* 35–51.

Pratt, Mary Louise. "Arts of the Contact Zone." *Profession* 1991: 33–40.

———. "Daring to Dream: Re-Visioning Culture and Citizenship." *Critical Theory and the Teaching of Literature: Politics, Curriculum, Pedagogy*. Ed. James F. Slevin and Art Young. Urbana, IL: National Council of Teachers of English, 1996. 3–20.

———. "Linguistic Utopias." *The Linguistics of Writing: Arguments between Language and Literature.* Ed. Nigel Fabb, Derek Attridge, Alan Durant, and Colin MacCabe. New York: Methuen, 1987. 48–66.

"A Progress Report from the CCCC Committee on Professional Standards." CCCC Committee on Professional Standards. *College Composition and Communication* 42 (1991): 330–44.

Raymond, James C. Rev. of *The Making of Knowledge in Composition*, by Stephen North. *College Composition and Communication* 40 (1989): 93–95.

Reconceiving Writing, Rethinking Writing Instruction. Ed. Joseph Petraglia. Mahwah, NJ: Erlbaum, 1995.

Resnick, Stephen A., and Richard D. Wolff. *Knowledge and Class: A Marxian Critique of Political Economy.* U of Chicago P, 1987.

Rewriting Literacy: Culture and the Discourse of the Other. Ed. Candace Mitchell and Kathleen Weiler. New York: Bergin, 1991.

Rhoades, Gary. *Managed Professionals: Unionized Faculty and Restructuring Academic Labor.* Albany: State U of New York P, 1998.

The Right to Literacy. Ed. Andrea A. Lunsford, Helene Moglen, and James Slevin. New York: Modern Language Association, 1990.

Rodby, Judith. "What's It Worth and What's It For? Revisions to Basic Writing Revisited." *College Composition and Communication* 47 (1996): 107–11.

Rose, Mike. "Narrowing the Mind and Page: Remedial Writers and Cognitive Reductionism." *College Composition and Communication* 39 (1988): 267–302.

Rouse, John. "The Politics of Composition." *College English* 41 (1979): 1–12.

Royster, Jacqueline Jones. "Perspectives on the Intellectual Tradition of Black Women Writers." *The Right to Literacy* 103–12.

———. "When the First Voice You Hear Is Not Your Own." *College Composition and Communication* 47 (1996): 29–40.

Russell, David R. "Activity Theory and Its Implications for Writing Instruction." *Reconceiving Writing* 51–77.

———. "Romantics on Writing: Liberal Culture and the Abolition of Composition Courses." *Rhetoric Review* 6 (1988): 132–48.

———. *Writing in the Disciplines 1870–1990: A Curricular History.* Carbondale: Southern Illinois UP, 1991.

Schell, Eileen E. *Gypsy Academics and Mother-Teachers: Gender, Contingent Labor, and Writing Instruction.* Portsmouth, NH: Boynton/Cook, 1998.

Schutz, Aaron, and Anne Ruggles Gere. "Service Learning and English Studies: Rethinking 'Public' Service." *College English* 60 (1998): 129–49.

Scott, James C. *Domination and the Arts of Resistance: Hidden Transcripts.* New Haven, CT: Yale UP, 1990.

Scribner, Sylvia. "Literacy in Three Metaphors." *American Journal of Education* 93 (1984): 6–21. Rpt. *Perspectives on Literacy* 71–81.

Scribner, Sylvia, and Michael Cole. *The Psychology of Literacy.* Cambridge, MA: Harvard UP, 1981.

Seitz, James E. "Eluding Righteous Discourse: A Discreet Politics for New Writing Curricula." *WPA* 16.3 (1993): 7–14.

———. "The Rhetoric of Curriculum: Where to Go Beyond the First-Year Course?" Penn State Conference on Rhetoric and Composition. State College, PA, 7 July 1997.

Shaughnessy, Mina P. *Errors and Expectations: A Guide for the Teacher of Basic Writing.* New York: Oxford UP, 1977.

———. "The Miserable Truth." *Journal of Basic Writing* 3.1 (Fall/Winter 1980): 109–14.

Shor, Ira. "Our Apartheid: Writing Instruction and Inequality." *Journal of Basic Writing* 16.1 (Spring 1997): 91–104.

Sidler, Michelle, and Richard Morris. "Writing in a Post-Berlinian Landscape: Cultural Composition in the Classroom." *JAC: A Journal of Composition Theory* 18 (1998): 275–91.

Simon, Roger I., and Donald Dippo. "On Critical Ethnographic Work." *Anthropology & Education Quarterly* 17 (1986): 195–202.

Slevin, James F. "Connecting English Studies." *College English* 48 (1986): 543–50.

———. "Depoliticizing and Politicizing Composition Studies." *Politics of Writing Instruction* 1–21.

————. "Disciplining Students: Whom Should Composition Teach and What Should They Know?" *Composition in the Twenty-First Century* 153–65.

————. "Genre as a Social Institution." *Understanding Others: Cultural and Cross-Cultural Studies and the Teaching of Literature.* Ed. Joseph Trimmer and Tilly Warnock. Urbana, IL: National Council of Teachers of English, 1992. 16–34.

Smith, Jeff. "Against 'Illegeracy': Toward a Pedagogy of Civic Understanding." *College Composition and Communication* 45 (1994): 200–19.

————. "Students' Goals, Gatekeeping, and Some Questions of Ethics." *College English* 59 (1997): 299–320.

Soley, Lawrence. "Big Money on Campus." *Dollars and Sense* March/April 1997.

Soliday, Mary. "From the Margins to the Mainstream: Reconceiving Remediation." *College Composition and Communication* 47 (1996): 85–100.

Solsken, Judith W. "The Paradigm Misfit Blues." *Research in the Teaching of English* 27 (1993): 316–25.

Sommers, Nancy. "Responding to Student Writing." *College Composition and Communication* 33 (1982): 148–56.

Stuckey, J. Elspeth. *The Violence of Literacy.* Portsmouth, NH: Boynton/ Cook, 1991.

Stygall, Gail. "Resisting Privilege: Basic Writing and Foucault's Author Function." *College Composition and Communication* 45 (1994): 320–41.

Sullivan, Francis J., Arabella Lyon, Dennis Lebofsky, Susan Wells, and Eli Goldblatt. "Student Needs and Strong Composition: The Dialectics of Writing Program Reform." *College Composition and Communication* 48 (1997): 372–91.

Tannen, Deborah. "Oral and Literate Strategies in Spoken and Written Discourse." *Literacy for Life* 79–96.

Tate, Gary, John McMillan, and Elizabeth Woodworth. "Class Talk." *Journal of Basic Writing* 16 (Spring 1997): 13–26.

Thompson, Karen. "The Ultimate Working Condition: Knowing Whether You Have a Job or Not." *College Composition and Communication Forum* Winter 1998: A19–24.

Totten, Samuel. "Educating for the Development of Social Consciousness and Social Responsibility." *Social Issues in the English Classroom*. Ed. C. Mark Hurlbert and Samuel Totten. Urbana, IL: National Council of Teachers of English, 1992. 9–55.

Traditions of Inquiry. Ed. John Brereton. New York: Oxford UP, 1985.

Traub, James. "P.C. vs. English: Back to Basic." *The New Republic* 8 Feb. 1993: 18–19.

Trimbur, John. "Consensus and Difference in Collaborative Learning." *College English* 51 (1989): 602–16.

———. "Whatever Happened to the Fourth C?: Composition, Communication, and Socially Useful Knowledge." Conference on College Composition and Communication. Phoenix, 14 March 1997.

———. "Writing Instruction and the Politics of Professionalization." *Composition in the Twenty-First Century* 133–45.

Tuell, Cynthia. "Composition Teaching as 'Women's Work': Daughters, Handmaids, Whores, and Mothers." *Writing Ourselves* 123–39.

Tuman, Myron C. "Class, Codes, and Composition: Basil Bernstein and the Critique of Pedagogy." *College Composition and Communication* 39 (1988): 42–51.

Vandenberg, Peter. "The Work of Composition for Teachers: Time, Practice, Place and the Ideology of 'Research.'" Conference on College Composition and Communication. Chicago, 2 April 1998.

Varnum, Robin. *Fencing with Words: A History of Writing Instruction at Amherst College during the Era of Theodore Baird, 1938–1966*. Urbana, IL: National Council of Teachers of English, 1996.

Wall, Susan, and Nicholas Coles. "Reading Basic Writing: Alternatives to a Pedagogy of Accommodation." *Politics of Writing Instruction* 227–46.

Walters, Frank D. "Writing Teachers Writing and the Politics of Dissent." *College English* 57 (1995): 822–39.

Watkins, Beverly T. "Issues of Racial and Social Diversity Are the Centerpiece of Revamped Freshman Writing Courses at U. of Mass." *Chronicle of Higher Education* 19 December 1990: A13–14.

Watkins, Evan. *Work Time: English Departments and the Circulation of Cultural Value*. Stanford UP, 1989.

Ways of Reading: An Anthology for Writers. David Bartholomae and Anthony Petrosky. 3rd ed. Boston, Bedford, 1993.

Wells, Susan. "Rogue Cops and Health Care: What Do We Want from Public Writing?" *College Composition and Communication* 47 (1996): 325–41.

Wiley, Mark. "Reading and Writing in an American Grain." *Rhetoric Review* 11 (1992): 133–46.

Williams, Joseph M. "The Phenomenology of Error." *College Composition and Communication* 32 (1981): 152–68.

Williams, Raymond. *Keywords: A Vocabulary of Culture and Society.* New York: Oxford UP, 1976.

———. *Marxism and Literature.* New York: Oxford UP, 1977.

———. *Problems in Materialism and Culture: Selected Essays.* London: Verso, 1980.

Willis, Paul. *Learning to Labor: How Working Class Kids Get Working Class Jobs.* Morningside Edition. New York: Columbia UP, 1977, 1981.

Working Classics: Poems on Industrial Life. Ed. Peter Oresick and Nicholas Coles. Urbana and Chicago: U of Illinois P, 1990.

Writing Ourselves Into the Story: Unheard Voices from Composition Studies. Ed. Sheryl Fontaine and Susan Hunter. Carbondale: Southern Illinois UP, 1992.

Writing the Community: Concepts and Models for Service-Learning in Composition. Ed. Linda Adler-Kassner, Robert Crooks, and Ann Waters. Urbana, IL: National Council of Teachers of English, 1997.

Writing Theory and Critical Theory. Ed. John Clifford and John Schilb. New York: Modern Language Association, 1994.

Young, Richard. "Arts, Crafts, Gifts and Knacks: Some Disharmonies in the New Rhetoric." *Reinventing the Rhetorical Tradition.* Ed. Aviva Freedman and Ian Pringle. Ottawa: Canadian Council of Teachers of English, 1980. 53–60.

Zeichner, Kenneth. "Contradictions and Tensions in the Professionalization of Teaching and the Democratization of Schools." *Teachers College Record* 92 (1991): 363–79.

Zuboff, Shoshana. *In the Age of the Smart Machine: The Future of Work and Power.* New York: Basic, 1984.

Index

Coercion, 84–85. *See also* Power
Cognitive psychology, 33–34
Coles, William E., Jr., 51–53, 58,
  115, 183
  Bartholomae, David, and,
    187–202
  style of, 190–91, 193
  on writing as art, 213, 219
Collaborative pedagogy, 43–46,
  100–102, 211. *See also*
  Pedagogy
Collective bargaining, 23–24, 179
Collins, Terence, 123
Commodification, 2–4. *See also*
  Alienated labor
  of academic discourse, 106
  exchange/use value and, 4–5,
    155, 211, 219–20
  Marx on, 219–20
  of pedagogy, 81–90
  resistance to, 185, 211
  of scholarship, 225–26
  of teaching, 5–6, 9–11, 17–21,
    32–33
  of work, 2–11, 60–61, 217–18
  of writing, 9–10, 15, 173, 211,
    219
Community(ies)
  academy versus, 160
  classroom as, 114–15
  collaboration and, 44–46
  discourse/speech, 107, 113
  homogeneity of, 61–63, 135
  literacy of, 69–71, 232
  methodological, 196
  volunteer work for, 161–62
Community service-learning (CSL)
  programs, 157–64
Composition
  in academy, 101–102
  Bartholomae, David, on, 15,
    202–203
  capital and, 146
  class identity and, 175
  culture of, 243–44
  definition of, 255, 264n. 1

  as discipline, xvi, 127, 133–56,
    172, 206
  discourse community of, 225
  extracurriculum of, 17, 117, 119,
    162
  "feminization" of, 1, 19–20
  history of, 168, 171
  literary studies and, 15–16, 141,
    147–51, 215
  lore of, 167, 176–79, 196–98
  mainstreaming and, 20
  at Michigan Technological
    University, 203–205, 207
  minority tradition in, 59
  as missionaries, 61
  as "mothering," 146–47, 268n. 8
  politics in, 73–77
  practitioners in, 176–77
  praise by, 60
  professionalization of, 15, 17, 95,
    166–67, 202–203
  proletarianization of, 13–15, 22,
    98, 173, 179–80
  remedial, 20, 28
  results of, 18
  service learning in, 66–71, 131,
    157–64
  subject of, 145–46, 212, 232
  teachers of. *See* Teachers
  textbooks for, 108–109, 171–72
  theories of, 200–202, 225–28
  tradition of, 167–79, 199–202
  Trimbur, John, on, xii
  value of, 15–16, 27–28, 138,
    218–20
  work in, 2–3, 14–15, 172; re-
    defining of, 202–208
  workshops for, 20, 28
  Writing across the curriculum
    (WAC) programs and, 151–56
  See also English Studies; Writing
Connors, Robert, 168
Consciousness
  critical, 238
  practical, 216, 242–43, 246
  social production of, 215–17

Unionization
  managerial control and, 23–24
  of teachers, 22, 52, 179
University of Texas at Austin, 78,
  266n. 9
University of Wisconsin–Madison,
  88
Upward mobility, 13

Value, exchange/use, 4–5, 155, 211,
  219–20
Vandenberg, Peter, 26, 51–52
Varnum, Robin, 204, 205
  Fencing with Words, 180–86

WAC. *See* Writing across the curriculum
Wall, Susan, 194, 269n. 10
Watkins, Evan, 1, 27
  on English studies, 135–36
  on value of literature, 4
Williams, Joseph, 220
Williams, Raymond, xvii, 1, 59,
  175, 247
  on aesthetic response, 115–16
  on authorship, 215, 221, 222
  on craftsmanship, 217–18
  on practical consciousness, 216
  on sociality, 26–27, 36, 52
  on tradition, 165–66, 172
Willis, Paul, 58
Woolf, Virginia, 244–49, 252
Work
  in academy, ix–xi, 3–7, 105–
    106
  alienated, x, 3, 4, 131, 179–80,
    213
  classroom, 43, 222
  commodification of, 2–11, 60–61,
    217–18
  in composition, 2–3, 14–29, 172,
    209, 270n. 1; redefining of,
    202–208
  control of, 133
  conversion of, 27
  definitions of, 1–2, 209

division of, 7–8
in English, 10–14
holy, 60
ideological, 27
paid, 1, 161
sociality and, 37–38
societal needs and, 4
of student writing, 58–71
text and, 253–54
traditional, 179–80
"unskilled," 117, 131, 155, 169
volunteer, 161–62
"women's," 53
writing and, 1, 209, 255
See also Intellectual work
Writing
adult, 58
ambiguity of, 209, 255, 270n. 1
as art, 52, 213–15, 217
authority in, 52–53, 220–22
commodification of, 9–10, 15,
  173, 211, 219
as craft, 215
about difference, 78
examination, 120
experimental, 221, 229–30,
  250–52
Jameson, Fredric, on, xix, 247
liberatory, 83, 235–38
oral tradition and, 169
for own sake, 218–19
as process, 40–41, 49, 209–10,
  215
production of, 211
reading and, 150–51
research on, 175, 223, 230–32,
  252–53
scholarship on, 223–32
standardization of, 38, 72
student. *See* Students
teachers of. *See* Teachers
as technique, 213–15, 219
traditions of, 167
transgressive, 252
value of, 15–16, 27–28, 138,
  218–20